Jean Tschumi Architecture at Full Scale

For Alice and Heide

Jacques Gubler

Jean Tschumi
Architecture at Full Scale

SKIRA

Cover
Nestlé headquarters in Vevey, double-spiral central staircase seen from above, with *trompe-l'œil* effect of two staircases fused into one. Photograph by Eric Ed. Guignard, 1960

Back Cover
Portrait of the architect by anonymous photographer, circa 1960

Editor
Luca Molinari

Art Director
Marcello Francone

Design
Luigi Fiore

Editorial Coordination
Eva Vanzella

Editing
Laura Guidetti

Layout
Tarmac Publishing, Mendrisio

Translation
Jasmine Benyamin
(from French into English)

First published in Italy in 2008 by
Skira Editore S.p.A.
Palazzo Casati Stampa
via Torino 61
20123 Milan
Italy
www.skira.net

All rights reserved by
Jacques Gubler, Bernard Tschumi
and Catherine Wegener-Tschumi, ACM
© 2008 Skira editore

All rights reserved under international copyright conventions.
No part of this book may be reproduced or utilized in any form or by any means, electronic or mechanical, including photocopying, recording, or any information storage and retrieval system, without permission in writing from the publisher.

Printed and bound in Italy. First edition

ISBN: 978-88-5720-071-2

Distributed in North America by Rizzoli International Publications, Inc., 300 Park Avenue South, New York, NY 10010, USA.
Distributed elsewhere in the world by Thames and Hudson Ltd., 181A High Holborn, London WC1V 7QX, United Kingdom.

Photograph Credits
Archives de la Construction moderne, Federal Institute of Technology, Lausanne
Page 6, Plates 1–4, 6–20, 35–36, 38, 40, 42–45, 48–52, 54, 56–61, 70, 72–73, 75, 78–81, 83–92, 94, 97–98, 104–111, 114, 116–119, 121–129, 134–135, 137–151, 153–165, 168–171, 177–203, 205–214, 216–224, page 212, page 223

Archives of the City of Lausanne
Page 216

Arcurio, factory of wooden models, Germany
Plate 53

Bonell and Gill, Barcelona
Plate 74

Jaak De Koninck, Leuven
Plate 136

J. Joedicke, Bürobauten
Plates 172, 174-176

Nestlé Historical Archives, Vevey
Plates 152, 166

Library of Congress, Washington
Plate 31

Novartis Archives, Sandoz files, Basel
Plates 77, 120, 130–133

Private collection, Basel
Plates 55, 173, 215

Private collection, Paris
Plates 5, 21–30, 34, 37, 39, 41, 46–47, 62-69, 71, 82, 93, 95–96, 99, 112–113, 115

Robert Castellana, Nice
Plates 32–33

Robert Monnier, Neuchâtel
Plate 204

Sandoz Family Office
Plate 76

Service de l'urbanisme, City of Vevey
Plate 167

Jean-Daniel Chavan (Lausanne), Marco Bieglin (Basel), Alexis Toureau (Paris): Jean Tschumi drawing archives

Table of Contents

7	Foreword
9	Architecture at Full Scale
29	A Swiss in Paris
49	From Furniture to Architecture
71	*La Variante*, a Dialogue within the Project
81	High Points of Corporate Architecture: Sandoz and Nestlé
181	Teaching at EPUL
213	Epilogue
217	Acknowledgments
217	Chronology

Nestlé headquarters in Vevey, Switzerland, 14 December 1957, contruction of portico.
Photograph by De Jongh

Foreword

Most histories of twentieth-century architecture describe the period as a battleground of ideological oppositions, among them modernism vs. classicism, Bauhaus vs. Beaux-Arts, regionalism vs. rationalism and, more recently, postmodernism vs. modernism and even digital vs. analog. While these breaks, ruptures, and polemics have often served the purpose of energizing an architectural thought all too ready to take refuge in successive dictionaries of received ideas, they have also masked a profound reality: Architecture, even when most ephemeral, deals with the long-term.

What strikes me about the work of Jean Tschumi is the implicit overview it proposes, as if there were a higher plane of understanding what architecture is, a sort of meta-history of the discipline that goes beyond mere oppositions or stylistic battles. A strange and haunting continuity permeates the work, from the large urban projects of his early "utopian" period to the small but luscious pieces of furniture, from his first building in Orléans, completed in 1953, to the projects in planning at his death in 1962 at the age of 57. The seven buildings for which he is best known today were all completed in the very short span of twelve years.

Jean Tschumi's work suggests that the art of building is inseparable from concerns with construction and materiality. Whether using the most traditional or the most technologically innovative materials of the time, his work seems as if informed by thousands of years in the art of building, from which it achieves a singular timelessness. Its critical function is implicit rather than explicit. It does not use words (Mies and Saarinen also did not write much), but conveys a sense that the built work, in the relationship that it proposes between materials and form, is the point of the demonstration.

The issue at stake is not about opposing puritanical modernity to the pleasure of materials and proportions, but rather an uncanny sensibility in combining sensuous surface and rigorous depth, in exploring the larger palette of what architecture has to offer rather than the narrow confines prescribed by ideologues. Hence the variants and their seemingly endless play of possibilities, as if each project were as much about permutations and combinations as about composition. Jean Tschumi's work suggests that there are numerous ways to arrive at an architectural solution. Ultimately, the art of architecture is about resolution.

My father died on my eighteenth birthday. As a young child I often heard him alluding to the continuum of architecture, with its play of possibilities and grounding material resonance, in his repeated declaration that architecture, even if it was "*un métier de…*(expletive)," was still "*le plus beau métier du monde* (the most beautiful craft in the world)." In his penetrating research on Jean Tschumi, the architectural historian Jacques Gubler takes us through an investigation that tells equally about the history of the period and the work of the architect. His insights into "*l'échelle grandeur*," or full scale, and the strategy of the "*variante*," among many other practices, possess the dimension of a detective story, in which carefully laid-out clues lead us to another, fuller understanding of what architecture can be.

Bernard Tschumi
October 2008

1
Flagpole for the Nestlé Pavilion, Paris World's Fair (1937), 1936, pencil and charcoal on tracing paper, full-scale drawing, reinterpretation of Roman bucranium

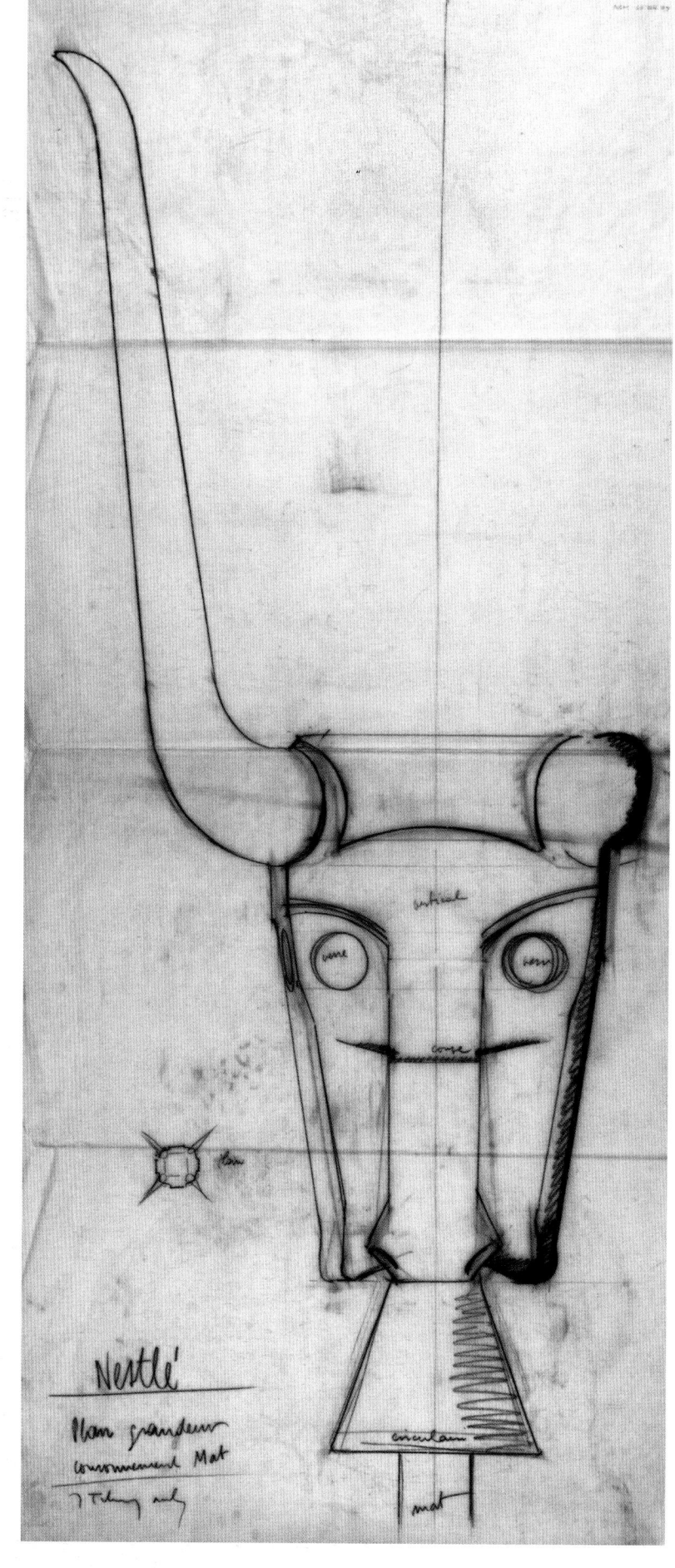

Architecture at Full Scale

The following chapters may read like a "success story," but I have no interest in that literary genre. If Jean Tschumi achieved posthumous international recognition, it is because of his creative energy during his lifetime. The roughly 4,400 drawings that today reside in Lausanne, Switzerland are proof of his passion, intelligence, and will to create and succeed. When Tschumi found himself in economic difficulties, he hunted out assignments and entered numerous competitions. He sought out every available opportunity for construction, even on the ground floor of his apartment building. While working with furniture makers as a student he came into contact with prominent industrialists. He would later have the opportunity to meet Edouard Marcel Sandoz, a polyedric artist and captain of industry, and become the official architect for the pharmaceutical giant Sandoz France SA. Additionally, while in Paris, he came in contact with Nestlé. As a student at the Ecole Nationale Supérieure des Beaux-Arts he was hedonistic in his use of time; his schedule was full. He discovered the creative power of capitalism in the American model of "corporate architecture" and put the competitive work ethic he discovered at the Beaux-Arts to use in his engagement with business. He lived through World War II without physical losses or career setbacks, taught in Lausanne, and built in France and Switzerland. As president of the International Union of Architects (UIA) he cultivated global contacts. He received several accolades shortly before his death, including the Reynolds Prize, then the architectural equivalent of an "Oscar," which was awarded to him by the American aluminum industry in 1960. That same year he won an international competition for the headquarters of the World Health Organization in Geneva, edging out Eero Saarinen. Tschumi's death came suddenly, on a night train from Paris to Lausanne. The funeral ceremony at the Lausanne cathedral took on the significance of a national memorial service. His death would cut short three sizable projects designed for Paris. Only one was built. Tschumi's ambition included a steady dialogue with prominent examples of modernism, including the auditorium for Massachusetts Institute of Technology (MIT) in Cambridge, Massachusetts and the UNESCO headquarters in Paris.

The majority of Jean Tschumi's drawings are at the Archives of Modern Construction (ACM) at the Federal Institute of Technology in Lausanne (EPFL). The American psychoanalyst Louise Kaplan warned against Jacques Derrida's "archive fever." She devoted an entire chapter of *Cultures of Fetishism* to the concept of biography, which she defined as an analytic transference from the subject's consciousness to the author's own imagination; in this manner, the artist was summoned to a kind of re-birth through the act of writing.[1] The danger is the writer's shipwreck in the archives, from which ensues the sacrificial drowning of the very person intended to be saved from oblivion. If our consumerist society fetishizes things, the biographer who resides in the midst of all that paper ends up by borrowing both the face and the body of the other. The subject becomes the object. Do archives merely create primitive masks of a contemporary world lost in globalization?[2] The power of the archival act, a relatively new force in architecture, would then be re-situated in a game of mirrors and seduction. This game would reduce the traces left by the artist to a kind of polychromatic powder, a commercial substance. But I enjoy tattooing myself in Tschumi's pigments. I will not ignore my own superficiality or my fantasies. I will move by following the example of those neurons that inhabit all physiological organs, including the feet, hands, stomach, and brain. I will aim at exceeding the brute accumulation of facts as well as hagiographical reverence.

This study is divided into seven thematic chapters. The narrative does not adhere to any chronological order, but instead takes leaps forward and backward. In Chapter Two the question of Tschumi's educational upbringing allows a biographical trajectory that feeds into subsequent chapters focusing on the architectural themes developed by Tschumi. These themes expand beyond his *oeuvre* to intersect with the history and theory of modern architecture. Questions regarding the scale of drawings, furniture, the variant, the city, and teaching are isolated into separate chapters. The fundamental and often mediating role of the client takes shape in the chapter titled "Corporate Architecture." My journey through the collection of drawings archived at ACM prompted numerous impressions, both qualitative and quantitative. Why did Tschumi propose so many varying solutions to studies with the same program? Was it to illustrate his aphorism "There is no good solution; only one is the least bad"?[3] Why so many small and minute sketches? At the other extreme, why are so many drawings rendered at full scale? It seems that this primordial and obsessive question of scale constituted one of the central themes of Tschumi's work. The evaluation of these drawings might thus be considered in relation to the attention to detail and dimensionality needed to achieve a controlled materialization: hence this chapter's title, "At Full Scale."

Point of Departure

Let's start from a provocative springboard, the Polish scientist Alfred Korzybski's famous statement from 1931 that "a map is not the territory."[4] Physics describes nature (the territory) through the invention of mathematical propositions (maps) that elude common sense. What would happen if we tried to introduce this statement into the practice of architecture, where mapmaking has a foundational role? Let's read the sentence that follows next in Korzybski's text: "If the ideal of the map could be correct, the map would include, at a smaller scale, a map of the map, a map of that map, and so on *ad infinitum*."[5] What does this romantic descent into the vertiginous vortex of fractals illuminate? Perhaps the optical metaphor of that descriptive onomatopoeia of filmmaking, namely, the "zoom." But doesn't architecture proceed from an empirical model—one that nevertheless does not renounce the use of theoretical models? Euclidean geometry and its graphic emanation, perspective, constitute a theory of representation linking Vitruvius to Alberti and Piero della Francesca to CAD software. In the twentieth century physicists were occasionally astonished or amused by the archaic geometric operations of "*costruzione operativa*." With respect to the city, modern physics could conclude that contemporary architecture was aiming to prove a piece of medieval dogma—that the earth was flat[6]—even if Euclid, the great pillar of industrialized society, viewed his postulates as philosophical entities. Yet even without their philosophical attributes, the laws that feed into the graphic conventions of plan, section, and elevation remain.

Architecture tackles the question of map and territory in metaphoric terms. The most-cited aphorism is that of a progression "from the spoon to the city." For its author, Hermann Muthesius, the analog of "zoom" expressed a model of practice.[7] Architecture shrinks and dilates into a microcosm and a macrocosm. There should be a part that can be held and touched, as if taking the thermal pulse of materials. Concrete, metal, and glass all differ in temperature and temperament. The feel of smooth or rough materials, of silky curtains or wool rugs, conveys contrasts. At the other extremity of scale lies the urban dimension of the large or "grand" project, perceptible as if from a plane or a moving vehicle. In the Weimar Republic, Muthesius's watchword converged with "*Gestaltung*," a holistic design concept that applied to both large and small scales, provided that both perspectives reinforced the unbreakable totality of the project. Wood studies at full scale were not uncommon in industrial design, particularly in the automobile industry: the bodywork of the Fiat 500 was developed from a massive mahogany prototype.[8]

At what point in history did full-scale working drawings appear? Did they exist before the twentieth century, apart from the covert military operations of naval construction? The Eiffel Tower might be the largest edifice ever designed and drawn at 1:1 scale. Its iron members were fabricated and drilled to the closest millimeter in Gustave Eiffel's workshop, then assembled and riveted on site. Later, standardized steel sections produced in factories in T and double-

2
Cartoon for a carpet commissioned by Sandoz, fragment, 1939–1942, watercolor and gouache, orthogonal geometry of the frame

3
Profile of a cornice, Sandoz Laboratories, Orléans, circa 1952, red chalk, "postage-stamp" sketches combined with a working drawing at full scale

4
Sandoz Laboratories, Orléans, west facade, winter 1952–1953, photograph taken by the architect, sequence of a report on the building site, verification of reinforced-concrete profiles through medium of the camera

5
Roman Corinthian frieze, copy of a plaster cast at full scale, school exercise at the *Technicum* in Biel, 1919, charcoal and stump

6
Standing ashtray for Sandoz headquarters in Paris, July 1951, pencil and ink on tracing paper

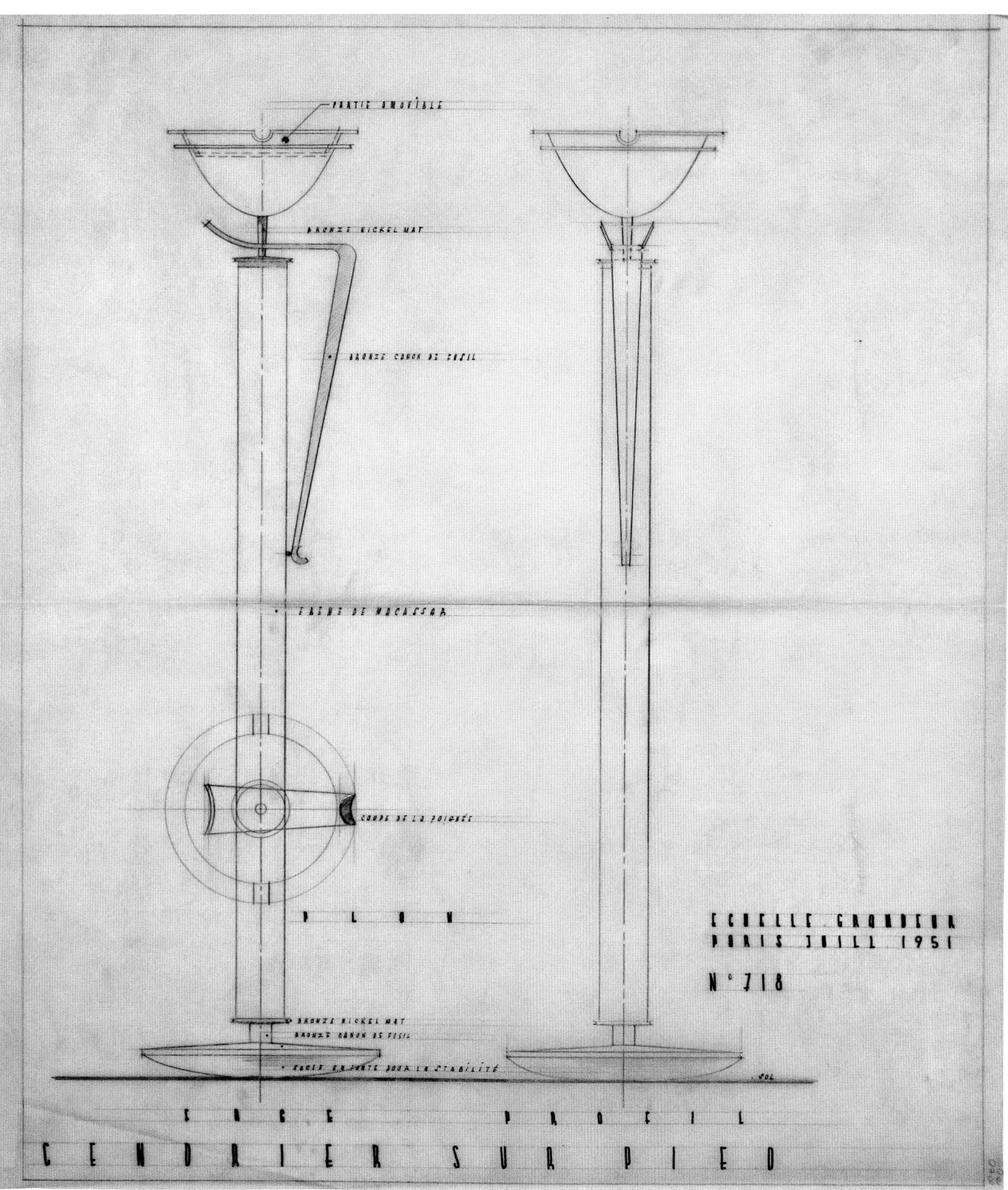

T forms were made available by mail order. In the twentieth century architecture produced numerous cases in which the design of a project, whether built or not, was verified by developing 1:1 scale models. Ludwig Mies van der Rohe's models for the unrealized Kröller-Müller Villa present a well-known example.[9] Mies set up a wooden chassis wrapped in sailcloth and installed on rails in a meadow in order to simulate the effects of the project in different site locations. But this *mise-en-scène* doesn't correspond to the type of 1:1 experimentation we are pursuing. Nor am I thinking of the common, fairly inexpensive wood models of classical orders that date from the nineteenth century.[10] Instead, examples that explore the actual mechanics of building are key. Engaged by the Hilton company to study the bedroom type, Skidmore, Owings and Merrill developed a kind of mock-up that tinkered with the form at full scale.[11] Examples from the later half of the twentieth century seem to have been devoted primarily to the study of light inside buildings. In 1955 Mies and his project architect Gene Summers tested variations on steel-frame structures for the facade of the Seagram Building in New York City.[12] In 1960, working from his office in Cambridge, Massachusetts, Josep Lluis Sert designed early versions of demi-vaulted roof forms for the Maeght Foundation in Saint-Paul de Vence. Similarly, Le Corbusier's team designed the unconstructed plan for Venice's hospital, and fabricated a prototype for sky-lit tunnel rows that would have allowed reclining patients to gaze out at the moonlight. More recently, Robert Venturi and Denise Scott Brown made use of mock-ups in two cases: first, the ceilings in Sainsbury Wing at the National Gallery in London; second, the windows in the assembly room of the Haute-Garonne District Hall in Toulouse.

Imagine my surprise at finding in Tschumi's work a different kind of technical case-study: two examples of concrete support structures. The first dates from 1953, from the beginning of construction on a building for an insurance company, the Mutuelle Vaudoise Accidents in Lausanne. The architect and contractor fabricated a complete span of reinforced concrete to test the impact of various wooden forms and different color additives. The other example, the Nestlé headquarters in Vevey, dates from 1957. The reinforced-concrete floor plates were submitted for testing at the materials laboratory in the Polytechnic School at the University of Lausanne (EPUL).[13] Full-scale models were also built on-site to simulate the building's exterior span. Glass and aluminum, the industrial components chosen for the curtain wall and the detachable office partitions, were tested during assembly. These experiences illustrate Tschumi's empirical methodology of "learning by doing."[14] His architectural training was shaped by his furniture designs, for which he built 1:1 scale models, as exemplified by a gouache-and-watercolor study, 1939–1942, for a carpet (Plate 2). But is it possible to master the discipline of architecture simply through full-scale models? Despite the unrealistic nature of this demand, Tschumi developed his abilities through 1:1 design, folding aluminum into an awning or making use of reinforced concrete for the profile of a cornice (Plate 3).

One could argue that such attention to detail was characteristic of Swiss architecture from the 1950s and 1960s, when the development of innovative solutions to technical problems embodied in details generated design signatures for architects.[15] The part, indeed the particle, became the whole. The watchmaker's call for precision was especially applicable to issues of joinery and assembly. Fritz Haller's skeletal system of cylindrical tubing and ball joinery, distributed through the USM Company, provides a prime example. However, Tschumi's ideas seem to have evolved outside of this design tendency. For him, the construction of an angle, the use of heterogeneous materials, and the logic of plan and section originated from the same calculation. As the Italian Swiss architect Livio Vacchini put it, "In architecture, there are no details: all things are of equal importance."[16] Equal intensity of precision could be found in both minutely scaled sketches and full-scale working drawings. Muthesius' axiom could be modified in this context to move "from the ashtray to the city" (Plate 6). I bring up the ashtray for two reasons: first, because of the social importance of smoking across all economic strata in industrial society, and second, because Tschumi and his team smoked throughout the design process, leaving indelible brown lesions from their cigarette embers on the tracing paper.

Competition in Stockholm

In 1932 an international competition was announced for the redevelopment of the Nedre Norrmalm district in central Stockholm. Located northwest of the Royal Palace, this commercial district is made up of many small islands. The initiation of the project by the City of Stockholm coincided with the planning stages for a subway system located in a difficult geological and marine subsurface. Three hundred and fifty European and American firms entered the field, but the immediate effect of the competition was negligible. Its more general impact on the public reinforced the willingness of local politicians to engage in infrastructure and housing developments, among other projects, in a coordinated manner.[17] The underground tunnels would not be completed until after World War II, when they would be coordinated in tandem with city planning.[18] Prominent urban design projects in the city center would have to wait until the 1960s. Nevertheless, the impulse extending from this international effort attracted entries by the likes of Alvar Aalto and Le Corbusier. Erik Gunnar Asplund presided over the jury.

At the age of 27, the young, still-unknown Tschumi was immersed in his studies at the Institute of Urbanism at the University of Paris, where he had established relationships with a few mentors, including Jacques Gréber. Tschumi pursued his own academic apprenticeship by entering several competitions.[19] For the Stockholm competition, he drew his proposal at a reduced scale using a favorite tool: a large soft-lead pencil. Highlights were rendered in black, blue, or green pencil or in

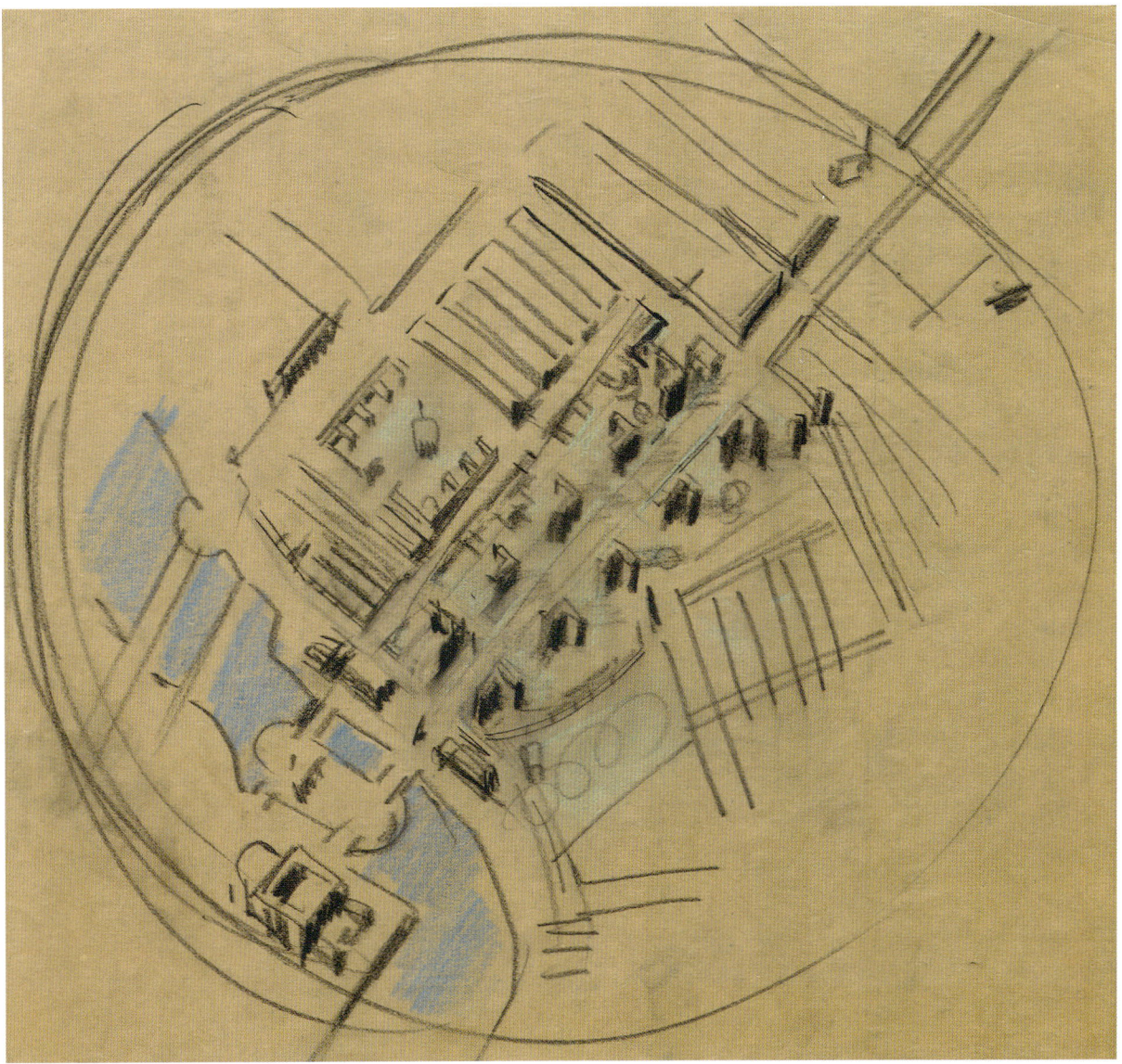

7
Competition for Stockholm master plan, 1932, "postage-stamp" sketch, pencil on tracing paper. The poetry of the city grasped through the porthole window of the plane

gouache. The earliest sketches show Tschumi's efforts to integrate perspectives with plan studies. The competition brief stipulated that the plan views be superimposed over an aerial photograph of the site. In his final version, Tschumi rendered the drawings in gouache and ink wash, approximating the look of a re-touched photograph (Plates 11, 12). More than 20 drawings on tracing paper remain, including the three examples shown here.[20] One of them locates the plan as if in a horizontal window-frame (Plate 8). This framing device recalls Le Corbusier's *Plan Voisin* (1922) and reiterates the centrality of the airplane as a conceptual model for modern architecture. A second sketch is drawn from an elevated position, as if from a bird's eye view (Plate 7). Here, the circular framing outlines a porthole window. The diagonal from the central axis uses the Palais Royal as a precedent, with its infinite perspective toward the midnight sun. However quickly drawn, the sketches still articulate a clear architectural typology: the "New Avenue" is flanked by symmetrically arranged L-shaped towers whose angles, in turn, reinforce the urban fabric. This grid accommodates slabs and includes a square framing a church. The poetics of speed permeate the drawing, as if to illustrate the option of an urban freeway. As Tschumi noted, the avenue served as a "dorsal spine for the layout of the financial district."[21] The office buildings ascended to 23 stories, and the elevated vehicular artery above the avenue was designed with the location of underground parking garages in mind. Following his conceptual habit, Tschumi submitted two variations to the jury. The alternate version is the more ambitious; it shows the avenue elongated to accommodate two additional towers and a roundabout (Plate 10).

What were Tschumi's architectural sources? Certainly the *Plan Voisin* was among them. Ludwig Hilbersheimer's notion of *Hochhausstadt*, which he outlined and developed in 1927, was also a precedent.[22] In Tschumi's proposals, Le Corbusier's jagged edges are streamlined by Hilbersheimer's persistent orthogonality. Another model from which Tschumi drew was Jacques Gréber's proposal for Benjamin Franklin Parkway in Philadelphia. These three references are not "influences" *per se*; the word "influence" carries allusions to alchemy and the unconscious that I reject. In contrast, the word "reference" allows for a

8
Competition for Stockholm master plan, 1932, "postage-stamp" sketch, pencil on tracing paper, perspective in south-north axis toward the midnight sun

9
Competition for Stockholm master plan, 1932, pencil on tracing paper, final study before rendering

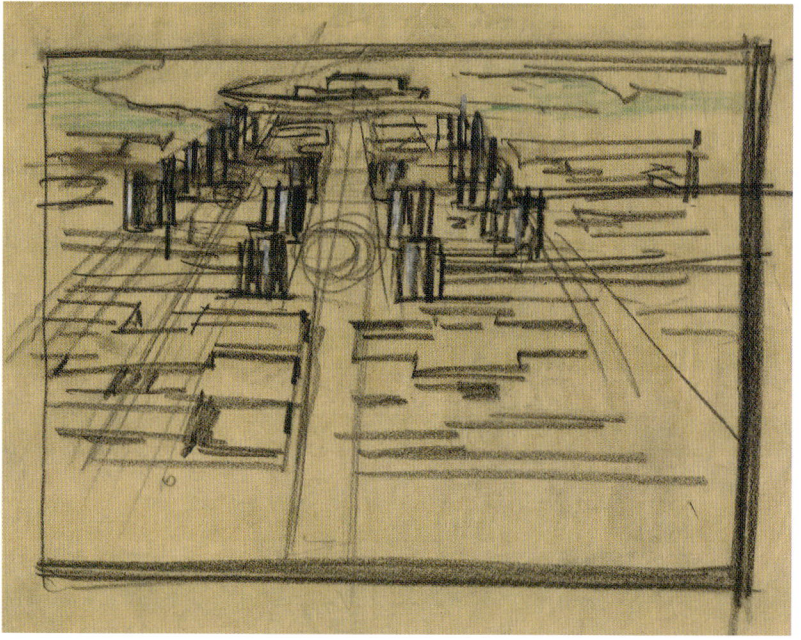

10
Competition for Stockholm master plan, 1932,
final rendering, photograph of second *variante*
with five pairs of towers

more reflective reading, one that consciously allies itself with examples. The impulse is that of a challenge, which is inscribed in the very institution of architectural competitions. For the first time, Tschumi, "a Swiss in Paris," found himself in the midst of an international debate. He worked at home in partnership with another Swiss architect, Henri Vermeil. Competitions at this global scale were few and far between, and were occasions that provoked young architects to throw themselves into the unknown. In this setting, consciousness mingled with unconscious desire. Indeed, there is at least one statistically proven fact about architecture: one must learn how to win competitions. This education can last a lifetime; in Tschumi's case, it included his winning entry for the World Health Organization shortly before his death.

What was the jury's response to the Stockholm competition entries? The jury report came out under the authorship of two members, Asplund and Ragnar Östberg.[23] I will highlight only responses to two of the 350 entries. Unsigned plans sent by Le Corbusier were easily recognizable, and the jury put its gloves on to describe the project as "the most logical of all the utopian concepts presented." Asplund even referred to "the Green City spirit." The jury's conclusion: the project was situated "beyond the realm of all possibility." Tschumi and Vermeil's proposal (Plates 11, 12) did not make it past the second round. The jury opined that "the project could be considered utopian." But the mere fact that they found themselves in the same utopian orbit as Le Corbusier must have been flattering to the two young designers setting foot on the international stage.

11
Competition for Stockholm master plan, 1932, final rendering, *variante* with five pairs of towers, India ink and gouache on photographic print. Wooden panel later used as drawing board in Tschumi's office

12
Competition for Stockholm master plan, 1932, final rendering, *variante* with four pairs of towers, India ink and gouache on photographic print. View of the diagonal toward south

Paris Underground

Let's return to the notions of micro, macro, and zoom. In Stockholm Tschumi was confronted with a site at the scale of the city. He teamed up with the Armenian architect Edouard Utudjian, a fellow student who was the founder and chief ideologue of the Study and Coordination Group for Underground Urbanism (GECUS or Groupe d'Etudes du Centre Urbain Souterrain). Utudjian devoted himself to the study of underground spaces, which he fondly referred to as "magnificent, pure volumes."[24] At the 1937 Paris Expo of Arts, Crafts, and Sciences in Modern Life (Exposition des Arts et Techniques), Utudjian's research on "urban undergrounds" was endorsed by prominent members of the Institute of Urbanism at the Sorbonne. Among its advocates were the heads of the Expo, Jacques Gréber and Marcel Poëte. For Poëte, the novelty of Utudjian's research lay in its demonstration, for the first time, of a systematic understanding of urbanism not only as surface or elevation, but also in its depth.[25] Tunnels are spaces with a long history of theoretical and technological evolution that, in modern-day France, was introduced by the Ecole des Mines.[26] In 1937, the urban problem generated by questions of circulation was an integral part of everyday life in cities like Paris, Milan, and Buenos Aires.[27] For many years, a principal aim of urban designers has been to resolve the problem of congestion. The question, how do underground tunnels connect with larger vehicular arteries? was addressed by Gréber, who nevertheless acknowledged that "underground urbanism is not a utopia."[28] Gréber had in mind a number of classic examples that were still little known in France, such as the underground connection between New Jersey and the island-city of Manhattan or the tunnels buried under Philadelphia's city center. During the Expo Utudjian and GECUS organized the first international conference on "Underground Urbanism."

The affiliated exhibition was installed strategically in the underground basement of Paris's new Museum of Modern Art. Within this subterranean space the visitor encountered a collective shelter equipped with all of its screens, filters, electrical generators, and "cylco-ventilators," as well as a labyrinthine cross-section of safes from the Bank of France. Infrastructure for the city's subway and sewage systems was also on display. GECUS took over a bare, 100-meter vaulted space. Here Tschumi introduced two objects—a triptych titled *Proposal for Underground Circulation* and a model of "Underground Paris" (*Paris Souterrain*). In Tschumi's proposal, a deep-sunk grid of highways was placed in relation to the principal street intersections located above ground (Plates 18, 19). The orthogonal geometry of the design challenged the meandering natural geometry of the river basin. In the architect's terms, the "rigid simplicity" of the proposal offered an alternative to the radial and concentric structures of the existing city. Underground, the north-south axis reinforced the importance of such above-ground sectors as Denfert, Sébastopol, and the junction created by the two interconnected railway stations, Gare de l'Est and Gare du Nord. The subterranean east-west axis similarly corresponded to the "exposed" sites of Nation, the Champs-Elysées, and the Pont de Neuilly. The intersection of these vectors generated a 45-degree grid that located the competing interfaces. Tschumi threw his energies into a large perspective depicting a subterranean crossroad with helical access-ramps, all of it rendered in a twilight ambience. This large "machine" was presented as if suspended under a parabolic dome (Plate 17). The rendering of the space is powerful, even shiver-inducing, and it recalls English painted depictions of the Sublime in

13
Project for an antiaircraft shelter in Bern, August 1936, published in the *Bulletin du GECUS*. Bunker as a polemical counter-project to the underground garage built under the new Casino Square

14
Paris Souterrain, 1937, study for model with neon tubes, color pencil on tracing paper. Superposition of networks and underground highway grid in red neon

15
Paris Souterrain, 1937, photograph of model showing existing networks (sewers and subways)

16
Paris Souterrain, 1937, photograph by René-Jacques of model showing underground network of new highways

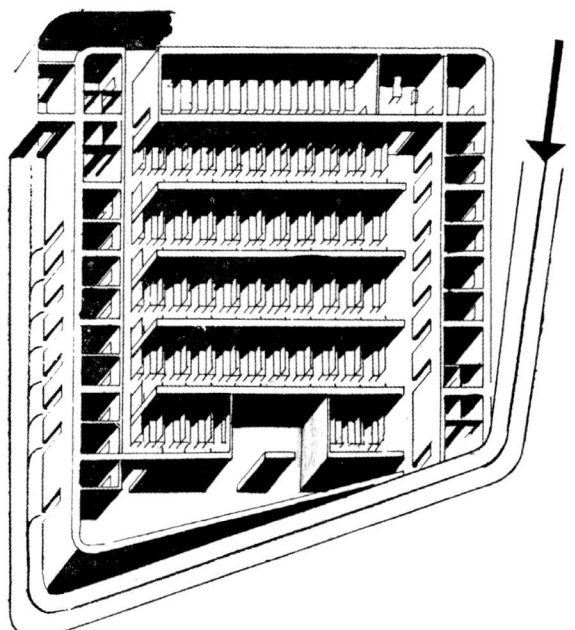

209. bleu. 3 m.
222 jaune. 5 m.
205 vert. 3 m.
227 rouge 1 m.
210. orange 1 m.
215 vert 2 m
570
299
1200.
8
12
5
neon
6
rouge
Egout bleu
metro vert
100 mètres
150 mètres
50 mètres

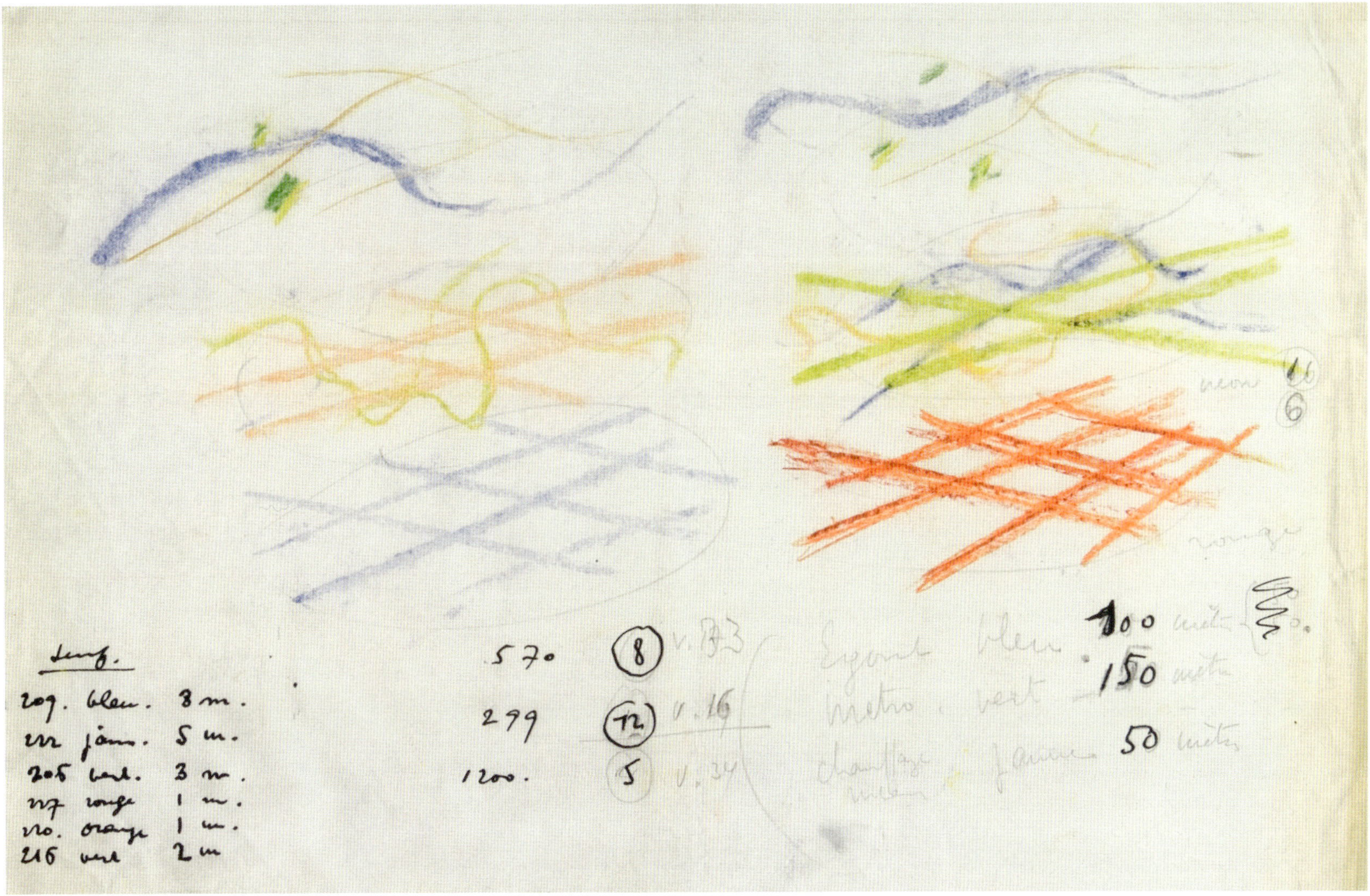

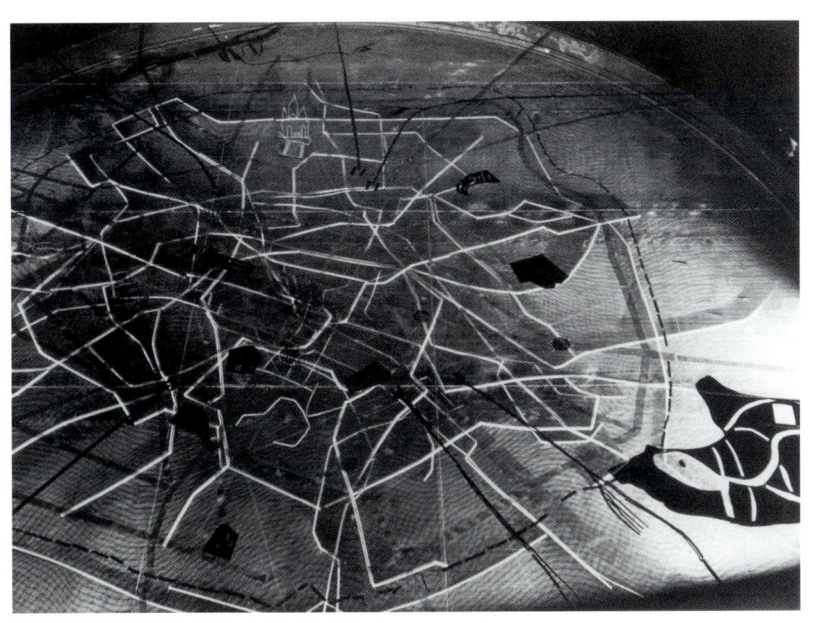

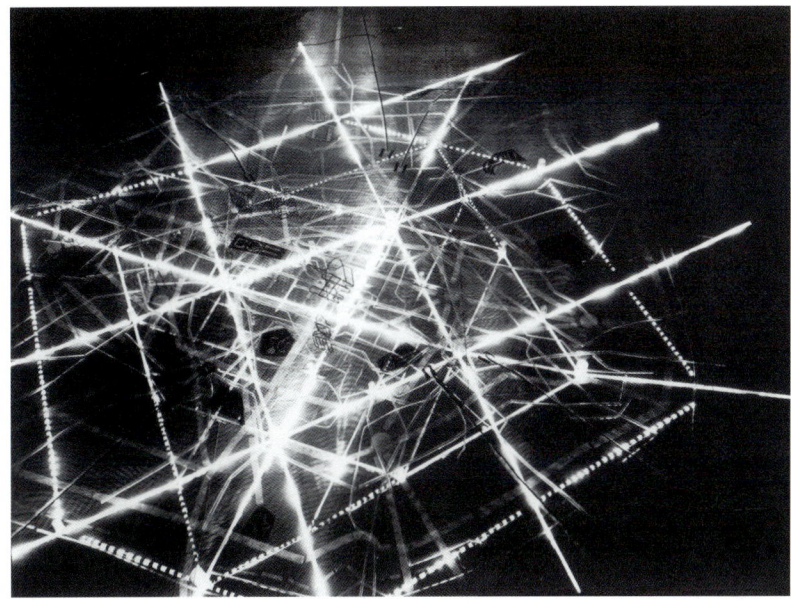

which grottoes are transmuted into caverns—a hellish vision projected onto the landscape of the Industrial Revolution.²⁹

Tschumi also presented a masterful, less conventional effort—an illuminated circular model. Not a diorama—the model offers no perspectives—it appeared instead as a kind of sandwiched assemblage in bird's eye view. The model was displayed suspended above the major stairway descending from the main hall. Three layers were superimposed: the lower grid, the infrastructure (including subway and sewers), and the ground plane of the city. Tschumi aimed for two distinct readings: on one hand, he wanted to stage a manifesto and, on the other, to seduce the public with a play of shadows and multi-colored light. Sketches for the project show the use of polychromy to distinguished the different networks (Plate 14). Black-and-white photographs of the installation succeed in dramatizing these chromatic effects (Plates 15, 16). However, this photographic documentation—all that remains today of *Paris Souterrain*—barely registers the curi-

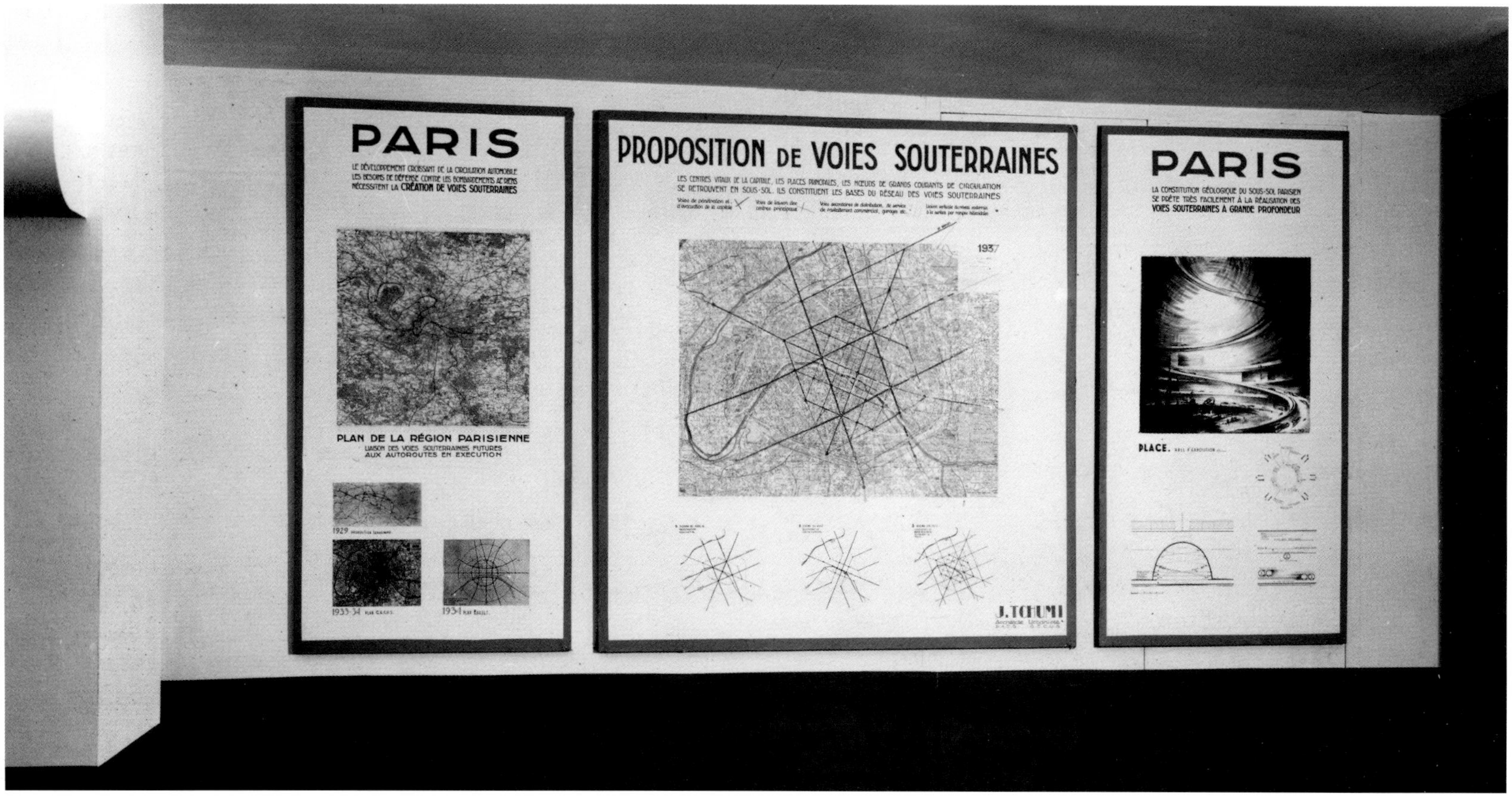

17
Paris Souterrain, 1937, perspective of spiral crossroads under a parabolic cupola

18
Triptych of *Paris Souterrain*, 1937, installation photograph

19
Cover of special issue of *Le monde souterrain, Paris 1937*, edited by Edouard Utudjian, showing "Underground Paris" as a central and diagonal system with four interfaces

osity, even stupefaction, of the viewing public at the time. The technical description of the project, which was presented under the signature of "Ed. Utudjian-Jean Tschumi," explains that the model was made out of superimposed metal trellises and a kind of Plexiglas. The shallowest programmatic layer housing the metro, sewage, and other servicing was represented using violet fluorescent tubing. The deepest layer was illuminated by wider red-neon lights. Electric power switches allowed for effects of effacement and intermixing.[30]

Tschumi and Utudjian insisted on the contemporaneity of their subject, given its historic date; in 1937 the project proclaimed a sense of urgency. The heavy weight of Hitler's German Pavilion had entailed expensive and complex foundation work, all subsidized by the French government. War had already broken out in Abyssinia and Spain. *Paris Souterrain*, contemporary accounts suggest, evoked the impending catastrophe, "the dangers that threaten the population of Paris and its public service sector…. The most unfavorable outcome…[was] also the most probable one: an aerial attack launched without a declaration of war and perhaps even without any diplomatic tension."[31] In wartime, we create shelters and hospitals; in times of peace, we generate automobile congestion. At street level, historic monuments are preserved. The plan's technical feasibility was taken for granted. The major works proposed by the architects would virtually eliminate unemployment. Toll collection would insure a secure return on capital investment. Utudjian and Tschumi proclaimed, "We are carving into the Depths,"[32] using a Dantesque capital "D." How could this underground poetics be understood or interpreted apart from catastrophes, volcanic eruptions, or earthquakes? The model for the GECUS project adopted the vigor of a manifesto and inserted itself firmly within the avant-garde tradition.

The age of romanticism is over. As a project, *Paris Souterrain* can be located in the literary and cinematic realm of H. G. Wells. *Things To Come*, a film based on a Wells screenplay and directed by William Cameron Menzies, debuted in England in 1936. Its story is a journey into the future that presents chronological markers. The film is set rather prophetically in London around 1940, in a city besieged by aerial bombardment. The bombs are chemical. Those who survive them are subjected to the regime of a capricious dictator. Several decades later a futuristic airplane appears from out of the sky, piloted by an alien messenger sent by a group of Freemason scientists. The dictator then commits suicide. Technological advances govern the city's reconstruction under the generic name of "Everytown," and by 2036 the city moves underground. Neither the Shakespearian play of the protagonists nor Wells' dialogue matches the empirical and enduring vision of Utudjian for underground urbanism.[33] Menzies' filmic imagery both revives and cancels Fritz Lang's earlier sets (in Berlin) for *Metropolis*, a city of stone skyscrapers in the manner of Manhattan. Yet Lang's and Menzies' imaginary cities are dominated by a new urban paradigm, the "rule of the air." Tschumi was himself a collector of airplane photographs. Ironically, the first aircraft highlighted in *Things to Come* was the disarmed "Tiger Moth" biplane designated for flight schools—not exactly the most technically advanced model available at the time. Later, at the outburst of the war in 1940, a new generation of double-deckers hovers over the city. I wonder if these images could be compared to Tschumi's underground circulation dome with its helical ramps. The scenes from Menzies' underground city similarly recall Eugène Freyssinet's parabolic vaults with glass panels manufactured by Saint-Gobain and dynamic ellipses and cupolas. The question remains: to what extent can the poetics of a film resonate on the poetics of an architectural project? Menzies' film was known in Paris. As the engineer André Basdevant exclaimed in the GECUS journal, *Le Monde Souterrain*, "What a veritable epic journey—man's triumphal march toward the center of the earth."[34]

Menzies' film and Tschumi's illuminated model for *Paris Souterrain* bring us back to the reality of 1937. The Paris Exposition of the same year welcomed a show of military force on a platform of national propaganda that sought to operate through the power of seductive slogans. A year earlier, the Berlin Olympics crystallized nationalist alliances and antagonisms. In the same way, the propaganda for GECUS was likely to rally around a provisional cease-fire between sworn enemies. The first "International Congress on Underground Urbanism" convened a group of engineers who touted their beneficent deeds: the drying-up of marshlands in Italy, Mussolini's urbanist forays, the boring of the Moscow subway under Stalin, and the large-scale projects in Lyon undertaken by the radical Socialist mayor, Edouard Herriot, including drainage of the Fourvière hill west of the city. Tschumi was not an engineer-surveyor-topographer, but truly an architect-urbanist. How did he act upon his deepening interest in the underground city? He had already approached regional authorities in Bern about converting the underground parking lot of the casino into a reinforced concrete bunker, seated on a mortar blast from the Federal Palace (Plate 13). Living and working in Paris in proximity to Utudjian, Tschumi refined his *Paris Souterrain* utopia, working at a scale of 1:10,000 meters. The geological cuts through the basin of the Seine river were reproduced so as to accommodate their project precisely. In fall 1939 Tschumi wrote to the French Ministry of War to enlist in the *Défense Nationale*—given Switzerland's neutrality, he thought he could instead be of some use to the French war effort.[35] Tschumi was acknowledged to be fit for the task, but the unanticipated French defeat in summer 1940 changed the narrative. Beginning in winter 1940–1941 he began his bifurcated life between Paris and Lausanne. During two decades, the theme of the tower would stay at the core of his architecture (Plates 216–224). The question of "map" versus "territory" manifested itself at the very moment the war began and destroyed all maps, revealing in their stead the lethal reality of conflict for those who survived.

Notes

[1] Louise Kaplan, *Cultures of Fetishism*, Pallgrave Macmillian, New York, 2007, p. 108.
[2] Paraphrase of statement made by Pierluigi Panza, *Corriere della Sera*, 17 March 2008.
[3] I am referring to a transcript written in 1956 by Alex Gerber, a student at EPUL and intern at Tschumi's office in Lausanne, and to an oral account from 11 January 2008.
[4] Citation from a 1931 conference of the American Mathematical Society held in New Orleans. I insist on maintaining a distance from Korzybski's ulterior motives in his *General Semantics*, from the racist and elitist ideology in which his unacceptable psychotherapeutic hypotheses originate.
[5] Alfred Korzybski, *Science and Sanity – An Introduction to Non-Aristotelian Systems and General Semantics* (1933), reprinted by the Institute of General Semantics, Fort Worth, TX, 1973, p. 38.
[6] See the lively and incisive remarks on the subject by Mario Ageno, Enrico Fermi's pupil, in *La Costruzione Operativa della Fisica*, Boringhieri, Turin, 1970, pp. 24–47.
[7] The aphorism attributed (without concrete evidence) to Muthesius would later be linked to Gropius, Le Corbusier, Rogers, Albini, and Gregotti as a way of proving their "rationalist" value.
[8] Designed by Dante Giacosa, the *Nuova Cinquecento* rolled off the Fiat assembly line starting in 1957.
[9] Mies worked on this project from 1911 to 1912. See Franz Schultze, *Mies van der Rohe, A Critical Biography*, Chicago University Press, Chicago, 1985, and Sergio Polano's essay, "Rose-shaped like an Open Hand, Helene Kröller-Müller's House," *Rassegna*, vol. 15, no. 56, 1993, pp. 23–27.
[10] See, for example, the Philadelphia Water Works designed by the engineer Frederick Graff in 1819–1922.
[11] Betty J. Blum, *Oral History of Natalie de Blois*. De Blois recalled her work from the 1950s while at SOM in New York.
[12] See Philip Ursprung, "Douleur fantôme," *Tracé* no. 9, 2007, p. 12. Ursprung discusses the German term *Raumprothesen*.
[13] As recounted by the engineer Maurice Cosandey, 5 March 2008.
[14] The pedagogical method of "Learning by Doing" was developed by the founder of the World Scout Movement, Robert Baden-Powell, then theorized in relation to art production by John Dewey.
[15] The Lausanne National Exposition from 1964 presented a multitude of innovative details and ingenious systems.
[16] "*Non c'è dettaglio in architettura: tutte le cose sono d'uguale importanza*," a remark made at the Accademia di architettura, University of Italian Switzerland, Mendrisio, 17 October 2003.
[17] A thick dossier on the competition was published later as *Förslag till ny stadsplan för Nedre Norrmalm i Stockholm M. M.*, Department of Urbanism, Stockholm, 1936.
[18] *Det Framtida Stockholm, Riktlinjer för Stockholms Generalplan*, K. L. Beckman, Stockholm, 1946. Summary in English.
[19] In addition to the Stockholm competition, Tschumi received third prize in 1931 for an urban expansion competition for the city of Renens; in 1932 he received third prize for an urban expansion competition for Lausanne. All three entries were submitted with Henri Vermeil. See Sylvain Malfroy, "L'axe et le 'Skyline' – Notes sur l'urbanisme de Jean Tschumi," *Faces*, no. 39, 1996, pp. 10–17.
[20] All that remains of the plans and elevations are a few gray photographs. The drawings are scaled at 1:600.
[21] Jean Tschumi, typed manuscript, ACM, Wegener-Tschumi Collection.
[22] Ludwig Hilbersheimer, *Groszstadtarchitektur*, Julius Hoffmann, Stuttgart, 1927. It is likely that this book was known at the Institute of Urbanism at the University of Paris, especially after Jacques Gréber made his proposal for Benjamin Franklin Parkway in Philadelphia. Tschumi also read German.
[23] Pamphlet titled *Concours de projets concernant le plan urbain pour la partie de Stockholm appelée Nedere Norrmalm, appreciations du jury*, K. L. Beckman, Stockholm, 11 January 1934. I would like to thank the architect Hans Matell from Uppsala for providing me with a copy of this material in 1988.
[24] Jean Tschumi, undated typed manuscript (circa 1953) for a conference titled "Les créations urbaines at la recherche de la *Ville idéale*" at the EPUL.
[25] "Paris 1937, Exposition Internationale, Classe 17ter, Urbanisme souterrain," *Le Monde Souterrain*, no. 15–17, Nov. 1937, p. 114. See also Sabine Brales, *City Planning and Underground Space in 20th and 21st Century France*, Laboratoire Théorie des Mutations Urbaines, Paris, 2006.
[26] Gabriel Chesneau, *Histoire de l'Ecole des Mines*, available on the Internet at www.annales.org/archives/x/ecole.htm.
[27] For the case of Milan, see Piero Bottoni, *Urbanistica*, Hoepli, Milan, 1938. He illustrates compelling images of urban congestion in the city around 1935.
[28] Jacques Gréber, "L'urbanisme souterrain à l'Exposition de 1937," *Le Monde Souterrain*, Special issue, 1937, p. 113.
[29] Enrico Castelnuovo, "Arte e rivoluzione industriale (1972)," in *Arte, industria, rivoluzioni*, Edizioni della Normale, Pisa, 2007, pp. 118–120.
[30] Rhône-Poulenc developed the technological innovation of fluorescent-tube lighting.
[31] *Le Monde Souterrain*, Special issue, 1937, p. 136.
[32] Ibid., p. 137.
[33] Ibid., p. 132. In his last address to the Congress, Utudjian remarked on the "anticipation" and "dream" of Wells. He saw the film in France, where it was distributed under the title *Vie Future*. I am assuming that Tschumi also saw the film.
[34] Ibid., p. 177.
[35] Letter from Jean Tschumi, ACM, Wegener-Tschumi Collection.

20
Fun Palace, from a "sketch-sketch" competition at Pontremoli's studio, circa 1928, pencil, chalk, gouache, and India ink. Pictorial virtuosity aimed at seducing the jury in a glance

A Swiss in Paris

Baby Boom in Geneva

Tschumi was born near Geneva, in the adjacent commune of Plainpalais, on February 14, 1904. His mother, Maria, originally came from a village near Lucerne. His father was from Bern. The baby was given a name that corresponded to the French translation of the name of his father, Johann, who was a cabinetmaker by training. In 1896 Plainpalais was host to the Swiss National Exhibition, a spectacular show presented under the modern banner of the electrical industry. Plainpalais had the advantage of being a suburb of Geneva, and thus a beneficiary of the city's rapid urbanization. The expansion of middle-class and workers' housing encouraged the development of flour mills, slaughterhouses, stables, printmaking workshops, and numerous *ateliers* for iron- and woodworking. Workers came from all over Switzerland, but also from Italy, Germany, and France.

In 1848, after a cascade of revolutions throughout Europe, Geneva had attracted an elite group of refugees from Poland, Germany, and Italy. By the end of the century the situation was quite different. Some patriots nostalgically remembered Switzerland's picturesque stature, along with the official church in Geneva and its doctrine of "new Rome" Calvinism. The younger, more modern generation recalled the glorious past of the country's banks and industries and its contributions to literature and natural science. The printing presses grew in large and small numbers without interruption. The university library was replete with economic and political treatises, magazines, pamphlets, and newspapers. All the political and economic "-isms" took root and flourished in Geneva: capitalism, liberalism, socialism, communism, internationalism, and anarchism. Class struggle was evident in the street and in commerce. The local government was kept busy. Vladimir Uljanov, later known by the name Lenin, read, wrote, lectured, and rode his bicycle in Plainpalais while Tschumi was still a baby.[1]

Among the other architecturally notable children raised in Geneva at the turn of the century, three names come to mind. The first, William Lescaze (1896–1969), was eight years Tschumi's senior. Forty years later, as an established International Style architect in New York, Lescaze would provide Tschumi with essential visual references that were imbued with a quality of elegance in the realm of design.[2] The second, Pierre Jeanneret (1896–1967), was the son of a surgeon and raised in a wealthy neighborhood that overlooked the hospital. In Paris Jeanneret entered a partnership with his more famous cousin, Le Corbusier, and co-authored the *Œuvres Complètes*. At the beginning of the 1930s Tschumi familiarized himself with Le Corbusier's architecture and urban planning proposals. Lastly, Alberto Sartoris (1901–1998) was born in Turin but raised in Geneva, where his father was a sculptor. Sartoris became involved with the avant-garde movement at the end of the 1920s and published several visual anthologies that became standard-bearers for the Modern Movement in Italy. Copied from the Futurists, Sartoris' anti-academic rhetoric would offer little inspiration for the Beaux-Arts trained Tschumi.

Tracing this rather improbable Geneva-based constellation of Lescaze-Jeanneret-Sartoris-Tschumi, the reader might wonder if birthplace holds a particularly meaningful place in history. In fact, I would be inclined to question the notion of generation as used in reference to architects. Henry-Russell Hitchcock, best known as the co-author of the International Style and for his foundational studies of nineteenth- and twentieth-century architecture, distinguished between two generations of pioneers—first Berlage-Behrens-Wright, then Gropius-Mies-Le Corbusier. Only a decade separates these two groups, and using a similar logic based on birth dates, one could argue that even a separation of five years would suffice. And yet looking at the members of the Bauhaus, Kandinsky (b. 1866) and the younger Breuer (b. 1902) worked together within a progressive structure and mutual inspiration. In fact, the notion of generation seems irrelevant if one considers the heterogeneous multiplicities and tendencies that constitute any given historical "moment" as a collection of anachronisms, breaks, and continuities. George Kubler's *The Shape of Time* demonstrates this fact. Historical periods do not necessarily coincide with generations. Whatever the parameters for periodic divisions—revolutionary dates or economic crises—the pluralism of trends remains. Today, what is the primary challenge to architecture if not the project of the present? This project distinguishes among architects according to their affinities and differences, regardless of their ages.

In 1919, after the millions left dead on the battlefields of World War I (known in Europe as the Great War), the Nobel Peace Prize was awarded to Woodrow Wilson. His political agenda was promoted by the Treaty of Versailles and founded on the utopian ideal of establishing an international body, the League of Nations, dedicated to the negotiation of conflicts. Wilson played an integral role in choosing Geneva as the location for the institution's headquarters. Switzerland's history of political "neutrality" provided one plausible explanation for such a choice. Another hinged on Wilson's strong Protestant convictions; Geneva celebrated its Calvinist roots and, for Wilson, embodied a "citadel of Protestantism."

In 1927, after the official launching of an international competition for the League of Nations, Le Corbusier used his proposal as a way to present and promote the superiority of his work on an international platform as well as to challenge the Parisian academic establishment. After World War II, Harry Truman supplanted the League with the United Nations, reinforcing the internationalist role of the organization, for which Geneva remained one headquarters. In 1960 Tschumi won the competition for the World Health Organization's headquarters, also in Geneva. He died shortly after this victory, leaving behind a posthumous edifice.

21
Worker's bedroom, April 1920, pencil and watercolor, one of two winning entries (at age 16) in competition sponsored by the Industrial and Commercial Society of Lausanne

Renens and Lausanne, along the Paris-Milan Rail Route

Let's return to the beginning of our story. In 1906 Johann Tschumi moved his family to Renens in order to establish his own cabinet-making workshop. This working-class area two miles west of Lausanne was expanding along the railway line, and in the same year the Simplon tunnel opened, making way for a direct Paris-Milan route. A city known for its private schools and hotels overlooking the lake, Lausanne would now occupy a strategic position because of its proximity to the transportation link. The subsequent growth of industrial production offered new hope for small enterprises. The family's relocation to Renens, then, established the possibility of upward mobility.

Young Jean was raised amidst the combined and alternating scents of coal, sawdust, glue, lilacs, sewers, milk, and chocolate. As an independent artisan, his father hoped that his son would attain a higher status within the established corporate hierarchy. It was under Johann's tutelage that the younger Tschumi developed his skills in drawing and woodworking. In 1918 and at the age of 14, Tschumi received his elementary school certificate and was employed as an apprentice by one of the few architects in Lausanne whom the construction crisis of 1917–1922 had spared; Charles Braun would go on to complete one of the new convention halls for the city's commercial exhibition, known as the "Comptoir Suisse." At Braun's office Tschumi learned to copy the canonical orders. He also took professional courses under the supervision of Frédéric Gilliard (1884–1967), an architect engaged in the cooperative housing movement as well as in historic preservation. Gilliard expected his students to measure and draw the entry gates to Lausanne's City Hall. At the age of 16, Tschumi received a certificate of distinction from the Industrial and Commercial Society of Lausanne for two low-cost furniture proposals, one for workers' sleeping quarters and the other for a living room (Plates 21–23). Tschumi left Renens and relocated to Bienne. He had spent his childhood and adolescence between Renens and Lausanne. Later, this area would host a social and professional life shared between two cities along the Simplon rail line. His death, too, took place on the express night train.

22
Living room, April 1920, pencil and watercolor, one of two winning entries in competition sponsored by the Industrial and Commercial Society of Lausanne

23
Living room, April 1920, pencil and watercolor, detail showing the pictorial abilities of the designer

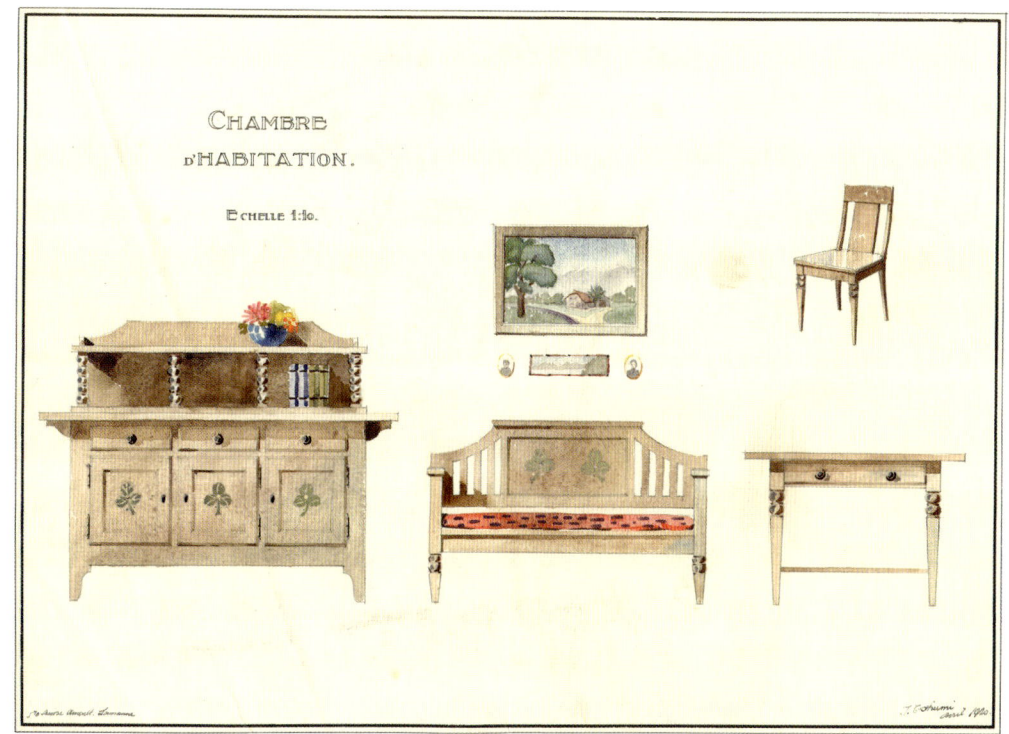

In Bienne, near Bern

Johann Tschumi's decision to enroll his son in Bienne's *Technicum* begged the question: why not send him to Geneva's Ecole des Beaux-Arts? This remarkable institution subsidized by the city functioned as a training ground for the designers who were employed by the most prestigious firms of the day. Jeanneret and Sartoris' fathers had sent their sons to the Beaux-Arts in Geneva because they lived in the area. But times were difficult throughout Switzerland. The end of World War I precipitated an often-violent social crisis. The majority of the country's population was affected by low wages and a high cost of living. Part of Johann's family came from the canton of Bern and lived in Bienne, so the choice of the *Technicum* was a logical one. Home to Omega and Rolex, Bienne was officially recognized as a bilingual French-German city, and it had taken part in the industrial developments initiated in the eighteenth century. In 1935 the Socialist mayor of Bienne, Guido Müller, successfully convinced General Motors to establish an assembly plant there. A year later, the first Buicks rolled off the line. With their six cylinders, they were the vehicles of choice for the butchers as well as the "rich peasants." But Bienne also had its lake and its vineyards, which overlooked the island of St. Peter, the patron saint of fishermen. This landscape was well-trodden in Jean-Jacques Rousseau's writings: one need only recall Rousseau's status in France as the patron of carpentry. In his pedagogical treatise *L'Emile ou de l'éducation* (1762), the little boy is initiated in the art of woodwork. This physical and artisanal practice was seen as the pathway to good hygiene, utility, dexterity, and taste.

From summer 1919 to spring 1922, Jean Tschumi studied architecture at the *Bauschule* division of the *Technicum*. This education roughly corresponded to the state-funded institutes of technology in Zurich, Paris, or Berlin, where practical training was the objective. In Berlin a former student from the *Technicum*, the architect Otto Rudolf Salvisberg (1882–1940), was leading a prolific practice. In the 1930s he was invited to teach the diploma studio at the Federal Institute of Technology in Zurich (ETH), and from that point on would be known as one of the first professors in Europe to foster functionalism as a formal design methodology. He also became the architect for the chemical company Hoffmann-La Roche in Basel, designing their laboratories and office spaces.[3] These corporate projects for the pharmaceutical industry served as a model for Tschumi's later work. In the meantime Tschumi, now 15, was busy copying casts of Roman friezes and cornices (Plate 5). He also had to render perspectives of local monuments. Two semesters were devoted to intense drills in the representation of curves, geometrical solids, hyperboles, cycloids, and cut cylinders (Plates 24, 25). He also developed an interest in rendering watercolor landscapes. For six semesters, the stu-

24
Hyperbola, exercise in descriptive geometry, Biel, 1919, black and red India ink

25
Cycloid, exercise in descriptive geometry, Biel, 1919, black and red India ink

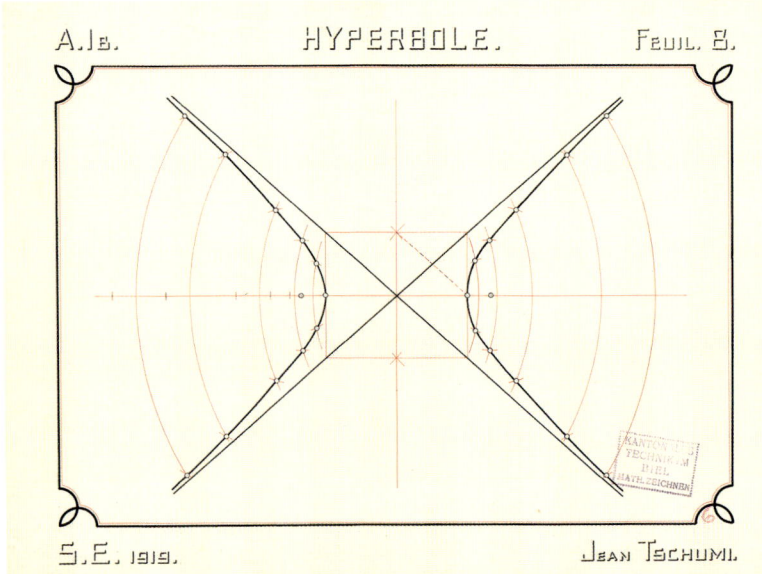

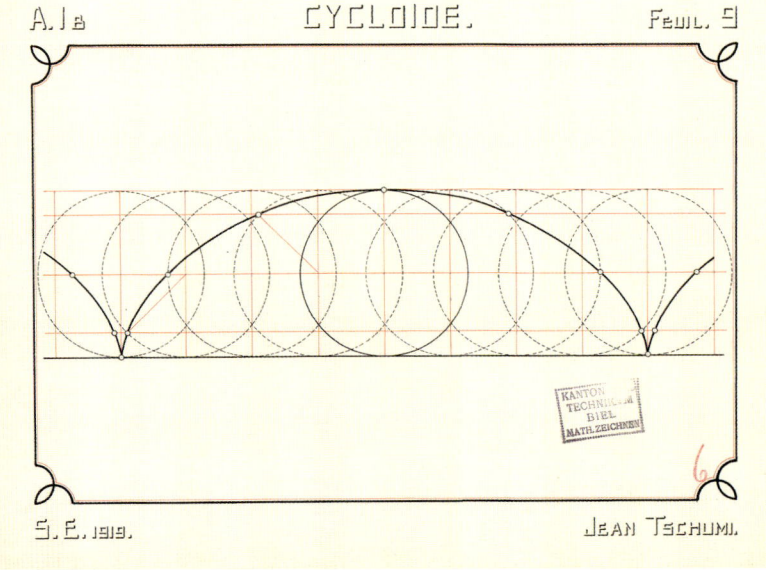

dents were asked to draw plans, sections, and elevations at the same scale on one board (Plate 30), a method that replicated J. N. L. Durand's lessons in his *Précis* (See chapter 4). Large- and small-scale programs were assigned, and attention was given to both urban and rural sites. The few drawings that remain from these years illustrate not only Tschumi's level of taste, but also the pleasure that he took in his work (Plates 27–29).

After receiving his diploma in spring 1922, three career possibilities lay before the young architect. The first was to find a job in some well-known professional practice. However, an economic downturn triggered by the war made this prospect risky. Building production was reduced to a few high-profile projects—largely the reconstruction of banks, since financing monumental palaces permitted them to avoid war taxation. Another solution would have been to work in a smaller office, but again, work opportunities in Switzerland were rare. The final possibility was to study at a higher level. Tschumi had been an excellent student and his training at Bienne prepared him to face the selection process for admission into the most prestigious schools. This last scenario prevailed.

Why did the Swiss Tschumi not go to Zurich and attend the Federal Institute of Technology? In that school, continuity of classwork, semester after semester, was required. Since there were no scholarships available to students at the time, only those with financial backing from their families could afford to attend. At the ETH some engineering students came from the countryside where their fathers operated lucrative businesses. The fact that the Ecole des Beaux-Arts in Paris had developed a more "egalitarian" system appealed to Tschumi. In order to advance, students did not have to take all their exams at predetermined dates; they could suspend their studies so as to earn money. Many firms in Paris approached Beaux-Arts students and offered them employment.[4] This system had two advantages. It was a method of self-support for those who did not have independent means. It also meant the discovery of a professional life, allowing students to work part-time as apprentices while completing their academic training. Before long, Tschumi was bound for France.

26
African elephant, copy of a sculpture in the round, Biel, winter term exercise, 1918–1919, pencil and charcoal on blue paper

27
Decorative frieze, Biel, 1919, India ink and gouache on paper, pattern suitable for wood carving

28
Alpine landscape, 1921, pen and India ink

29
Project from class on rural architecture, detail, Biel, 1920–1921, pen and India ink

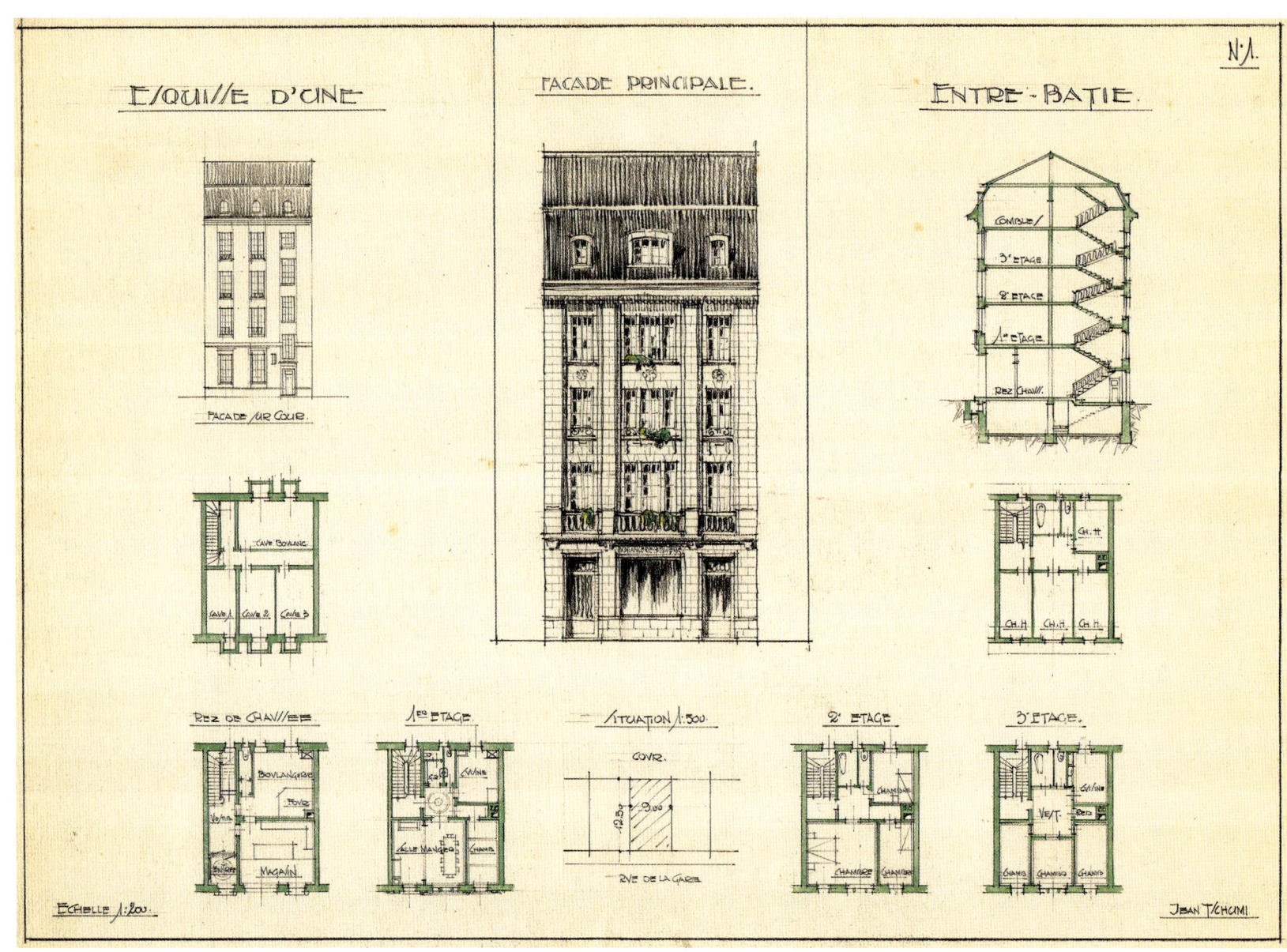

30
Project for an apartment house on Railroad Station Street showing a realistic approach to local urban typology, Biel, 1922, pencil and watercolor

Arras, then Paris

Before landing in Paris and going through the examinations that would open the door to the Beaux-Arts, the young architect had to find a job. Tschumi went to Arras, one of Vauban's classical citadels in the region of Pas-de-Calais. The city had been flattened in 1915 by the Kaiser's artillery (Plate 31). Other cities and towns in northeastern France had also been destroyed during the war; indeed, it was in this region that focus was put on "national reconstruction," which was funded by Germany according to the 1919 Treaty of Versailles. The young Sartoris went to the city of Reims in this area after receiving his degree from the Geneva Beaux-Arts. The master plan for the reconstruction of Reims was designed by the American architect George B. Ford (1878–1930), who had studied at both MIT and the Beaux-Arts in Paris.[5] Sartoris was employed for a year by one of Ford's French colleagues working on a design for a new wheat mill. The year was 1920 and Sartoris was 19.[6] For much of the war, the front line of battle was simply in Arras' eastern suburbs; the city's great public squares, town hall, and cathedral experienced widespread devastation. The principle of "identical reconstruction" was espoused for rebuilding arcaded properties and the town hall, although concrete was widely used for internal structures.[7] We do not know who employed Tschumi, but it was probably an architect trained at the Beaux-Arts and licensed by the government. All we know is that the Swiss architect worked in Arras for ten months.

Afterwards Tschumi arrived in Paris in February 1923 and found a hotel room. It would take him nine full years to obtain his diploma at the Beaux-Arts. During this period he moved seven times from one hotel room to another and from temporary accommodations in Paris and the outer suburbs. He could afford a permanent address only after receiving his diploma. In spring 1923 he contacted the Swiss embassy because foreign students had to be formally presented by their ambassadors. Such a letter of introduction played a decisive role in the selection of the degree candidates; the French government guaranteed the supreme quality of the degree. The ensuing title was DPLG (*Diplômé par le Gouvernement*) and thus sponsored and recognized by the State. Tschumi had already undergone three years of training in Bienne and was a talented draftsman. He passed the exams in June and a month later was admitted to the Beaux-Arts to work under the tutelage of Emmanuel Pontremoli (1865–1956).[8]

31
Town Square, Arras, February 1919, Schutz Documentary Mission, courtesy of Library of Congress, Washington, DC

Emmanuel Pontremoli

One must remember that Beaux-Arts students were expected to develop their studies in the same atelier. The same advisor or *Patron* supervised them. The complete cycle was divided in two successive ranks, from second to *première classe*. Examinations were organized as a seasonal exhibition in which drawings were pinned up anonymously and the various studios were placed in overt competition. The jury was the gathering of the professors teaching design. They defended their own students. Emulation, competitiveness, and fair play were the moral principals needed to bring improvement and progress to architecture. The renderings pinned up without names were inseparable from the graphic style of one particular studio (Plate 20). Students were quite literally associated with the name of their *Patron*. During his studies Tschumi would refer to himself as a "Pontremoli." This designation remained with Tschumi throughout his career, and the atelier was nicknamed "At. Pont." At the Beaux-Arts the jury distributed credits (*valeurs*), honorable mentions, medals, and prizes (Plate 35). The distribution acknowledged both the personal aura of the studio masters and the collective identity of their students.

What lessons did Tschumi learn from his time with Pontremoli? Undisputed is that he was an insightful student, ready to work for all immediate and practical advantages. He had to secure the future of his life in Paris. The first lesson was short and perhaps trivial: gaining the confidence of wealthy clients. A second lesson: an architectural project should be a complete work of art, not only walls and windows but also furniture and technical equipment. A third was that architectural history offers a large reservoir of ideas that could be utilized in response to contemporary programs. The fourth important lesson had to do with the method of composition. Variables had to be tested during the study of the project. To sustain these hypotheses I will first sketch a brief presentation of the master and then open two further chapters.

It was often rumored at the Beaux-Arts that Pontremoli had built his practice and reputation on one mythical project, the Villa Kérylos.[9] Somewhat in the manner of the *chef-d'œuvre inconnu* or unknown masterpiece, the villa was an inaccessible, well-protected private house located some 900 kilometers outside of Paris; Pontremoli published his project only in 1934, a quarter of a century after its

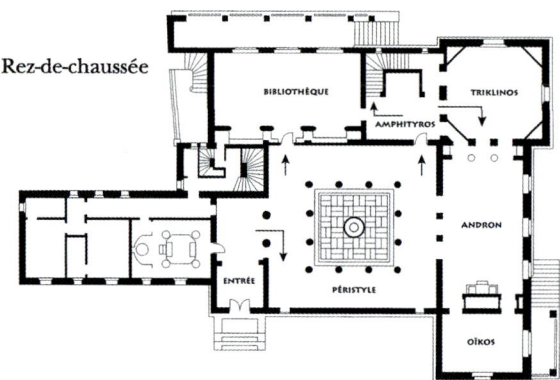
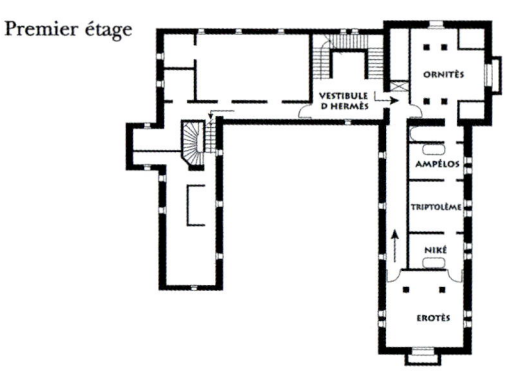

32
Emmanuel Pontremoli, Villa Kérylos, Beaulieu-sur-Mer, 1902–1908, three views of the peristyle as published by Robert Castellana, 1998

33
Emmanuel Pontremoli, plan of the Villa Kérylos, Beaulieu-sur-Mer, 1902–1908, first and second floor as published by Robert Castellana, 1998

34
Detail of project for the lobby of a corporate building, exercise at Pontremoli's studio, 1929, pencil and charcoal on tracing paper

construction. Born in Nice and the son of a rabbi, Pontremoli received the French government's Grand Prix de Rome in 1890. This major prize was awarded to those individuals who represented the best in scholarship. Its recipient was deemed the best in his discipline. Winners were given a residency in Rome at the expense of the State. In return, they were required to send the results of their postgraduate achievements to Paris. They generally worked on the restoration of Greek and Roman monuments and cities built in Italy and the Eastern Mediterranean. The word "restoration" implied a drawn hypothesis of the initial conditions of the monument, a dream of perfection. Pontremoli focused his interest on Greece and its archeology. He took part in excavations. He collaborated with the archeologist Maxime Collignon on the publication of their research on the architecture of the Acropolis in Pergamon, which was shown in Paris at the World Exhibition of 1900.

Pontremoli's research closely paralleled the work of the French historian, antiquarian, and numismatist Théodore Reinach (1860–1928), who also had a passion for Greek antiquity. Pontremoli was commissioned to design his luxurious house, which was named after the Greek word for sea swallow. Built in the years 1902–1908 in a town near Nice, it was a creative exercise in the use of modern archeology.[10] Villa Kérylos reflected Pliny's description of his Laurentian villa overlooking the Mediterranean. The latest developments in sanitation, heating, lighting, and technical equipment were employed. Reinach was lucky to be able to use his wife's fortune. The final cost of their project amounted to nine million francs.[11]

A major design source for the architect was the reinterpretation of the Greek house described by Vitruvius in Book VI, Chapter VII: "The Greeks, having no use for atriums, do not build them, but instead make passageways for people entering from the front door....From it one enters the Peristyle."[12] Pontremoli had examined an archeological example at Delos that corresponded to Vitruvius' description. Pontremoli bypassed the difficulty in building a closed patio flanked by Doric porticos. His peristyle commanded the entrance to the reception rooms (Plates 32, 33). On the first floor the same orthogonal disposition in long perspective combined in a suite the Pompeian-red *chambre de monsieur* and the blue *chambre de madame*. The rooms' decoration emulated mural painting according to instructions laid out by Vitruvius. Inventive solutions had to be found for bathtubs, radiators, and the Pleyel piano. The house had a living area of almost one square mile (1,500 square meters). Nevertheless, it was said to be "modest"[13] in comparison with the antique models.

It might be amusing to recall that when a Beaux-Arts professor pronounced the name Vitruvius, all students repeated in chorus, "the Father of us all."[14] Jokes were a ritual in the atelier. Pontremoli himself wrote: "Each studio is like a little republic...where cutting caricature corrects the most absolute of temperaments." His students shared a distinctive taboo. They had banned a word the *Patron* considered to be inappropriate: "The word *corridor* was forbidden. Rather, students had to create a *gallery*."[15] This theoretical insistence on the contemporary relevance of the gallery was inherited from Durand, whose centennial textbooks were recognized as authorities on the subject. On the other hand, Villa Kérylos was an example that respected the nobility of the peristyle gallery and denounced the triviality of the corridor. The conviction that historical buildings, when observed with accuracy and in response to contemporary programs, could be primary sources for design was not exclusive to the Beaux-Arts. On the contrary, the two major inventors of the "anti-academic" tradition, Viollet-le-Duc and Le Corbusier, shared this sentiment. Their polemical campaigns against the educational monopoly of the Beaux-Arts were founded on a notion of "truth" found in architectural history, whether in the brilliant rationality of Gothic structure, the geometrical and industrial order of the Doric temple, or the Roman solidity of mass and volumes in the form of primary geometries. Viollet-le-Duc and Le Corbusier waged their battles on the hostile field of history.

Pontremoli expected his students to become virtuosos in architectural rendering, in both monochromy (Plates 34, 36) and polychromy, mixing pencil, charcoal, pastel, gouache, tempera, liquid gold, and vaporized colors. Pontremoli's students learned to create the underlay for their perspectives. As Robert Camelot notes, tracing paper was moistened in a bowl of tea, which would give it a particu-

35
Postage stamp for the 1930 Exposition Nationale des Beaux-Arts, Rougevin competition at the Ecole, 1928, India ink simulation of a woodcarving with three monuments, diagonal superposition. Second prize was awarded to Tschumi's entry, which was then reproduced as a photo-lithograph.

36
Commercial building on a boulevard, exercise at Pontremoli's studio, pencil and charcoal on tracing paper. Later dated 1928

37
The *bar américain* at La Coupole on Boulevard Montparnasse in winter rain, anonymous photographer, circa 1933

38
Café Le Rouquet, 188 Boulevard Saint-Germain, three sketches on tracing paper. Research into order, proportions, polychromy

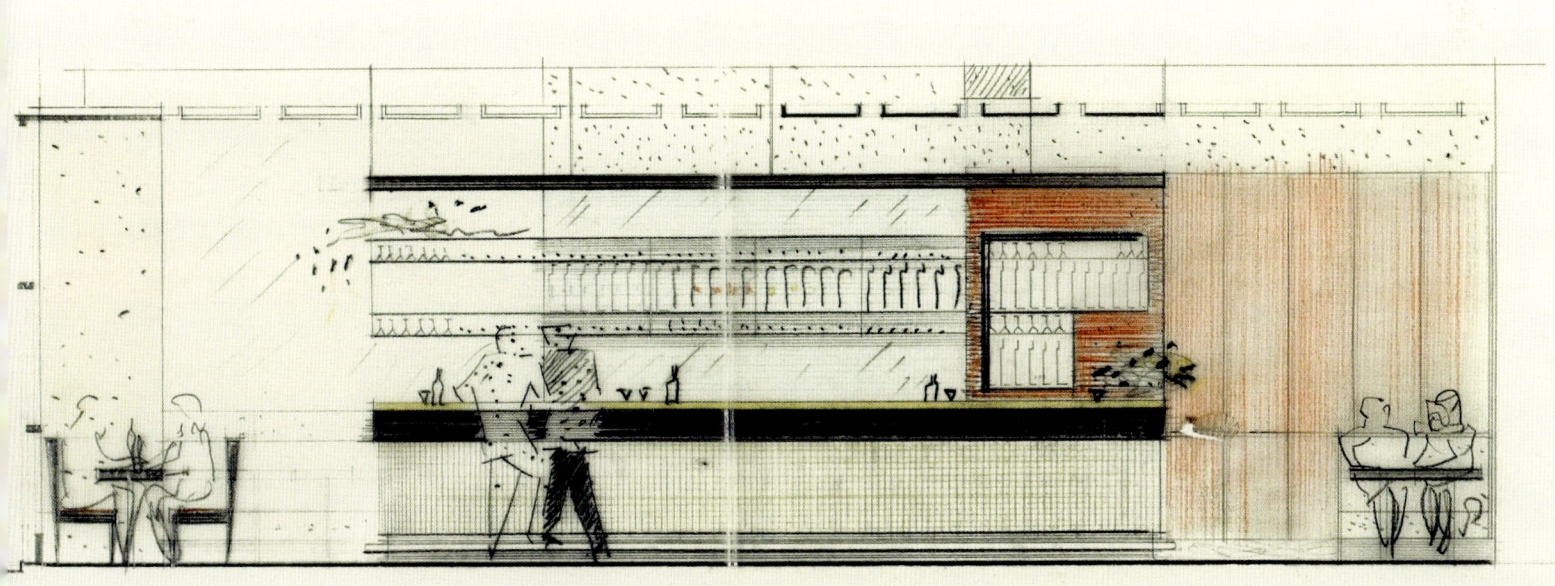

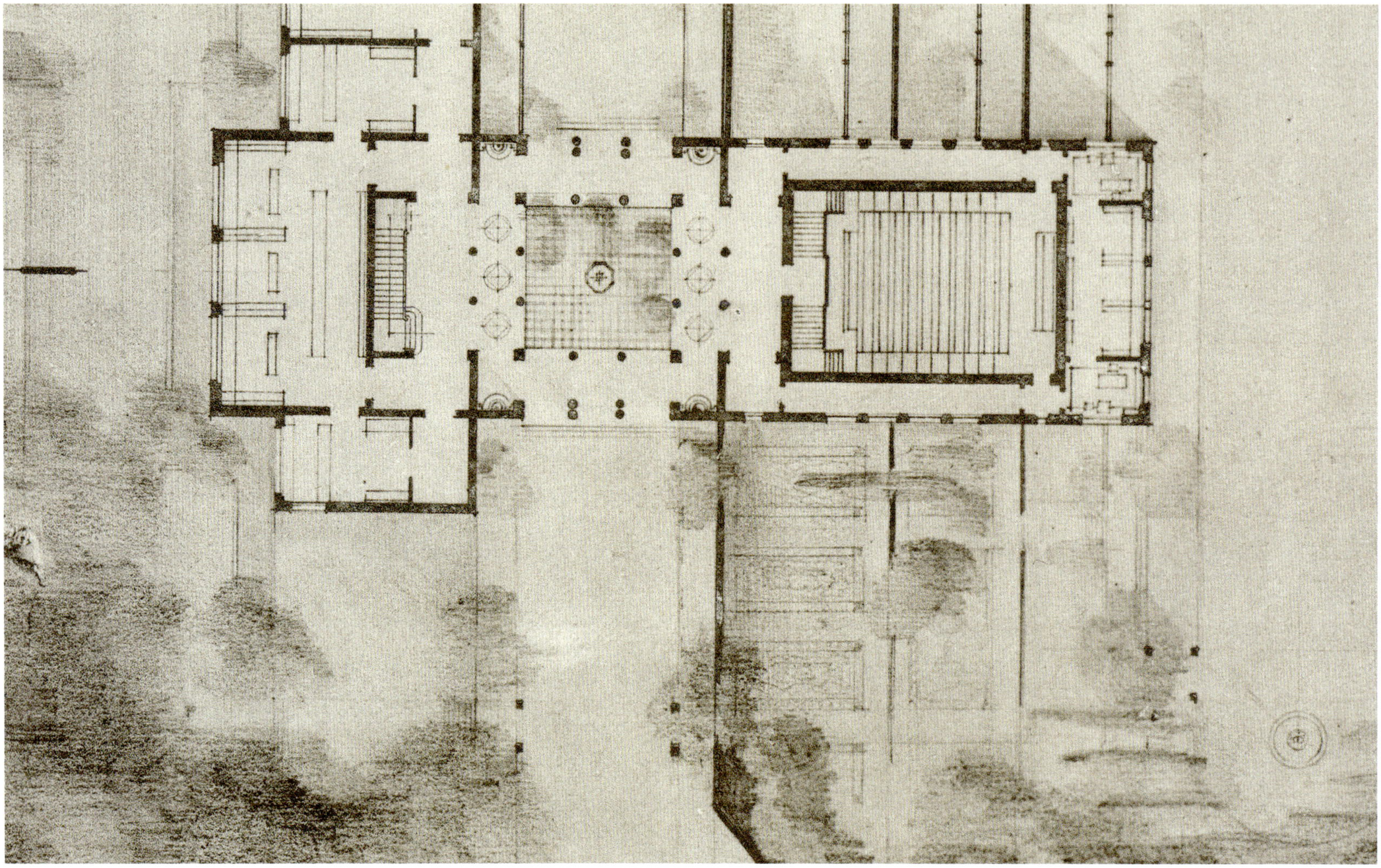

46

40
Alpine landscape, 1927, pencil and watercolor, reflecting pleasure found in painting during a family visit in Switzerland

lar patina and materiality.[16] Before leaving the *Patron*, I will recount an episode etched into the collective memory of "*les Pontremolis*." Tschumi was one of Eugène Beaudoin's *nègres*[17] on the charrette[18] of his winning entry for the Grand Prix de Rome in 1928.[19] The success of such charrrettes depended on the collective labor of the many additional hands, and Beaudoin's victory showed that the Swiss architect had succeeded in mastering the spectacular Pontremolian *tours de force* in rendering. Remember that in order to survive in Paris, Tschumi had to earn money; he would have no problems finding work as a draftsman. Remember also that he was familiar with the field of furniture design. It was in the field of Art Deco furniture that he would work with two other masters.

39
School of horticulture and viticulture, project from Pontremoli's studio, circa 1926. Awarded a *mention* by the jury, then published as a photo-lithograph

Notes

[1] Maurice Pianzola, *Lénine en Suisse*, Libraire Rousseau, Geneva, 1965.
[2] See Christian Hubert and Lindsay Stamm Schapiro, *William Lescaze Architekt*, Wiese Verlag, Basel, 1994.
[3] The standard work on Salvisberg is Claude Lichtenstein ed., *Otto Rudolf Salvisberg, Die andere Moderne, Werkkatalog und Biographie*, gta Verlag, Zurich, 1995. Salvisberg's programs at the *Technicum* in the years 1901–1904 and those followed by Jean Tschumi between 1919 and 1922 are essentially the same.
[4] The colloquial expression was *faire la place*, meaning that a student would find a job prospecting the city as a central staging ground, thus *la place (de Paris)*.
[5] Hugh D. Clout, "The Great Reconstruction of Towns and Cities in France 1918–1935," *Planning Perspectives*, London, vol. 20, no. 1, 2005, pp. 1–33. Clout is my main source for the "Reconstruction" period.
[6] Jacques Gubler and Alberto Abriani, *Alberto Sartoris, Dall'autobiografia alla critica*, Electa, Milan, 1990, pp. 34, 45–46.
[7] Hugh D. Clout, "Rebuilding Northern France after the Great War," *CHS Newsletter*, no. 70, Dec. 2004, p. 8.
[8] I am greatly indebted to Marie-Laure Crosnier Leconte for assisting me in accessing all relevant material on Jean Tschumi housed at the Beaux-Arts archives.
[9] The house received acclaim after the owner's death in 1928, when it was bequeathed to the Institut de France, and after its publication in 1934 by Joseph Chamonard: *Emmanuel Pontremoli, Kérylos, la villa grecque*, revised edition, Jeanne Laffite, Marseilles, 1994.
[10] On the villa, see the website *villa-kerylos.com/en/kerylos/261-history*.
[11] Hervé Duchêne, "Kérylos ou les charmes de la Grèce à la Belle Epoque," http://www.u-bourgogne.fr/STIMULUS/D001/200/300.htm.
[12] Vitruvius, *The Ten Books on Architecture*, translated by Morris Hicky Morgan, Harvard University Press, Cambridge, 1926, pp. 185–186.
[13] Duchêne, op. cit.
[14] "Notre Père à tous." This credo was ironic, given the comparison to other mythical fathers, including Adam, Abraham, Chronos, or even the Great Apes.
[15] Paul Malo, 3 December 2001: "In Emmanuel Pontremoli's Beaux-Arts studio, the word 'corridor' was forbidden. Students had to create a gallery or something else. No corridors allowed." www.DesignCommunity.com/discussion/11054.html.
[16] See Gilles Ragot, *Robert Camelot*, Mardaga, Liège, 1988, p. 13.
[17] Literally "the nigger," the *nègre* was a student willing to help another co-disciple complete the work required for competition deadlines. On Eugène Beaudoin, see Colette Raffaele, *Une école d'architecture et son système d'enseignment (1942–1968), Eugène Beaudoin et Gêneve*, Thesis II 2942, Federal Institute of Technology (EPFL), Lausanne, 2004.
[18] The word *charrette*, which has passed into English-language usage, originated from the nineteenth-century practice of bringing the drawings on a little cart in a carnival ritual of *Charivari*.
[19] The charrette for the Prix de Rome lasted 100 days. Beaudoin had compiled a stellar team of distinguished hands who were also fellow Pontremoli students: Robert Camelot, Paul Herbé, Jacques Marmey, and Jean Tschumi.

41
Bar at Sandoz headquarters in Paris,
1949–1950, detail, pencil, charcoal, pastel,
and tempera on tracing paper

From Furniture to Architecture

One narrative of architecture would have as its origin the making of a chair, a textile, a table, or a bed; such a hypothesis is rooted in many readings of modern production. The seminal value of furniture is reinforced by the phenomenologies of comfort and posture. For social history as much as for the archeology of the house and everyday life, the evaluation of domestic objects is a first step toward a theory "taking command." In his *Mechanization Takes Command*,[1] Sigfried Giedion traces the "anonymous history" of pre-industrial societies that merged into the Arts & Crafts tradition to ultimately reach the status of industrial design. Giedion opposed the traditional practices of craftsmanship, its collective origin, its relative permanence as a *règle de l'art*, to the impulses and breaks ushered in by inventors and engineers who patented their technical innovations. From 1850 to 1940 industrial design was inseparable from technical experimentation. Using the trope of furniture, Giedion is able to confirm his faith in technical progress as translated in the sciences as well as in the arts.

In his treatise *Emile ou de l'éducation*, Rousseau elucidates the founding value of furniture. Young Emile was raised through the practice of various physical and intellectual activities, including swimming, gardening, and land surveying. The development of wooden tools played a central role. Joinery would help the coordination of touch with other senses. Hence the manipulation of a saw and a plane entered Emile's education. Rousseau describes the craft of cabinetmaking as "clean and useful. It can be practiced at home....It requires skill and industry from the worker. Elegance and taste are not excluded from the objects made for utility."[2] One century after Rousseau, Viollet-le-Duc devoted a monumental six-volume dictionary to French furniture (*mobilier*).[3] He used the French term in a juridical sense, distinguishing between mobile (cattle, clothes, furniture) and immobile goods (property or "*immobilier*"). Throughout his analysis he describes the "common uses" of more or less ephemeral objects and, in so doing, merges his research on architecture and furniture. Furniture may even precede architecture in the teaching of arts and crafts. Such a belief is at the core of Viollet's educational novel, *Histoire d'un Dessinateur*, copies of which were given to schoolboys as "prizes in excellence."[4] The two main characters are "Little John" and his mentor. Under his mentor's watchful eye, the student begins with an observation of nature divided into vegetal, animal, and mineral. Geography is the field that discloses nature. Nature must be drawn with due regard for Euclid's basic figures. *Manufacts* are then observed, and drawing becomes design: Little John builds a table. In a parallel fiction, Viollet-le-Duc tells the story of another boy, "Master Paul," who built a family house for his sister on her honeymoon.[5] While Little John was a gifted craftsman who wanted to teach design to cabinetmakers, Master Paul became an architect with the help of his anti-academic mentor, an expert in "modern dwelling."[6]

These allusions to Rousseau and Viollet-le-Duc are not meant as digressions. On the contrary, I see Tschumi's identity as an amalgam of "Little John" and "Master Paul." The assumption that architecture has its roots in the fabrication of a stool or a bed could lead us into further excursions into Art Nouveau and the Modern Movement.[7] Ultimately, the direct connection between furniture and modern architecture is confirmed by the personal trajectory of leading protagonists of the twentieth-century avant-garde; one need only recall Gerrit Rietveld and Marcel Breuer as two of many examples.[8] While Rietveld began his career as a joiner in his father's workshop, Breuer illustrated Gropius' original program for the Weimar Bauhaus, a call to all craftsmen to join in a collective movement of social reform.[9]

**Jacques-Emile Ruhlmann:
The Standard-bearer of Art Deco
and the "Lesson of the Postage Stamp"**

In Paris, the city that brought us Citroën, Renault, Jacques Doucet, and Paul Poiret, the Exposition Internationale des Arts Décoratifs et Industriels Modernes of 1925 was a spectacular effort on a national scale. Given the rapid economic ascendancy of the United States, the organizers of the Expo wanted to revive domestic industrial production and strengthen France's political influence in Europe and its colonies. The local press began referring to the objects on display as evidence of *"le style 1925."* The patriotic image of "Victory" had a new focus: colonialism in the arts and through the arts. The age of Versailles and the Napoleonic empires, when France had been the arbiter of taste and Paris the center of fashion, needed to be revived. The Expo presented a seductive counterpoint to the New World. Melodic echoes of the Jazz Age were heard in fringe theaters and cabarets beginning in 1917. European car manufacturers adopted an assembly-line model that was first launched in Detroit. Paris had to reassert its cultural supremacy. French labels needed to be secured through copyright and branding, justifying the use of government funds. Fashion and modernity were presented in tandem. One of the goals of the exhibition was to pinpoint the production of middle- and large-size retailers (*établissements*) that specialized in furniture, since many small shops had disappeared as a consequence of the war.

In 1925 the arrival of Jacques-Emile Ruhlmann (1879–1933) on the stage of the Expo became a media phenomenon.[10] His fame crossed the Atlantic just as his fashionable *salon de thé* was launched on board the ocean liner *Ile-de-France*. His name was established through its association with a wide range of products. Ruhlmann quickly became synonymous with luxury and modern elegance. In 1925 his own exhibition at the "Art Lover's Mansion" (*Hôtel du collectionneur*) epitomized the Art Deco phenomenon—luxury and thinly veiled eroticism. Ruhlmann's role as a designer and contractor was to lead a team of roughly one hundred craftsmen.[11] Much in the same vein as a fashion designer, his

42
Competition for Veterinary Hospital at the University of Zurich, 1944, pencil on tracing paper, studies of the *parti* at "postage-stamp" scale

43
Competition for Veterinary Hospital at the University of Zurich, 1944, black and green pencil on tracing paper, studies of the *parti* at "postage-stamp" scale

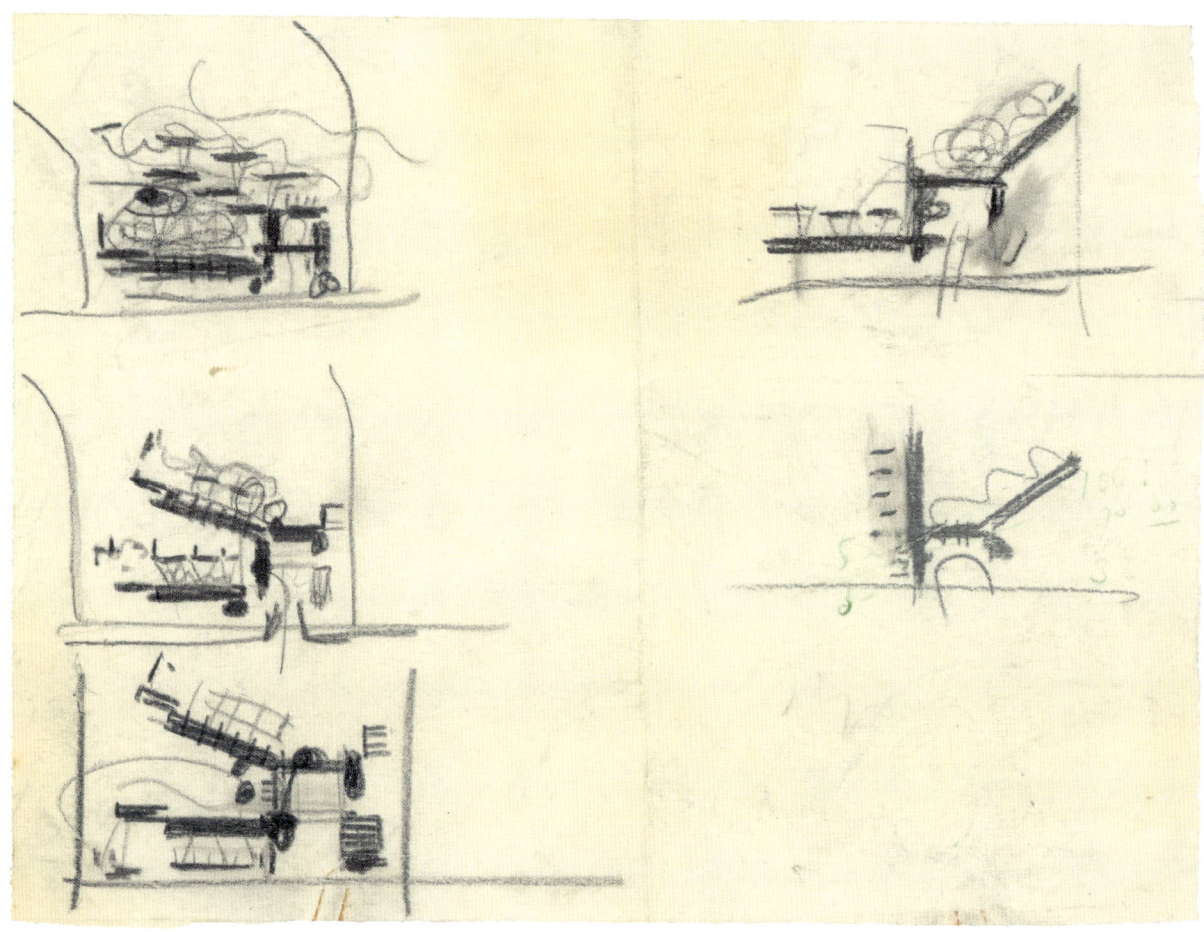

52

44
Table adapted for business machines, Sandoz Laboratories, Orléans, circa 1952, pencil on tracing paper, "postage-stamp" scale and streamlining

45
Armchairs for Sandoz headquarters in Paris, circa 1948, pencil on tracing paper. The frame as philosophical essence of the profile

sketched ideas were transformed into models by his team. A new French word circulated in 1925 to identify this kind of working methodology: *ensemblier*.[12] In French, the word hovers between two connotations: managing a group of people on the one hand, and assembling decorative elements together on the other. This term substituted for the more vague designation of "*meublier*," another neologism of the 1920s.

Looking for work, Tschumi successfully found a position in Ruhlmann's production factory. Here, the intensity and graphic acumen of Pontremoli's students were revered; Tschumi's life-long friend, Henry-Jacques Le Même (1897–1997), also passed through Ruhlmann's doors.[13] Junior employees like Tschumi and Le Même were hired to translate into perspectives the models that had appeared in the catalogue. The drawings were initially rendered in monochrome, but the graphite was only an underlay for the addition of the ink, gouache, and flecks of gold that followed. Those who worked at the office also employed another methodology: they made copies of the model at multiple scales, in plan, section, and elevation. Ruhlmann advocated the "principle of luxury."[14] His elite clients, those happy few, would shape the future of ordinary production.[15] What kind of lessons could be taken from his achievements as a designer? Certainly what might be called the "lesson of the postage stamp," in which small-scale sketches were the detonator of his ideas. In 1928 he gave a lecture at the Ecole Boulle,[16] a distinguished technical school that specialized in joinery, metal work, and decoration. He told the students: "I insist that you render your *parti* diagram[17] at the scale of a postage stamp. Only then will you be able to control the general impression generated from the interaction of volumes and from the main qualities and proportions of your architecture.…It is for me an absolute principle: I never leave aside the small sketch before it reaches its full potential, when my eye can no longer account for an advantage at that scale."[18] Tschumi, too, followed this "postage-stamp" principle throughout his life. Through the development of a variety of small perspectives, he designed furniture but also at the scale of buildings and the city (Plate 42, 43). While it was fairly common practice to sketch in pocket-size notebooks or *carnets*, Tschumi kept all his little drawings on tracing paper, not unlike a precious collection of butterflies. The fact that he did not abandon these fragile traces was not due to any kind of fetishism on his part. Rather, he used them as working documents that followed the trajectory of his analytical process. The drawings constituted elements of an archive that documented his reflections on program and his thoughts on projects to come (Plates 44, 45).

Edgar Brandt, an Entrepreneur in Ironwork and Artillery

Edgar Brandt (1880–1960) was a blacksmith whose elegant craftsmanship bridged two moments in the decorative arts, Art Nouveau and Art Deco. As the historian Joan Kahr notes, "The story of how Brandt, a young man from a middle-class French family, became an artist-blacksmith, an inventor, and an entrepreneur—in short, a self-made man—is also the story of the evolution of metalwork in the early twentieth century."[19] Brandt's first successes were in jewelry design. But his more brilliant industrial achievements were developed behind the scenes for covert military projects. During World War I he designed and produced his first mortar with a 60mm caliber. The second mortar, a 61mm caliber, was developed in 1934 and sold to 52 countries before World War II.[20] It is part of the arsenal of the French army to this day. Brandt's leadership in the auto and consumer electronics industries is tied to several established French trademarks, for example, Hotchkiss and Thomson. While Moulinex had also maintained production of Brandt's refrigerators and washing machines, recent restructuring enlarged the production of mortars and missiles. Originally an iron craftsman, Brandt was also known, especially after the Treaty of Versailles, in relation to war and death. In 1923 he designed the complex machinery for the "eternal flame" embedded in the Tomb of the Unknown Soldier at the Arc de Triomphe. In the Jazz Age this monument was viewed as one of the most sacred of the Fourth Republic. Patriotic commemorations gathered together politicians, officers, and disabled ex-servicemen alike. Very few people knew that the goldsmith of the flame had also produced a very effective mortar. A prominent example of his work, a dramatic staircase, was also on display in the famed department store, Au Bon Marché. Moreover, the photogenic balustrade that he designed for Paul Poiret's couture house came to serve as his trademark or *carte de visite*.

Brandt's extensive knowledge of metallurgy enabled him to achieve skillful decorative effects. He applied techniques first used in the production of industrial components (including bronze plating and electrical welding) to costly unique pieces. In

46
Table in director's office, Sandoz headquarters in Basel, 1938–1939, pencil and stump on tracing paper

47
Table in director's office, Sandoz headquarters in Basel, 1938–1939, pencil and stump on tracing paper. Bull sculpted by Edouard-Marcel Sandoz

48
Table manufactured by Edgar Brandt, 1932–1933, pencil, stump, and charcoal on tracing paper. Catalogue item

49
Table manufactured by Edgar Brandt, 1932–1933, pencil and stump. Catalogue item

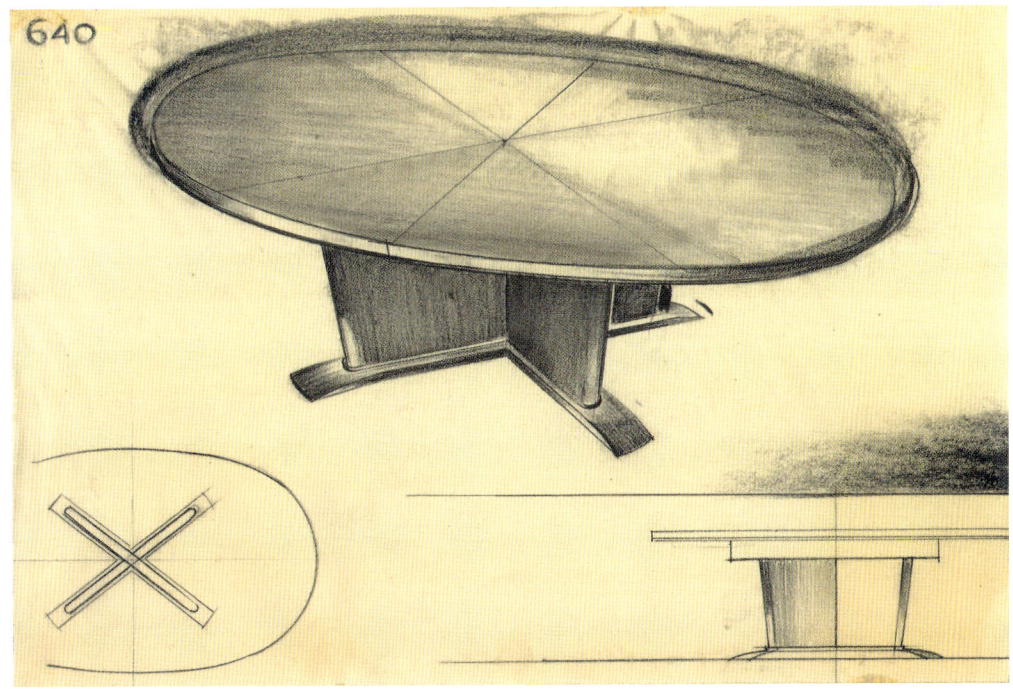

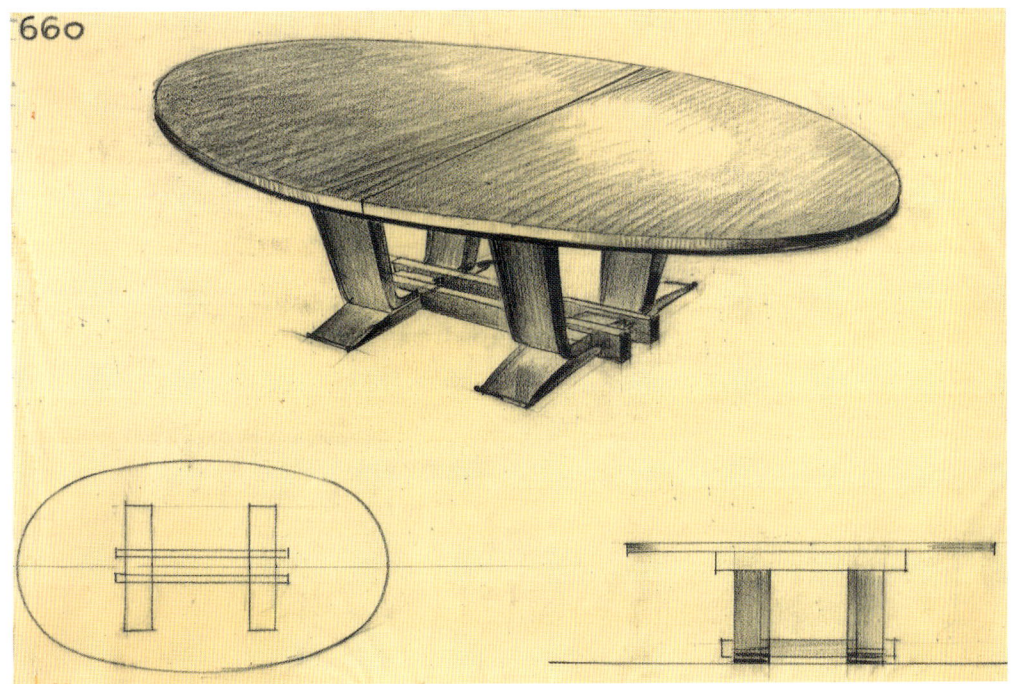

this manner, chrome, nickel, and aluminum entered the domestic sphere. Brandt also loved to combine metal with other materials like the milky and chiseled Lalique glass, alabaster, and marble. Electric floor lamps (*torchères*) were a major seller for the Brandt firm; since they could be moved easily from room to room, *torchères* were often preferred to chandeliers.[21] In 1925 two events made Brandt front-page news: his octagonal faceted pavilion at the *Exposition* and the opening of a permanent showroom located near the American Embassy. The latter space functioned rather like an art gallery, allowing his work to be shown alongside pieces made by fellow decorative artists, and at least 30 exhibitions took place there. Suffice it to say that La Galerie Brandt was an elegant menagerie for animal sculptors, among them Edouard-Marcel Sandoz, as well as a haven for leading furniture designers like Ruhlmann.

As Kahr notes, Brandt had gained an "impressive foothold" on the North American continent even before 1925.[22] She points to the patronage of the Toronto-born publicist and pedagogue George G. Booth, the founder of the Cranbrook Academy of Art in Bloomfield Hills, Michigan. Booth invited the Finnish architect Eliel Saarinen (a permanent U.S. resident since 1923) to design the campus of the new school. Saarinen's presence guaranteed doctrinal continuity between European Art Nouveau and further research in American craftsmanship and architecture. Booth's mediation explains why Brandt found high-profile customers in Montreal and New York. The Frenchman's first hit in Manhattan, the flagship store for the Cheney Silk Company, opened in 1925 at the eastern corner of Madison Avenue and 34th Street. Cheney imported silk from France, and it also imported the massive and elegant bronze doors used for its storefront. With the completion of this project, a true manifesto of Art Deco was born. As Andrew Dolkart notes, "You can (still) see…the frozen-fountain motif over the doors, a motif eventually used on many of the city's buildings."[23] The intrinsically European style's arrival in New York at the time of the 1925 Expo was not a sign of a unilateral French invasion of the United States in taste, fashion, and design. On the contrary, Brandt's story illustrates a continuous transatlantic interaction, a real traffic of patterns and ideas. I have already noted that

50
Reception room, Edgar Brandt headquarters in Paris, 1933, door to director's office

51
Edgar Brandt's office in Paris, 1933. The director's office as showroom, a symphony in wood, metal, glass, and fabric

American factories and assembly lines served as influential models for many European industrialists and mechanical engineers. Brandt was fascinated by the United States and had great admiration for America's technological superiority.[24] He fell in love with a luxury car from Lincoln, Michigan, a fast V12-powered sedan that he shipped back to Paris. It was the 1932 model, an object of concupiscence in Europe (Plate 53). The car was sold in the US for $4,300, a sum that represented over four years of the average worker's salary. In Europe, after the publication of Ozenfant & Le Corbusier's iconographical 1923 treatise *Towards an Architecture*, the automobile became a status symbol for those artists and architects who could afford it. The car was not only a sign of the coming Machine Age; its bodywork illustrated unique choices in plastic configurations and symbolic details. The 1932 Lincoln, for example, had a silvered greyhound leaping ahead of its radiator.

Tschumi's connection to Brandt is far from tenuous. In fact, for a few years the Swiss architect became one of Brandt's most faithful collaborators. He also shared his boss's fascination for American innovation. In 1949 he came up with the money for his first car and chose the V8-powered Ford Vedette. Its unified profile and compact streamlined volume, absence of superfluous effects, and new hubcaps echoed his architectural ideals. In the 1950s he told his colleagues at the International Union of Architects that they had to travel to the U.S. at least once a year. He sent his son Bernard to the United States as a reward for passing the *baccalauréat*.[25] Chicago must have been quite a cultural shock….

52
Unrealized project for André Citroën's office in Paris, photograph of drawing with added gouache and India ink. Commissioned by Brandt and developed by Tschumi, the design has the grandness of a chancellery and shows a Mercator projection of the world adjusted to the Paris meridian.

53
1932 Lincoln, wooden model by the German firm Arcurio

Tschumi's Tenure with Edgar Brandt

Tschumi financed his education by working at Ruhlmann's office on temporary assignments. After receiving his diploma from the Beaux-Arts he developed a more regular professional relationship with Brandt. From 1932 to 1934, Tschumi designed and produced furniture ensembles under the collective trademark and seal of Etablissements Edgar Brandt (Plate 48, 49). In a CV submitted to the University of Lausanne ten years later, he referred to his title at Brandt's office as "design manager" and "consulting architect."[26] Regardless of the emphatic nature of those titles, there is no doubt that he was a useful addition to the team. Floor lamps, radiator grilles, ashtrays, and inkstands, as well as other specialties of the firm, were not enough to make a reception room; tables, armchairs, and closets had to be part of the display. The firm kept a catalogue of models as a kind of commercial inventory of items that could anticipate and meet the client's needs. This collection of samples was presented as a beautiful array of perspective drawings. From the hundreds of graphic models in perspective, only a dozen are documented in the Lausanne archives and two have survived in the United States.[27] Such designs for Brandt's catalogue could have only been achieved by an accomplished draftsman capable of synthesizing the contrast of materials with a play of luminous effects. Drafts or rapid sketches were excluded. The polish of the flawless object was on view. It was a rational exercise in differential repetition; it conveyed the *variante* through a design methodology, not only the alternative options of rectangular or oval table shapes. This binomial configuration had to be replaced by polynomial combinations.

Between 1933 and 1934 Brandt asked Tschumi to design his own manager's office as well as a reception room for his "War Armament Society" (AMG) headquarters in Paris (Plates 50, 51). The two rooms for the AMG served as interconnected *ensembles*. They presented an orchestration in wool (carpets), fabric (curtains), precious wood (fixed and sliding doors, paneling), polished wood (closets and tables), colored leather (armchairs), glass and mirrors, not to mention the metal: door handles, table and armchair supports, floor lamps, inkstands, and rocking blotting paper holders. The quality of the ensemble had to reflect the precision of Brandt's new 61mm mortar, which would soon be sold worldwide. Under the Edgar Brandt name, Tschumi developed another important commission: a suite of two reception rooms for the Etablissements André Citroën in Javel. The project was never completed, and the original colored perspectives have probably been lost; only two black-and-white photographs remain. The reception room and the director's office were to be dominated by a mural-sized perspective. The carpet outlined the exact perimeter of an orthogonal stage. Tschumi loved to study color on 1:1 scale boards. The textiles would have been woven in thick wool, bordered by strict orthogonal patterns. The formality of the setting evoked the atmosphere of a chancellery. The carmaker's double chevron logo stood above two giant entrances, and the coffered ceiling was designed to reach a height of roughly 20 feet.

Behind the director's armchair and shoulders was a background Mercator projection of the world centered on the Paris meridian, from whence the Citroën cars conquered steppes, deserts, and cities in Africa and Asia. With its subtle easel strokes, the architectural rendering emulates photography in a realistic *trompe-l'œil* effect obtained through fine washes of gouache and India ink (Plate 52). The monumentality of the project belied Citroën's progressive mechanical engineering. In spring 1934 the famous "*Traction-Avant*," a front-wheel drive streamlined box without a chassis and foot board, was put on the assembly line, representing a true technological breakthrough.[28]

A Season in Furniture

Tschumi worked in Paris for ten years following his graduation from the Beaux-Arts. He established a private practice with another Swiss architect, Henri Vermeil,[29] with whom he started to work on competitions without immediate success. They also tried to obtain commissions for decorative projects, hence their business title as "*Architecture, Mobilier, Décoration.*" The office was located at 188 Boulevard Saint-Germain, not far from the Beaux-Arts and in close proximity to the city's famous brasseries. In fact, this elegant professional address was also the location of Tschumi's apartment. The contacts and reputation he had gained at Brandt's office proved useful; among some other small projects, he designed a showroom for a lamp manufacturer (Plate 54) and a display-stall for electric ovens at the Salon des Arts Ménagers.[30] A more interesting opportunity came in 1934 through Francis Huet, Ruhlmann's former design manager. Ruhlmann had died in 1933, leaving behind valuable furniture commissions for the transatlantic steamer *Le Normandie*. Huet joined forces with Vermeil and Tschumi on a small project. Designed in 1931, the ocean liner required four years of shipbuilding. The Compagnie Générale Transatlantique wanted to take the lead over German and British luxury liners for North Atlantic crossings. The *Normandie* (Plate 55) was to become the standard-bearer of French taste in modernity and magnificence. It generated a monstrous charrette that involved more than 20 architectural firms.[31] Huet, Vermeil, and Tschumi's design was for a first-class two-room apartment called Honfleur (Plates 56, 57) which entailed a bedroom and sitting room that were separated by a curtain.[32]

The interior design on board the *Normandie* followed two opposing trends. The first tendency could be called classical, featuring wood, plush armchairs, fabrics, and Aubusson carpets.[33] The second could rather be defined as modernist (Plate 61); it favored light metals, tubular stainless steel, aluminum alloy, steel containers, neutral and white enameled earthenware, and movable chairs.[34] Tschumi and his partners were enlisted to the first group. Their ensemble revealed a sober, late, or post-Art Deco taste. In the bedroom side of the Honfleur cabin, a generous paneled mirror created the allusion of a larger domestic space (Plate 59). The corner boudoir was placed alongside a flat polished-wood cornice in an L-shape, and had two protrusions: the horizontal plane of the inclined

54
Showroom for lighting shop on Boulevard Malesherbes in Paris, 1934–1935, pencil, chalk, charcoal, gouache, and wash

55
Liner *Le Normandie*, postcard, 1935, print published by the Compagnie Générale Transatlantique

circular mirror and a semi-oval table wide enough to accommodate two glasses and the champagne ice bucket based on a model by Brandt. The twin beds were designed to accommodate a Simmons fireproof standard mattress on flat springs. The new bedding system was called "tranquility" (*Quiétude*). Its structure consisted of several hundred small vertical steel coils, and was touted for its constant elasticity (Plate 60). While the beds were standardized, this was not the case for the chairs and armchairs designed by Tschumi. The bronze naval horse on the chest of drawers of the *commode* can be safely attributed to Sandoz (Plate 59), a successful *animaliste* who worked among Brandt's circle of friends.

In 1937 Tschumi broke his association with Huet and Vermeil. He then teamed up with Sandoz (Plate 68), who was to become his lifelong ally and guide. Meanwhile, on the ground floor of his apartment building on the Boulevard Saint-Germain, the café was sold to a new owner, Monsieur Rouquet. Tschumi offered his services to the native of Auvergne, transforming the space's kitchen equipment and designing the bar and furnishings. Le Rouquet, as it came to be known, was his first completed project as an independent practitioner.

56
First-class cabin on *Le Normandie*, perspective toward the lounge, 1934, pencil, chalk, and wash on tracing paper

57
First-class cabin on *Le Normandie*, perspective of bedroom, 1934, pencil, chalk, and wash on tracing paper. Color as erotic effect adapted to the comfort of the fireproof mattresses

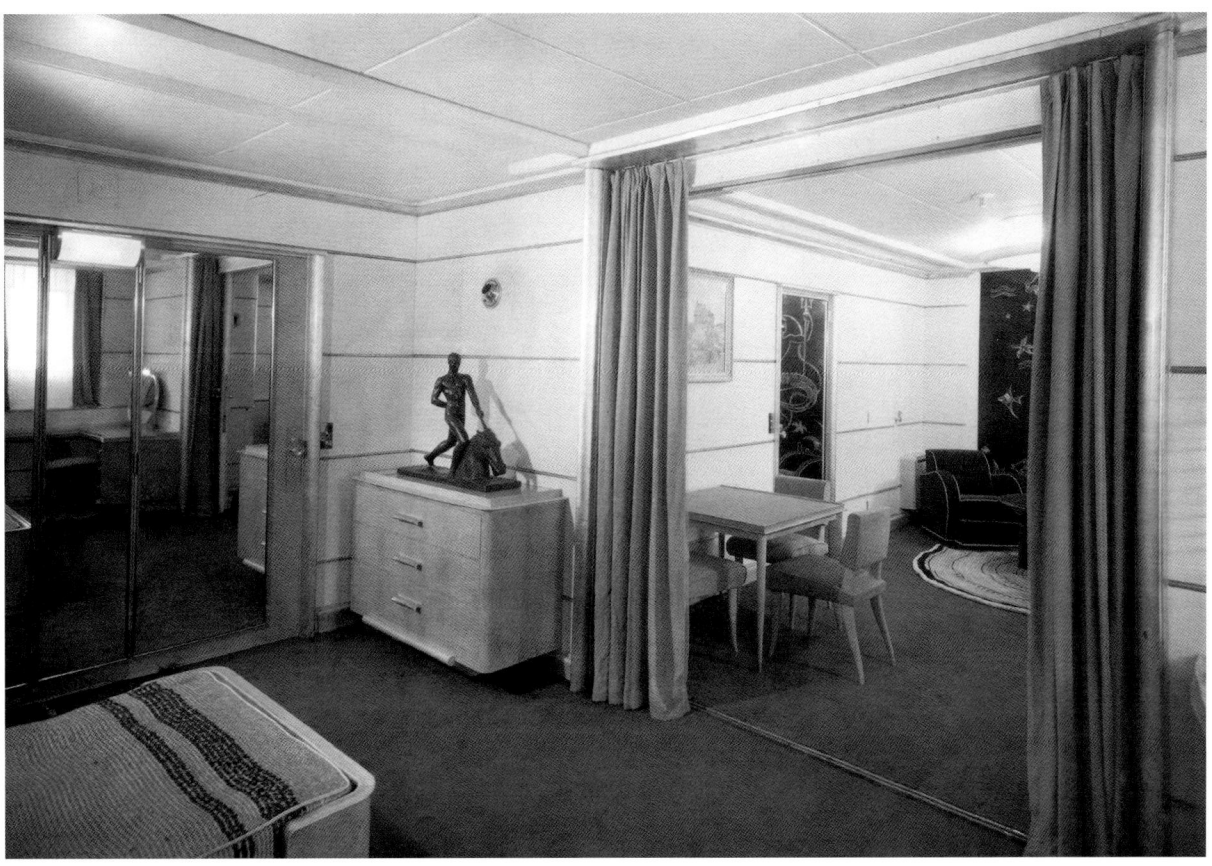

58
Bedroom, first-class cabin on *Le Normandie*, 1935, view toward windows, integration of boudoir in bedroom corner, lamp and champagne bucket by Brandt

59
Bedroom, first-class cabin on *Le Normandie*, 1935, mirrors as wardrobe doors, sculpture by Edouard-Marcel Sandoz on *commode*

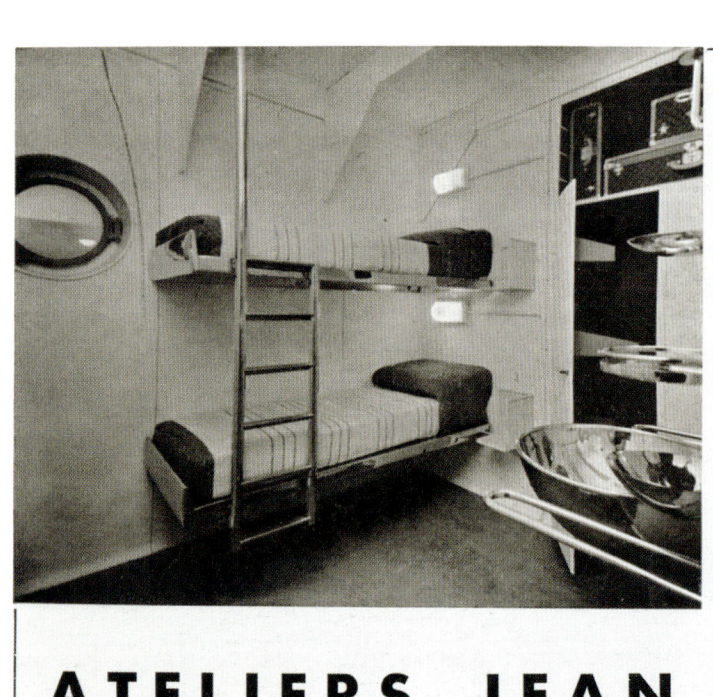

60
Publicity for fireproof Simmons mattresses, exclusive contract for all beds on *Le Normandie*, full-page advertisement in *L'Architecture d'Aujourd'hui*, no. 8, August 1935

61
Publicity for Ateliers Jean Prouvé, Nancy, in *L'Architecture d'Aujourd'hui*, no. 8, August 1935

62
Unrealized project, plan of veranda, music room, and living room commissioned by Sandoz director in Paris, circa 1950, pencil on tracing paper

63
Unrealized project for veranda and music room commissioned by Sandoz director in Paris, circa 1950, pencil, chalk, and pastel on tracing paper. Decorative study of the atmosphere

64
Unrealized project for veranda and music room commissioned by Sandoz director in Paris, circa 1950, pencil, chalk, and pastel on tracing paper

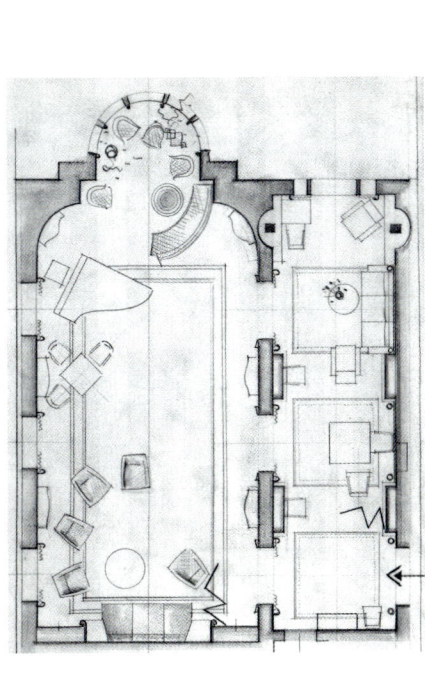

65
Boardroom, Sandoz headquarters in Basel, detail, 1938–1939, pencil, wash, gouache on tracing paper

66
Boardroom, Sandoz headquarters in Basel, detail, 1938–1939, pencil, chalk, tempera, and gouache on tracing paper

67
Boardroom, Sandoz headquarters in Basel, detail, 1938–1939, pencil, charcoal, stump, gouache on tracing paper

68
Boardroom, Sandoz headquarters in Basel, detail, 1938–1939, pencil, charcoal, stump, gouache on tracing paper. Sculpture by Edouard-Marcel Sandoz

Notes

[1] Sigfried Giedion, *Mechanization Takes Command: A Contribution to Anonymous History* (1948), Norton, New York, 1969. See part five in particular.

[2] Jean-Jacques Rousseau, *Emile ou de l'éducation* (1762), Garnier-Flammarion, Paris, 1966, p. 261.

[3] Eugène Viollet-le-Duc, *Dictionnaire raisonné du mobilier français de l'époque carlovingienne à la renaissance*, Gründ & Maguet, Paris, s.d. The six volumes were published at the beginning of the Third Republic. See the entry "Meubles" in vol. 1, part 1.

[4] Eugène Viollet-le-Duc, *Histoire d'un dessinateur*, Paris, Hetzel, s.d. (1879). The book has never been published in English. Viollet-le-Duc's pedagogical fiction was published the very year of his death and effectively contributed to the national effort in public education under the new French Republic.

[5] Eugène Viollet-le-Duc, *Histoire d'une maison*, Hetzel, Paris, s.d. (1874). Hetzel was also Jules Verne's publisher.

[6] Effectively a pattern book, *Habitations modernes* is the title of a thick folio published in 1877 by Félix Narjoux and printed by the *Encyclopédie d'architecture*. The publisher stresses that Eugène Viollet-le-Duc had collected these examples of urban and rural "Modern Dwelling."

[7] Adolf Loos designed his first matrimonial bed as a large mattress placed directly on the floor under the warm and supple texture of a white bed cover. Henry van de Velde designed sinuous dresses for curvilinear women to match his luxurious private residences. In opposition to *Art Nouveau*, Loos thought that tailors, not architects, were best suited to designing clothing. For a refreshing presentation of this debate, see Alan Colquhoun, *Modern Architecture*, Oxford University Press, Oxford and New York, 2002. I refer specifically to chapters one and four.

[8] One might also recall Alberto Sartoris' trajectory as traced by Jacques Gubler and Alberto Abriani in *Alberto Sartoris, Dall'autobiografia alla critica*, Electa, Milan, pp. 57–65.

[9] Andrea Gleininger, "Marcel Breuer," in Jeannine Fiedler and Peter Feierabend eds., *Bauhaus*, Cologne, 1999, pp. 320–331.

[10] My information on Jacques-Emile Ruhlmann comes directly from *Ruhlmann, un génie de l'art déco*, a catalogue for the exhibition at the Musée des Années 30 de Boulogne-Billancourt, Somogny, Paris, 2002. I rely specifically on essays by Colombe Samoyault-Verlet, Philippe Rivoirard, Michèle Lefrançois, and Pierre-Emmanuel Martin-Vivier.

[11] P.E. Martin-Vivier, "Les ateliers Ruhlmann," in *Ruhlmann, un génie*, op. cit., p. 118.

[12] Philippe Rivoirard, "Ruhlmann, l'architecture et les architectes," in *Ruhlmann, un génie*, op. cit., p. 82.

[13] See Françoise Véry and Pierre Saddy, *Henry-Jacques Le Même, architecte à Megève*, Mardaga, Liège, 1988; Maurice Culot, Anne Lambrichs, and Dominique Delaunay, *Megève: 1925–1950, Architectures de Henry Jacques Le Même*, Editions Norma, Paris, 1999.

[14] Colombe Samoyault-Verlet, "Ruhlmann, créateur de meubles," in *Ruhlmann, un génie*, op. cit., p. 33.

[15] P. E. Martin-Vivier, "Les ateliers Ruhlmann," in *Ruhlmann, un génie*, op. cit., pp. 120–121.

[16] See www.ecole-boulle.org.

[17] A magical and exclusive word in the Beaux-Arts tradition, *parti* could be roughly translated as the composition of the plan. The term encompasses the overlaying of architectural program onto an overall pattern related to the bilateral symmetry of wings and courtyards. The *parti* is the antithesis of *configuration*, a term proposed by Gestalt Theory and practiced at the Bauhaus. A foundational concept for the Modern Movement, the latter notion denotes the articulation of volumes joined in asymmetry.

[18] Quoted by Philippe Rivoirard in *Ruhlmann, un génie*, op. cit., pp. 82–83.

[19] Joan Kahr tells this very story in her outstanding book, *Edgar Brandt, Master of Art Deco Ironwork*, Harry N. Abrams, New York, 1999.

[20] See "Edgar Brandt-Leben und Werk" on www.galerie-claude.de. The same gallery published *Edgar Brandt, Kunstschmied des Art Déco*, Galerie Claude, Cologne, 1922.

[21] Kahr, op. cit., p. 79.

[22] Ibid., pp. 166–167.

[23] Andrew S. Dolkart, *The Architecture and Development of New York City: The Skyscraper City*, Columbia University Digital Knowledge Ventures, New York, 2003, p. 2.

[24] Kahr, op. cit., p. 166.

[25] In France and French-speaking Switzerland, the *baccalauréat* is a prerequisite for entry in the university system.

[26] *Dessinateur en chef, architecte-conseil*. See Olivier Robert, Francesco Panese, *Dictionnaire des professeurs de l'Université de Lausanne dès 1890*, Etudes et Documents no. XXXVI, Université, Lausanne, 2000, p. 1259.

[27] *Edgar Brandt, Master of Art Deco Ironwork*, illustration #216 of an oval table and # 217 of a rectangular table with U-shaped legs. Both tables are dated circa 1930–1933. The two drawings are in Robert Zehil's collection. Shall I resist temptation and bypass the attribution to Jean Tschumi? There is a family likeness between the two renderings in perspective, the subtle modulation of light, shade, and reflections on metal and marble, and other drawings of the same period in Tschumi's files. Nevertheless I shall leave it as an open question.

[28] On André Citroën, see www.citroen.com./CWW/fr-FR/HISTORY.

[29] Little is known of Henri Vermeil except for a *carton* containing his 1937 design of stained glass windows for a Protestant church in Villeret, near Bienne.

[30] Initiated in 1923 under the patronage of the French government to promote national industry, the Salon is held each year to present the latest domestic innovations. *Arts ménagers* literally means the "arts of the household." See www.museedelapub.org/virt/mp/arts-menagers/salons.html.

[31] Among them, R. Bowens de Boijen & Roger Henri Expert, Pacon & Patout, Laprade & Bazin, Magnani & Masera, Frantz Jourdain & André Louis, M. Gascoin & Jean Prouvé, Robert Mallet-Stevens, René Herbst, G. H. Pingusson, P. Montagnac, J. B. Klotz (the only woman). Care was given even to third-class cabins and berths, for which Robert Mallet-Stevens, Jean Prouvé & M. Gascoin, Franz Jourdain & André Louis designed metal tubular furniture. See the special issue "Evolution des transports," in *L'Architecture d'Aujourd'hui*, vol. V, 1935, #8, pp. 27–41. See also Louis-René Vian, *Arts décoratifs à bord des paquebots français, 1880–1960*, Editions Fonmare, Paris, 1992.

[32] Huet Vermeil and Tschumi's apartment on *Le Normandie* was never published in contemporary magazines.

[33] Such was, for instance, the contribution by Laprade & Bazin.

[34] These kinds of designs were produced by René Herbst, Jean Prouvé, J. B. Klotz, Robert Mallet-Stevens, and Magnani & Masera for first- and third-class cabins.

69
Boardroom, Sandoz headquarters in Paris, detail, 1949–1950, pencil, red chalk, watercolor, and gouache on tracing paper. Pictorial exercise in "sculpting light"

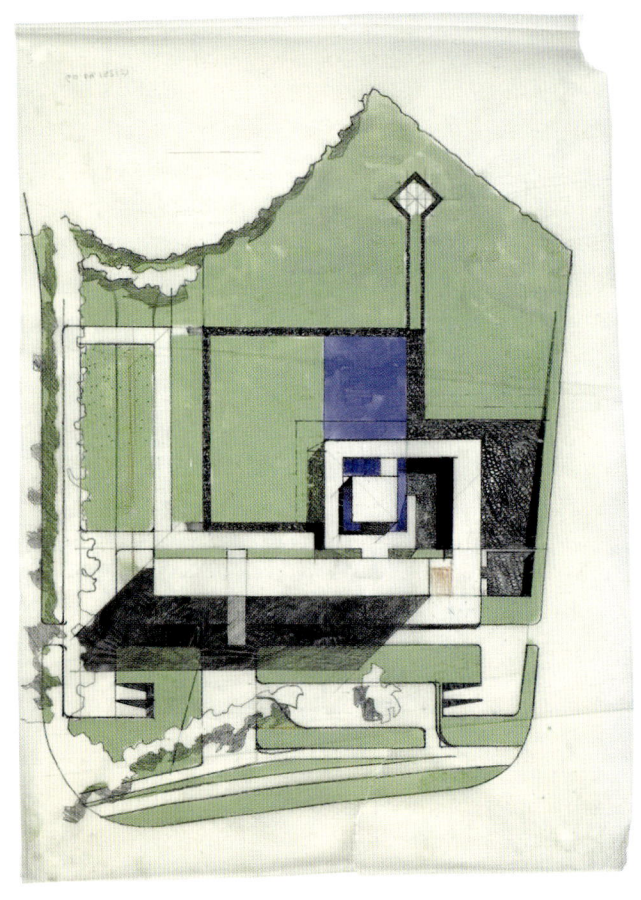

La Variante, a Dialogue within the Project

Does the Notion of a "Work in Progress" Exist in Architecture?

We return to Tschumi's apprenticeship at the Pontremoli *atelier*. As previously noted, Pontremoli insisted on the methodology of the *variante* during the design process. How should the notion of *variante* be defined?

In nineteenth-century France architectural education seized on a characteristic method used by the Ecole des Ponts et Chaussées during the period of the Ancien Régime, one that articulated the development of a project through a play of variants, versions, and variations. This method enabled the negotiation of alternative choices and solutions. In one example, the method could take on the bipolar logic of A/B, as in the relationship between positive and negative polarities outlined by Benjamin Franklin in a treatise on electrical properties published in the 1750s. But the logic of the variant could also be illustrated by the figure of the bridge; its design can respect a pre-established route while also offering multiple material and structural possibilities. This discussion is not exclusive to the construction of bridges and buildings; an analogous scenario is visible in philosophy, theology, or literature—at the precise moment when a questioning of the origin of the logos or word occurs. Both a text and the act of its reading provoke multiple meanings. For this reason a slight literary detour may provide the quickest link back to architecture. After all, aren't university libraries replete with treatises, journals, and monographs?

James Joyce published his "work in progress" in serial form in the journal *Transition*. This text eventually appeared in its final iteration as *Finnegans Wake* (1939). An ostensibly fictional novel, it also treads on the realm of autobiography. The act of writing becomes the embodiment of the continual flux of the self; it constitutes a collection of fragments.[1] A number of critiques make parallels between the book and the notion of the "stream of consciousness," as outlined by William James in reference to the literary process of introspection.[2] These analyses also occasionally look to philosophers like Giambattista Vico, Henri Bergson, and Edmund Husserl, as well as to novels by William James (*The Portrait of a Lady*), Marcel Proust (*Remembrance of Things Past*), and Virginia Woolf (*Mrs. Dalloway*). The latter books trace the dynamic flux of consciousness through the narrative practice of internal dialogue.

What would happen if we tried to introduce this term into the context of fine arts practices? Most often, attention is focused on painting, especially in respect to its central problem of representing nature. While painting and sculpture historically have their basis in imitation or *mimesis*, this precondition of artistic production entered a crisis period at the end of the nineteenth century. By way of synthesis, Phillipe Junod presents two opposing metaphors to address this centennial, if not millennial, problematic: transparency and opacity.[3] Transparency responds to the ancient ideal of imitation as well as to certain proclamations on the part of the later avant-garde; I am thinking here most specifically of Kandinsky and surrealism's efforts to project the spiritual or the unconscious onto the canvas. Isn't the concern in this case to reinforce the *a priori* status of truth and authenticity? In contrast, opacity conforms to an experimental approach that integrates the painted canvas with the reflexive adventure of its making. Beginning in the years 1919–1921, the point of departure for Mondrian's work was strictly regulated.[4] But the actual manual process of applying paint to canvas followed a tra-

70
World Health Organization (WHO) international competition, Geneva, 1960, pencil, India ink, and watercolor on tracing paper. Executed by Tschumi's draftsmen in the Lausanne office with occasional corrections by the Master, illustrating Tschumi's aphorism, "There is no good solution; only one is the least bad."

jectory that he discovered only along the way. Thus, the final result documented the pathway; meaning was discovered *a posteriori*. When applied to painting, Joyce's metaphor of the "work in progress" yields another consequence—successive readings of the work of art that are as diverse as they are contradictory, readings that secure the work's value. Accruing over years, the multiplicity of meanings and significations engendered by a work of art reinforces its weight and topicality. Today, polysemy infers a kind of iconoclastic blasphemy for those defenders of monotheism for whom the written word is divine and remains unchanged throughout millennia.

Does the term "work in progress" have a place in architecture? The question, not an easy one, is in fact a bit complicated. It is easy to see how the editorial genre of "complete works" (*oeuvres complètes*) lends itself to a quest for a multiplicity of meanings. Each catalogued work by an artist remains partial; without resorting to evolutionary models or stylistic ruptures, it still constitutes only a fragment open to a multitude of interpretations. But can one also defend the argument that the construction of a building presents a temporal sequence involving major decisions that were unknown only a few months earlier, at the time of the contract's signing? Doesn't the set of working drawings connecting builder to client constitute a series of quasi-legal rules and regulations that guarantee the interests of both parties? Arguably, Gothic edifices were constructed in the manner of works in progress. Building interruptions were common, whether due to a lack of funds or to the architect's disappearance from the building site. Over the course of decades, radical design decisions were often made *in absentia* or amid dissension. It could even be argued that these structures were susceptible to the Joycean term "pregross," that is, to an ongoing, never-ending quest for finality. The example of the colloquium organized by the *Fabbrica* of Milan's cathedral dome at the end of the fourteenth century in order to question how to proceed with its construction is now canonical.[5] A venerable working-class institution, the factory continues to insure the continuity of operations to this day. Nevertheless, the builders of the Milan dome could not have known that they were initiating a kind of pragmatic modernism.

Doubtless if we were to give ourselves the task of documenting historical case studies among the thousands of twentieth-century building sites (a frequently insurmountable task, due to lack of documentation), we would find examples of works in progress. However, this situation is somewhat rare in the case of civic architecture. In searching for an example, I choose the Picasso Museum in Barcelona, built in phases by the Catalan architect Jordi Garcés. Each successive stage of the project generated unforeseeable consequences for the previous one, so the building became a construction site in progress. At the large urban scale, the recent service sector district in Milan known as the Bicocca, designed by Gregotti & Associates and built on the industrial wasteland of the former Pirelli tire factory, illustrates a unique example due to its monumental size. Using the foundation of a master plan that was stopped in 1988, the program components were developed over the course of two decades. The architects maintain that changes in the site contents allowed them to approach the idea of "a continuous modification ... a permanent action of self-critique."[6] Based on these examples, I would hazard a preliminary, if general, conclusion: the contractual, economic, and technical considerations of building tend to block or at least preempt modification. This condition does not prohibit the kind of pragmatic changes that are known as "site decisions" (*solutions de chantier*). Often the geology of a site will incur costly surprises. I offer a second, corollary conclusion: the true work in progress in architectural terms is found in the early phases of a project, when studies and their variants still hinge on the reflection of open-ended choices. The necessity of deadlines, whether for the final competition submission or the mutually agreed-on construction documents, involves a kind of difficult and painful countdown that cuts into the present moment.

71
Villa on St. Peter's Island, circa 1921, exercise at the Bienne *Technicum* involving coordination of plan, section, and facade at the same scale, according to J. N. L. Durand's compositional method

The Academic Practice of the *Variante*

During the second half of the eighteenth century the soon-to-be engineers at the Ecole des Ponts et Chaussées worked under the direction of Jean-Rodolphe Perronet. They utilized the method of the *variante* to develop their projects. Roads were laid in response to topographic obstacles. Hills, gorges, twists and turns, and sandy soil mocked the Euclidean principle of the shortest distance. The choice of the path taken was dictated by public funds and technical performance; the type of the bridge would then adapt itself to this path. Ever since the eighteenth century, successive monarchies and Republics have funded the production of public works by making use of the institutional continuity of the Ecole des Ponts. Leaving aside the Vichy years, the school's various avatars have managed to transcend political change, perhaps driven by the superior laws of Reason, which interpret economy in both geometric and political terms. The optional play of the *variante* fosters an analytical talent in the service of theory and construction. In school, the study of a broad field of completed projects as well as work in the process of being built constituted an integral part of the educational process. Students were encouraged to maintain travel sketchbooks, developing architectural "autopsies" that would then play a role in their own designs. After the French Revolution, the Ecole Polytechnique would absorb and reinforce the role of the Ecole des Ponts.

The integration of the system of the *variante* with architectural theory occurred under J. N. L. Durand's teaching tenure at the Polytechnique.[7] Durand's architecture courses were intended for engineering students, and his teaching philosophy spanned the Republic, Empire, and Restoration eras. His successive volumes, titled *Compendium and Parallel of Buildings of All Kinds*, and his published *Précis* of lectures at the school are accompanied by a robust graphic component made up of engravings. The didactic success of the plates, along with their reprinting, telegraphed a drawing method that privileged comparative readings "in parallel" and in combination with each other. Durand was a polemicist *par excellence*; he enjoyed correcting his former colleagues' costly projects. For him, the *variante* signified a competitive site for counter-proposals. His *Précis* presented a compositional method according to the Cartesian division of a given spatial problem into smaller constraints so as to resolve the design of its recurring elements—door, window, stair, ceiling, vault, and roof. The student would then copy these invariable pieces of the puzzle and situate them in his own plans, sections, and elevations. Such conceptual operations were drawn at the same scale, on the same sheet, and organized within the secure logic of an orthogonal grid. This grid did not purport to predict standardization in fabrication, although it intuitively took into account material performance. Durand reversed the Palladian logic by which compositional axes corresponded to load-bearing zones. Durand was speaking as an architect to engineers, insisting on the solidity of walls and the primacy of their center distances (*entr'-axe*).[8] As a result, his grid located masonry openings. In fact, one of his first exercises focused on a "house with three openings" (*maison à trois trous*), in which three center distances determined the lateral and frontal location of three apertures. The design precondition involved memorization of the elements that form the basis for any large structure: porches, stairs, roofs, porticos, and courtyards. It was Durand's intention that, starting from the running inventory of possible solutions, the student would be able to choose the appropriate combination of elements for any given architectural program and register it in a symmetrical composition. Then would come the delicate moment of choosing a *parti*, a vehicle for exhibiting various building elements according to the use of a pivotal distribution moment: corridors arranged along the periphery of one or multiple courtyards that diffused light and air into the rooms.

Durand's *Précis* clarified a compositional approach that was also introduced at the Beaux-Arts. Who could believe that, 150 years later, Tschumi's students in Lausanne would be confronted with the problem of the "house with three openings"? As discussed earlier, the architectural projects at the Bienne *Technicum* were developed according to orthographic projection, following the same graphic model outlined in the *Précis* (Plate 71). Did Pontremoli expect his students to present him with design variants? It would appear so. One need only refer to a study titled "Vendôme" that Tschumi submitted in 1929 for a building for a large company. Five completed drawings remain, including two plan and facade variations each, along with a perspective of an interior courtyard (Plates 34, 72, 73). Otherwise, one could examine the work of another Pontremoli student from the 1930s, Robert Camelot, who developed his projects through variants presented to his clients.[9] Suffice it to say that Pontremoli encouraged the practice of a kind of conceptual gymnastics whose movements Tschumi would systematically reprise until his death. In 1951, while preparing a competition entry for the MVA building in Lausanne, Tschumi had his drafters compose the principal facade according to three solutions with 9, 13, and 15 bays, each of which included a small and a large center distance in three different dimensions. In total, eight facade options were submitted for consideration.[10]

The academic institution of architectural competitions, whether conducted within the confines of academia[11] or *extra muros*, for public commissions, can also be defined as the presentation of proposals as variations on a theme. The jury identifies and distinguishes among solutions according to a mechanism of promotion aligned with the academic method. The competition becomes a tournament; in fact, the same moral imperative of arbitration first established in the nineteenth century would inspire the founders of the modern Olympic games. Coubertin introduced the presentation of medals, a hierarchic notion of prizes that had originated at the Beaux-Arts. Participation in the competition would become as important as victory. But who among architects could subscribe to Gadamer's conviction that art is both a game and a celebration?[12] The realm of the *variante* belongs foremost to the architectural competition. This quixotic game succeeds in excluding all those passions that were denounced and mocked in seventeenth-century classical literature, namely jealousy, desire, and longing.

Let's return to Durand. As previously noted, his compositional dialectic would reverberate through 150 years of architectural education. Jean-Pierre Epron notes that his students had to tackle the necessity of learning and drawing a *corpus* of references.[13] Durand's *Compendium and Parallel of Buildings of All Kinds* had the status of a reference guide, indispensable for the legitimacy of any project.[14] In 1950 Tschumi required his Lausanne students to present around 300 drawings that copied preeminent examples from antiquity, the Middle Ages, the Renaissance, the Baroque, and twentieth-century architecture. As prerequisites for the Diploma, these drawings were viewed as "master exercises." A former student recalls that "it was perhaps a simplistic method, but a useful one in terms of forming an institutional memory, cultivating a classical culture."[15]

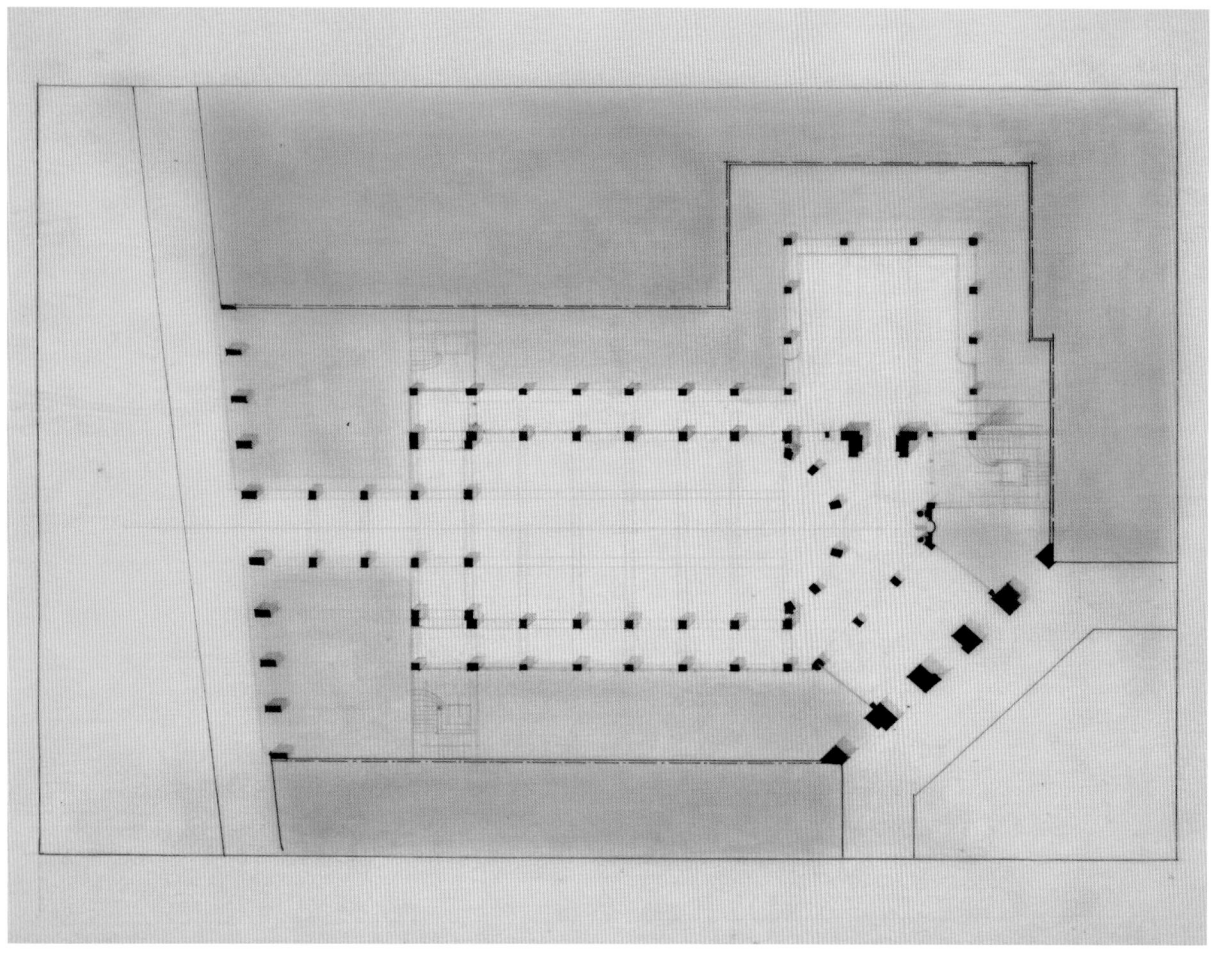

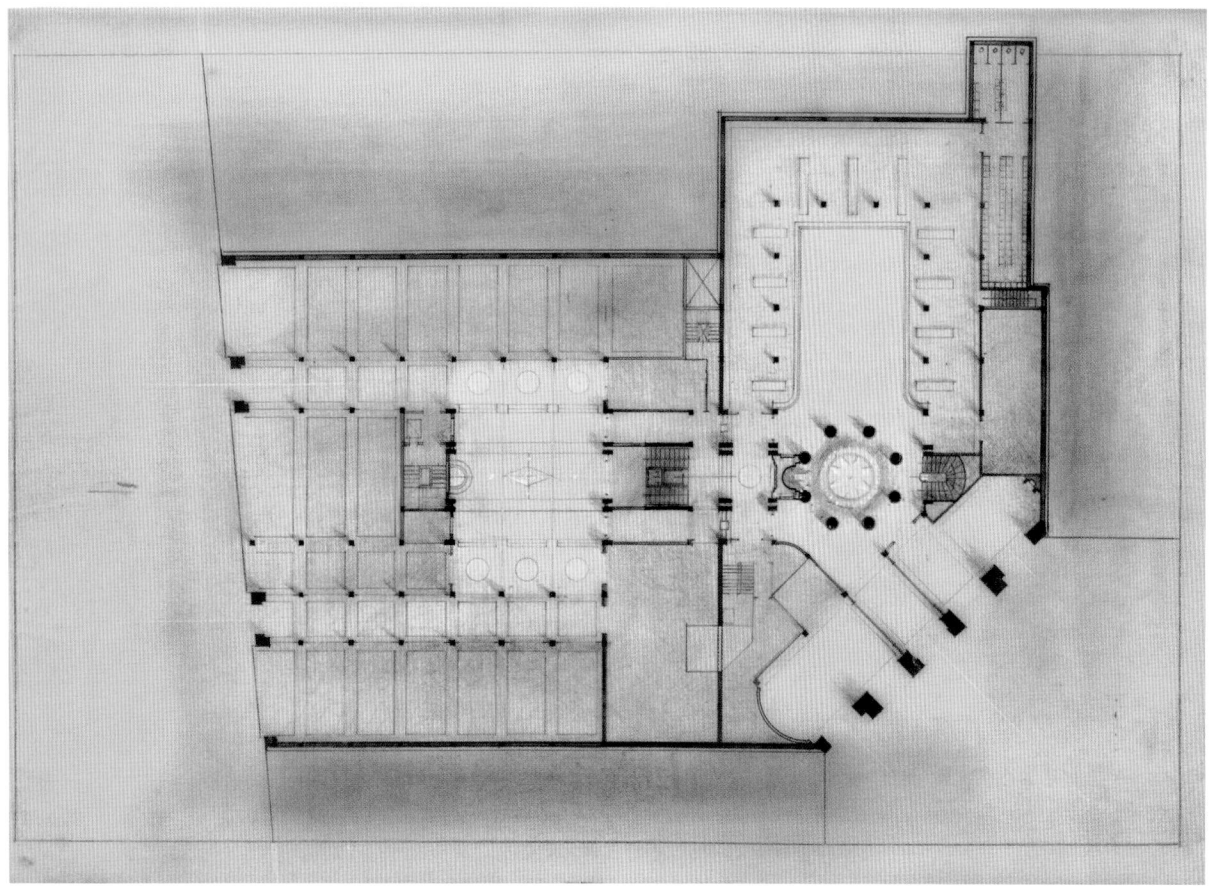

72
Head office of a large company in Paris near the Place de la République, exercise from Pontremoli's studio, 1929–1930, pencil, India ink, and gouache on tracing paper. Two variants showing geometrical play with diagonal entrance, peristyle, galleries, and the basilica type

73
Head office of a large company in Paris near the Place de la République, exercise from Pontremoli's studio, 1929–1930, pencil, charcoal, chalk, India ink, and gouache on tracing paper. Final rendering, with two variants for shop windows and mezzanine

Dialogue within the Project

Inasmuch as the study of any project can proceed from the confrontation and synergy implicit in an exchange of studies, evidence can be found in the practice of two Catalan architects, Esteban Bonell and Josep Maria Gil. Bonell and Gil developed their own particular graphic vocabulary while often working at the scale of a postage stamp. From one set of hands to the other, they moved their process along from scribbles to sketches, from doodles to drafts.[16] Taking turns leaving their Barcelona office to teach in Switzerland, they shuttled back and forth from school to construction site. The large entrance portico for a university library in Lerida and the furniture for its reading room were sketched in two different scales on the same piece of paper (Plate 74); the cantilever confronts the load-bearing frame. The working dialogue between the two men was based on the notion of the *variante*, as if a competition had been opened up inside the project. Once basic options of formal configuration were determined, the development of the program, its refinement, and its technical completion were driven through the confrontation of potential solutions. This internal debate occasionally centered on the choice of a structure, in particular when the spanning of a large distance was called for (as in a stadium), and sometimes on the study of openings between plinths and cornices, when the window module defined the order of the elevation. Lastly, the practice of the *variante* revealed itself as fundamental to their studies for social housing.

The graphic method of Bonell and Gil reminds me of Tschumi's process. Also a commuter between two cities and the founder of a second firm in Lausanne, Tschumi had to coordinate the work of his designers. In his absence, they were asked to develop ideas he had sketched out at the beginning or end of the week; on his return to the office, he would resume control of the outcome. If a designer was on his way out of the office and knew that the boss was on his way in, he would write notes on the drawing, such as, "The framework for the south facade is not yet resolved, the single-occupancy rooms are still a little narrow." Making corrections in pencil, Tschumi would reply, "No, the load-bearing point should correspond to the dimension of the small room; then the facade will be better" (Plate 70). The remark would not resolve the problem of the width of the rooms, but it did introduce a structural principle that could be developed. This working dialogue was an empirical one that stemmed from past successes and earlier failures. Again, I am reminded of Tschumi's statement about good and bad solutions.[17] The ideal of unattainable perfection that he advanced illustrated his own rejection of self-satisfaction and the necessity for the pursuit of research.

Notes

[1] Erin O'Connor, "Work in Progress." See www.erinoconnor.org/writing/joycepaper.html.
[2] In *The Principles of Psychology*, Holt, New York, 1890, William James describes the method of the "stream of consciousness."
[3] Philippe Junod, *Transparence et opacité. Essai sur les fondements théoriques de l'art moderne: pour une nouvelle lecture de Konrad Fiedler* (1976), J. Chambon, Nimes, 2004.
[4] The art historian Yves-Alain Bois has argued that Mondrian's neo-plastic oils on canvas are not enlargements of preliminary small-scale studies, but rather the development of a series of decisions made along the course of the work. Yves-Alain Bois, "The Iconoclast," in *Piet Mondrian, 1872–1944*, Leonardo Arte, Milan, 1994, pp. 313–372.
[5] The dispute during the years 1399–1400 over the construction of Milan's cathedral dome is narrated by James S. Ackerman, "Ars sine scientia nihil est, Gothic Theory of Architecture at the Cathedral of Milan," *Art Bulletin*, XXXI, 1949, pp. 84–111.
[6] Guido Morpurgo, *Gregotti & Associati, L'Architetettura del dise-gno urbano*, Rizzoli, Milan, 2008, p. 9.
[7] Werner Szambien, *Jean-Nicolas-Louis Durand, 1760–1834. De l'imitation à la norme*, Picard, Paris, 1984.
[8] As recounted by Armand Brulhart, who had visited the papers of the Geneva-based Polytechnic graduate Guillaume-Henri Dufour.
[9] See also the three variants for the spectator stands designed for a sports arena in Sucy-en-Brie. Cf., Gilles Ragot, *Camelot*, Mardaga, Liège, 1988, p. 151.
[10] ACM file No. 60.04.195.
[11] This "pedagogy of confrontation" underlying the 200-year history of the Beaux-Arts is a central theme of Jean-Pierre Epron, *Comprendre l'éclectisme*, Editions Norma, Paris, 1997.
[12] Hans-Georg Gadamer, *The Relevance of the Beautiful and Other Essays*, Cambridge University Press, Cambridge, 1987.
[13] Epron, op. cit., p. 150.
[14] Published in the years 1799–1801, this luxurious body of work is also known as *le grand Durand*.
[15] As recounted by Alin Décoppet, who received his EPUL diploma in 1954, on 8 August 1997.
[16] Jacques Gubler, curator of the exhibition and catalogue, *Bonell e Gil, Architetti Barcellona, Il dialogo del progetto*, Mendrisio Academy Press, Mendrisio, 2001.
[17] Alex Gerber, a student at EPUL and draftsman in Tschumi's office, recalls this phrase: "There is no good solution; only one is the least bad." As recounted by Gerber on 17 March 2005.

74
Library for the University of Lerida
and furniture study, Bonell and Gil, 4 July 1996,
preliminary competition sketches showing
the four hands of the two partners
at "postage-stamp" scale

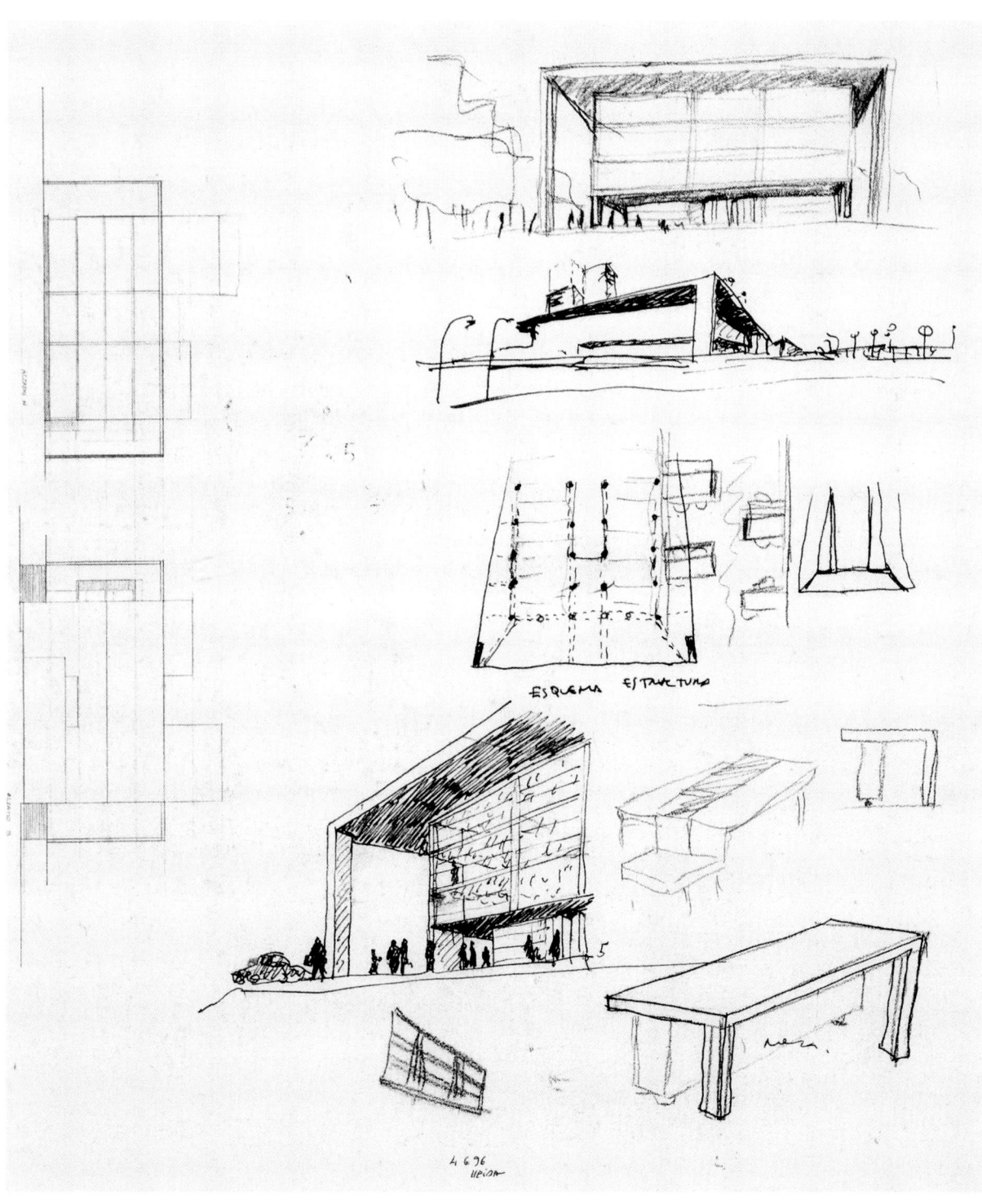

High Points of Corporate Architecture: Sandoz and Nestlé

While it recuperates a phenomenon evident in the nineteenth century, the notion of corporate architecture is relatively recent.[1] The adjective "corporate" derives from the noun "corporation" and indicates what belongs to a firm in the trajectory of its commercial progress. We are in the domain of private architecture. Capitalist competition encourages firms to distinguish themselves, to *appear* different. In this context, architecture takes on an iconic value of representation and participates in a strategy of identification. Developed in the 1980s, the sociological notion of corporate identity is multifaceted.[2] In the flux of marketing, the personification of a trademark is translated through the graphic display of the logo, becoming a visual identification of the product, hence the very portrait of a firm. Thus the "nest," a translation of the Nestlé family name. Similarly, paper industrialists during the Ancien Régime conceived of imprinting their sheets with watermarks, from which the primitive association with trademarks derives. The strategy of broadcasting products also enters the domain of communication, a term that has become a subject of study all its own in universities and high schools today. Finally, the notion of corporate identity takes on a moral dimension, expressing the modes of behavior, values, rituals, catch phrases, and even linguistic idiosyncrasies that make up the unique identity of a group—in short, a "corporate culture."[3] Without a doubt, architecture plays a role in this effort of differentiation, whether in the form of an urban sign or as a metaphor for the product's quality.

The function and power of architectural representation are registered in the costs that bind the master builder with his backer. The circumstances of the contractual agreement span the length of history itself. However, in industrial societies the connection between facilitators and clientele enters a new political and economic framework that opposes private architecture (or what Durand termed "*l'architecture particulière*") and public architecture. This leads us to the question of programs. Hospitals, prisons, schools, museums, and libraries are among examples of public institutions that represent the state. In the nineteenth century, whether in Europe or the United States, the department store, the café, and the large-scale newspaper printing press distinguished themselves among private programs anchored in the notion of corporate identity. At the beginning of the twentieth century, the factory, along with the large urban or suburban hotel, would become such a monumental and representative trope that it would be possible to rewrite the history of modern architecture through the lens of an iconology that opposed public and private property. We will see that the question of signs and images began to be argued in the late 1960s, when semiotic theories of visual communication replaced the classical dialectic of styles and models.

Beginning in the last decades of the nineteenth century, department store architecture established itself in urban areas either by incorporating the name of its owner (as in the case of the Philadelphia Wanamakers) or by using the enticing motto of a large bazaar (such as the one Emile Zola depicted in his emblematic *Au Bonheur des Dames* (1883), translated into English as "The Ladies' Delight"). In New York the *Tribune* newspaper headquarters flirted with vertically stacked floors[4] even before the metaphor of the "skyscraper" appeared in Chicago. In 1922 the international competition for a tower for the *Chicago Tribune* telegraphed to the world the idea that the tall building was an appropriate vehicle to represent the image of private business concerns even without the figurative send-up of Greek motifs and statuary. Previously, the image of a New York

75
Project for Nestlé Pavilion for Paris World's Fair (1937), June 1936, gouache, wash, and airbrush. Cylinder is corporate sign of the powdered-milk box. Presented under the names "Jean T. Chumy, architect, Edouard-Marcel Sandoz, sculptor"

skyscraper aping a Gothic cathedral had signaled the power of a department store. It was not uncommon in nineteenth-century Europe to adorn corporate letterhead with small vignettes depicting medals won at exhibitions, or factories or workers' housing. In the years before World War I, a refocusing of values took place in Wilhelmine Germany. Trade groups, manufacturers, store-owners, architects, and schools of applied art all came together under the banner of the Deutscher Werkbund, founded in 1907.[5] The aim of this organization was to coordinate the division of labor into primary and tertiary sectors within a unified *Gesamtkunstwerk*. Architects who were bold in their expressions shaped and built factories. The classic historiography of the Modern Movement, as written by Pevsner and Giedion, discovered this phenomenon and focused attention on the duo of Peter Behrens and Walter Gropius. Behrens had the opportunity to intervene in emerging historical and economic tensions. As AEG's *Berater für Kunst*,[6] or artistic advisor, he designed not only the industrial company's plants and products but also its hexagonal logo, which signaled the prominence of the enterprise in Berlin. That the same architect was commissioned to design AEG's logo, factories, products, posters, and catalogs would remain unique and even lead to some nostalgic memories. Behrens' work helps us understand what would later become known as "corporate design."

In Turin at the end of World War I, FIAT succeeded in building up the car factory and its Ford-modeled organization to the level of a modern monument in reinforced concrete. In the interwar years, designers arrived in force, and communication specialists offered their advertising and branding services. Ephemeral pavilions marked as "X" or "Y" flourished in the halls of trade fairs and international exhibitions. This "*architecture parlante*," often quite talkative, contrasted with the laconic methods of the avant-garde, for example, in the work of the Belgian Louis Herman De Koninck.[7] Transplanted to the United States, the Viennese architect Frederick Kiesler referenced contemporary theories of visual communication in his aphorism, "The shop window is a silent loudspeaker."[8] In the process, an intertwining relationship developed that, far from being silent, placed the sponsor in the position of the impresario, or even the director of the building itself.[9]

Our fast slalom along the terrain of corporate architecture and design aims to illuminate the consequences of one particular meeting. In 1936 the sculptor Edouard-Marcel Sandoz (1881–1971), then director of Sandoz France and Sandoz SA, whose world headquarters was in Basel, joined forces with the architect Tschumi.

1936–1937: The Singular Collaboration between Jean Tschumi and Edouard-Marcel Sandoz

That a 55-year-old sculptor and industrialist like Sandoz would embark on a joint venture with a 32-year-old architect posed a unique scenario. For Tschumi's part, the meeting did not transpire without asking existential questions à la Gauguin in Tahiti: Where do we come from? What are we? Where are we going? It is not surprising that when Tschumi received his French professional license (DPLG), he began wondering about the spelling of his artistic name. His doubts stemmed from his status as a Swiss in Paris. The German spelling of his Bernese surname caused disquiet in France: the "tsch" was hardly elegant. At the Beaux-Arts he had signed his drawings as "Tchumi." But he needed his Helvetic surname to participate in competitions in the cantons of Vaud, Bern, and Zurich. When he submitted his competition entry for the city of Stockholm, his signature became "Tschumy." The most graphic extravagance was thrust into his work between 1936 and 1937, during his association with Sandoz, when he was transformed into "Jean T. Chumy." One could assume an amusing scenario somewhere between irony and despair. Finally he settled on the diplomatic balance of dual membership. In Paris his letterhead bore the inscription, "*Jean Tchumi Architecture Mobilier*," while work destined for Switzerland was conducted under his registered name. The collaboration with Sandoz would exacerbate, then clarify, his dual status.

Born in 1881 in Basel, where his father managed a successful synthetic dye company in partnership with the chemist Alfred Kern,[10] Sandoz was a figure of many dimensions (Plate 76). His generalist aptitude reconciled the skills that the university system was used to separating. Sandoz would define his professional identity in these terms: "I am a painter and a sculptor, a physicist and a chemist."[11] He forgot to mention his talents as a financial manager in the service of capitalist enterprises. His scientific concepts emerged from the context of an excellent private high school in the Alps where both the humanities and the natural sciences were taught.[12] His immersion in the art and business worlds recalls the adventures of several self-made American millionaires who had inspired Edgar Brandt. It was through the School of Decorative Arts in Geneva that Sandoz had access to the practice of drawing and handicrafts. His father supported his artistic interests, and Sandoz settled comfortably in Paris. Enrolled at the Beaux-Arts, he developed an academic career as a sculptor. He chose Antonin Mercié's workshop. He became passionate about stone carving, but sculpting unique pieces out of melted wax interested him as well. From 1907 on he exhibited at the Salons and drew critical attention for his work.[13] There was no shortage of humor in his art, as exemplified by his piece titled "Thinking Monkey," which poked fun at Rodin. During World War I Sandoz organized a philanthropic workshop for the disabled that produced toys and trinkets, crafting stunning polychromatic *bricolages*.[14] At the same time he developed a singular bestiary made up of enameled porcelain pieces cast in large workshops like those of Limoges and Sèvres. He would become known under the artistic title of "*animalier*."

Sandoz led the life of a wealthy young man who, with one foot in Paris and the other in Lausanne, traveled far and wide to places that fed his interest in cultural geography. He practiced watercolor skills as a kind of logbook. In Paris, his studio on the Rue d'Alésia amused visitors with its wildlife: a family of birds and mammals. He loved the Saharan fox known as a fennec. He maintained a friendly correspondence with the biochemist Arthur Stoll, who was head of the research laboratories in the Basel headquarters. In addition to his famous work on ergotamine, Stoll developed an injectable form of calcium for Sandoz. For his own part, Edouard-Marcel Sandoz sought to colorize the group of white pigeons that had nested in his studio. Stoll provided Sandoz with appropriate food supplements, but the effect on their plumage color was unstable. (The sculptor, however, did get some red eggs!) He wanted to develop and patent a product that could determine the color of feathers and fur for domesticated animals. His obsessive desire to mutate the chromatics of animals translated successfully into porcelain enamel or mixed alloys of bronze with patinas of gold and silver and green granite. It was through sculpture that Sandoz succeeded in his agenda of zoological transformation. In Paris he exhibited his works with a group of *animaliers* in Brandt's showroom.

76
The sculptor and painter Edouard-Marcel Sandoz and his Sahara fox or fennec, 1930. Portrait by De Jongh

77
Edouard-Marcel Sandoz, *The Fennec*, circa 1930, bronze and white patina, nocturnal effect

78
Competition for Swiss Pavilion at Paris World's Fair (1937), joint entry by Tschumi and Sandoz, 1936, pencil, charcoal, and watercolor. Facade on the Seine, lakeside atmosphere

79
Competition for Swiss Pavilion at Paris World's Fair (1937), joint entry by Tschumi and Sandoz, 1936, pencil, pastel, and watercolor. Interior perspective of hall toward south, southern light

It was in this multifaceted environment, where art and technology joined hands with big business, that Tschumi and Sandoz met.[15] They shared common life experiences: they had both attended the Beaux-Arts, and could exchange memories of its jokes, rites, and rituals. Their age difference of 22 years did not prevent them from establishing a joint studio whose first products appeared in 1936. While Sandoz was well established in his social and professional *milieu*, Tschumi was still building up his own reputation. He focused on winning competitions and commissions. With Sandoz' support he met great captains of industry who had developed their businesses in France. The OSEC (Office of Swiss Business Development) had been founded in 1927.

Before turning to the Nestlé Pavilion at the 1937 Exposition des Arts et Techniques, a brief pause to mention the national competition for the Swiss Pavilion at the same exhibition is merited. Beginning in January 1936 and appealing directly to OSEC, Tschumi sought to anticipate future needs which, for him, meant building an extension to the Swiss Pavilion devoted to wines, cheeses, and meats to provide both an international meeting venue and a Swiss club in Paris. He began the competition in partnership with Sandoz, working under the springtime motto of "Switzerland alive and fresh" (Plates 78, 79). The project was eliminated, but it did permit Tschumi to explore a partnership that was unorthodox in the corporate sphere. The scheme and renderings showed Tschumi's hand. The architecture developed decorative events on a monumental plinth along the banks of the Seine, with wide beaches intended to be painted on a mural inside the glazed market hall; the latter would have been Sandoz' work were the project realized. The poetry was nautical, and a central marquee sheltered the pier. It would also have been possible to accommodate a terraced café or restaurant. The colors of the project recalled the southern light and the chromatic values of Roger Expert, one of the winners of the Colonial Exhibition of 1931. Their project's failure impelled the artists to pursue their efforts outside the bounds of competition. The Swiss industrial group of the small Parisian colony was called to attention. Switzerland's presence, it was suggested, could be strengthened if a second pavilion were built, namely a food pavilion located in a sector north of the Swiss Pavilion. The architect sketched out an alpine village, a large Bern-style farmhouse, and a mountain whose spiralling structure could accommodate a ski jump.[16] In the central courtyard, the geometry of a triangular pylon echoed the shape of the Toblerone bar—a specialty of Bern's notable *chocolatier*[17] (Plate 81). Perhaps the construction was intended as a counterweight to the major presence of Nestlé, which had entrusted its own pavilion to the Tschumi-Sandoz team.

80
Competition for Swiss Pavilion
at Paris World's Fair (1937), joint entry
by Tschumi and Sandoz, 1936, pencil, charcoal,
and watercolor. The main gate through north
facade

81
Competition for the Swiss Pavilion at Paris
World's Fair (1937), joint entry by Tschumi
and Sandoz, 1936, pencil, India ink,
and watercolor. Suggestion to jury in form
of a second "Swiss Food" pavilion

A Competitor of Le Corbusier

In 1928 Le Corbusier designed the Nestlé pavilion at the Paris Expo.[18] In 1937 it was Tschumi, now allied with Sandoz, who built the pavilion to advertise the business ventures of the same Vevey-based company at the Exposition Internationale des Arts et Techniques. This permutation provides a precise marker of the enduring rivalry between Tschumi and Le Corbusier.

Beyond Le Corbusier's campaign against the Beaux-Arts (a polemic that found many partisans in Switzerland) and his near-exclusive appropriation of the banner of modernity, Tschumi would have many occasions in 1937 to recall ideas that he had developed and Le Corbusier had then exploited. The 1937 exhibition would set a primitive stage for this competition. As Secretary of the GECUS Executive Committee, Tschumi worked on the presentation of the architectural project devoted to the Paris underground that was exhibited in the cellars of the Museum of Modern Art under the patronage of the exhibition's chief architect, Jacques Gréber. The Utudjian-directed GECUS project received a Grand Prize and Tschumi was awarded a diploma of honor. When in his later writings on urban planning Le Corbusier referred to the idea of "passive defense" in relation to the theoretical effect of the bombing of European cities, Tschumi felt dispossessed without compensatory recognition.

A cursory glance, often shared retrospectively by survivors, would conclude that the architectural "show" in 1937 set the stage for the inevitable arrival of war. In fact, the war had already begun in Spain; in April of the same year, the bombing of the Basque town of Guernica stirred the dark monochrome turmoil of Picasso's more than 20-foot-square canvas hung in the Pavilion of the Spanish Republic.[19] It might therefore appear merely anecdotal to report on the rivalry between a young colleague and an older one. However, the episode deserves mention—not because it meant much to Le Corbusier's work and life, but because it would leave a mark on Tschumi's work and teaching. Le Corbusier's impact was such that it might be possible to interpret Tschumi's subsequent work as a constant replica of the elder master, a fact that was unspoken or whispered in hushed tones, as some alumni still recall.[20]

82
Nestlé Pavilion at Paris World's Fair (1937), interior perspective of the cupola in the cylinder, 1936, pencil, color chalk, and watercolor. Entrance, diorama, and concave chart showing company's presence in the world

83
Nestlé Pavilion, 3 June 1936, at Paris World's Fair (1937), two options for more central and costly sites, rejected by client

The Nestlé Pavilion of 1937

The project for the Nestlé flagship, called "The Pavilion for All the World's Babies," was completed in June 1936 by J. T. Chumy (sic) and Sandoz. The architects proposed a series of variations. Initially, there was uncertainty about the site. Was the client ready to rent a prestige plot, or would it prefer a more economical location? The question provoked a range of possibilities. One can imagine that the architects' preference tended toward the first solution: the building would then be a signal visible to motorists during their acceleration along the Cours La Reine near the Concorde (Plate 83). But costs would have to be examined. The program had three basic elements: a coffee-tasting area where the house specialties (including condensed milk, homogenized cereal- and vegetable-based foods, nescao, and NPCK chocolates) would be consumed; a diorama illustrating the firm's global presence (Plates 82, 89); and, finally, the special "Cinéma Guignol Nestlé" invented by the architect himself. Tschumi illustrated the various possibilities for the pavilion in a book of colored vignettes, reducing them to four variants: a modern and dynamic solution based on the spiral, two compact and symmetrical compositions and, finally, an eclectic solution, dynamic on the south and classicist on the west, which enticed the sponsors (Plate 85). In all four cases, the major architectural "event" was the dominant plastic cylinder, a sign of the powered-milk box that was Nestlé's flagship product. Some colorful and bold details remained unbuilt, including an ornamental bucranium destined for the spike of the central pylon where it emerged from the cylinder (Plate 1)—a spot that would have provided Sandoz an animal motif. The latter would have to be content with painting dioramas on the walls of a Punch and Judy show.

The architect summarized the project chosen by the client in an imposing polychrome rendering (Plate 85). Vertical blades growing in height and arranged in an ascending spiral formed the bracing for the cylinder. These blades expressed "chocolate" through their color. The execution of the project retreated from earlier intentions. The surviving views exist in black-and-white only, so the polychromatic effect has been lost, but what remain are the dominant white volumes. The bird's nest logo adorns the cylinder that houses the model of the plant amid an alpine landscape in a kind of friendly reminder of the original products. The dome hosted a group of paintings by Sandoz. A virtuoso projection of the Four Continents was reflected in the field of a circular mirror installed at its focal point (Plate 89). One frieze depicted rotating colonial motifs in support of the slogan: "121 Nestlé factories spread health to the ends of the civilized world." The gabled pediment over the archways of the terrace on the west facade displayed the sign "Cinéma Guignol Nestlé." The discrepancy between the singular, expressive quality of the original drawn design and its rapid execution challenges us. The building was located midway between theater décor and permanence. The wood and plaster structure included a minimum of repeated elements. Each part aimed at uniqueness. The scenography governing the routes and flows of visitors illustrated a kind of dexterity.

Dated 1937, the Nestlé Pavilion marked the first individual commission for the young architect. Under the dome of the diorama, his signature read "Jean Tschumy." This spelling version had replaced "Jean T. Chumy," the name used for the competition's multicolored renderings. He finally settled on the spelling "Tschumi" in 1939, after completing a commission in Basel.

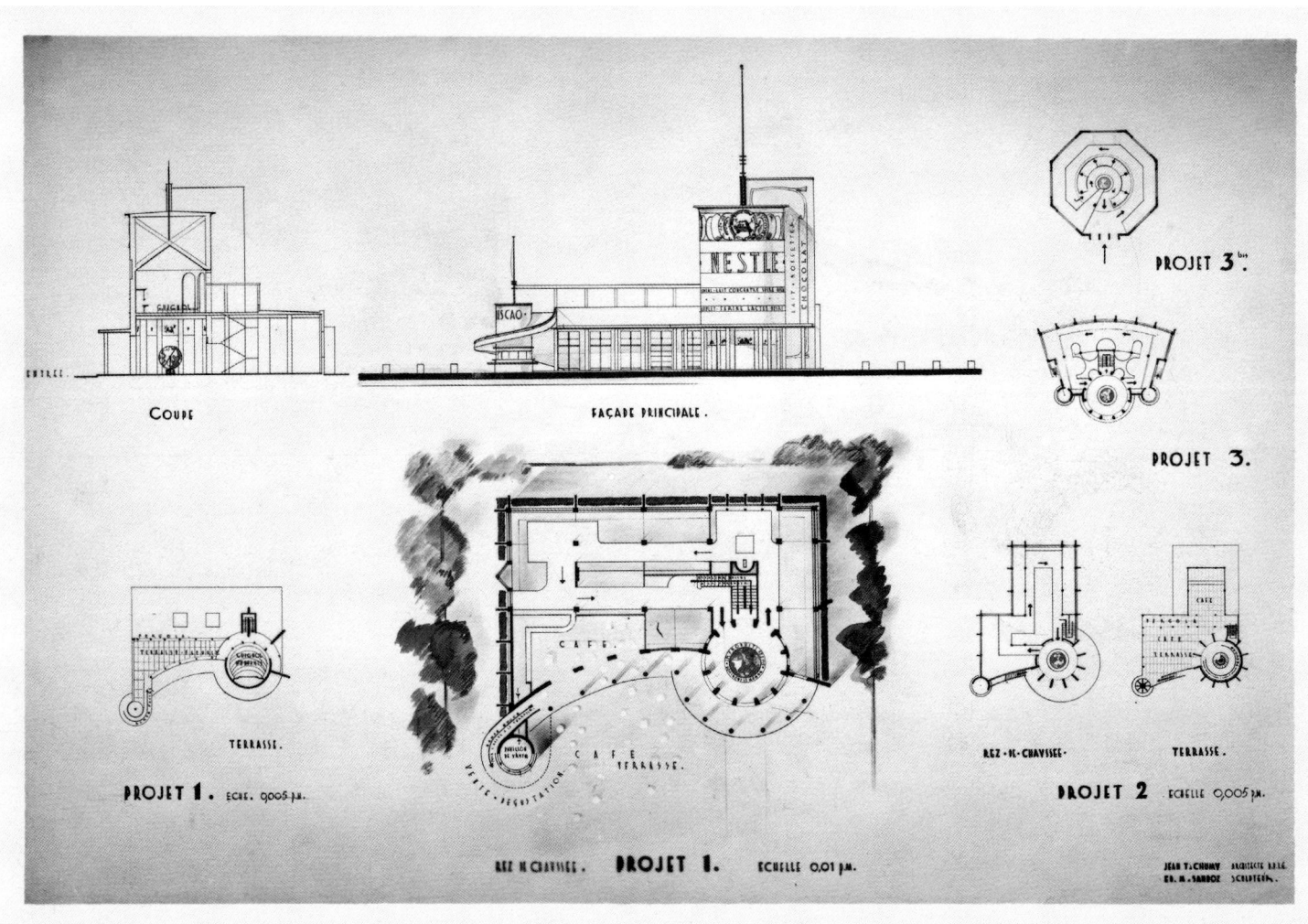

84
Nestlé Pavilion at Paris World's Fair (1937), June 1936. The first of four variants that will be accepted and developed

85
Nestlé Pavilion at Paris World's Fair (1937), 1936, pencil, gouache, washed drawing, India ink, and watercolor, tracing paper on wooden board. Attractive rendering preceding final project modification

86
Nestlé Pavilion at Paris World's Fair (1937), bar at southwest corner where coffee and chocolate were served

87
Nestlé Pavilion at Paris World's Fair (1937), southern facade, entrance through cylinder, staircase to upper terrace

88
Nestlé Pavilion at Paris World's Fair (1937), western facade, terrace and portico for movie and puppet theater

89
Nestlé Pavilion at Paris World's Fair (1937), dedicated to "all the world's babies," major space under cupola in cylinder with diorama showing powdered-milk plant in Switzerland

Miro-Mirage

Shortly after the end of the exhibition our two colleagues executed a patent filing for a transparent mirror under the banner of *Tchumi & Sandoz Décorateurs*. Sandoz was fond of photographic montages that played with mirrors. Like Alice in Wonderland, he had his daughter Nicole sit at a table to draw her portrait in multiple views—back, face, and profile. The transparent mirror was named *Miro-Mirage*. The device included a housing and a metal support; its surface was a two-way mirror. The bottom was a piece of polished metal onto which photographs could be adhered. As alternatives, one or two bulbs of 40 or 60 watts fit into the housing. Ventilation was provided through lateral holes, and a switch fit into a cradle. A tilted mirror when set on a night table or dressing table, the *Miro-Mirage*, once lit, would unveil the portrait of the beloved (Plates 90, 91). It was a magic lantern, a kind of *mise en abyme*, embracing the poetic theme of lovers meeting in a mirror. Tschumi had had the *Miro-Mirage* in mind for two years since the construction of his Honfleur suite aboard the *Normandie* liner. The transatlantic journey would have provided an effective advertising vehicle.[21] As usual, the architect studied a dozen variations on paper. In its optical principle, the project copied a wall mural devised by the firm of Baudet Donon Roussel, manufacturers of arms and metal works. It is possible that Tschumi and Sandoz contacted this factory to provide them with a limited number of prototype variants. In 1938 the product was presented at the Salon d'Automne, on a boudoir table with a pouf. Despite Sandoz' commercial and industrial know-how, this chic and expensive object found neither customers nor distribution.[22]

90
Miro-Mirage, 1938, rear front

91
Miro-Mirage, 1938, display of model in advertisement for a beauty cream, prototype presented at 1938 Salon d'Automne

1938–1942: First Projects for Sandoz in Basel, Noisy-le-Sec, and Orléans

In 1938, on the eve of a war enabled by Hitler, Sandoz secured a prestigious commission for Tschumi to design executive offices intended for the director, Fritz Imhoff, and the boardroom at the Basel headquarters of his family company. Sandoz SA occupied a large plot of land along the immediate Alsatian border. The calcium ampoules it manufactured entered France from a factory in Saint Louis, which was adjacent to the Swiss laboratories that provided the base material. At first Tschumi developed a decorative scheme in Paris on the basis of plans provided by the project architects. His study was detailed. One hundred polychrome designs offered a multitude of possibilities for assembling carpets, paneling, radiator covers, tables, chairs, and lighting. In a second step, the architect was sent to Basel to learn the operation of chemical plants. His mandate as an interior designer soon shifted to the interior of the construction site that had been opened in 1937.[23] Some traces of this work survive today.[24] Admittedly, the archival archeology of the project can relish in the virtuosity of the graphics. Several relics *in situ* still bear witness to aggressive decisions, for example, the metal radiator grilles. Also notable is Tschumi's use of paneling and bronze and aluminum lighting in the apse of the waiting lounge, which was reserved for Imhoff (Plates 99–101). Finally, the table and ceiling lighting in the boardroom remain, as well as models for a pedestal table with a tripod base whose legs reflect a late Art Deco taste (Plate 102).

The architect delegated to observe operations in Basel soon discovered chemical manufacturing and the complex machinery of laboratories. This mission allowed him to anticipate by a few months the decommissioning of the Saint-Louis plant located on the border of Alsace and Switzerland, which would be evacuated in September 1939.[25] The reservoir of pharmaceuticals, equipment, and machinery was transported to the Noisy-le-Sec site in Seine-Saint-Denis, whose location close by a national highway allowed medicines to be transported rapidly to hospitals in the French capital. In Paris Sandoz had befriended some doctors and introduced them to his recent products: ampoules of calcium and optalidon, a powerful painkiller.[26] The architect monitored the rapid reassembly facilities, which were operational by 1940. He also studied the expansion of the company's laboratories.[27] Indeed, until his death nearly a quarter-century later, Tschumi would direct all projects for all divisions of Sandoz France. The second site chosen by the Swiss firm was located in Orléans. The architect went there for the first time in September 1939 to meet his colleague André Masson, who under Tschumi's leadership would monitor the expansion of a first plant at Rue de Tudelle.

In 1940 Sandoz employed about 40 people in its Orléans branch, but its enlargement was difficult because of the Nazi invasion: Orléans was part of the occupied zone. Cement became a material of strategic importance, and its transportation was closely monitored. The plant would allocate three floors for the production of coatings for pills and the filling of vials. The architect announced to the board what he wanted to finish construction by December of that year.[28] The multiple and tragic circumstances of war did not inhibit the production of Sandoz France. The architect and his patron presented as

92
Sandoz Laboratories, Orléans, 1940–1941, first location at Rue de Tudelle

93
Sandoz headquarters in Basel, 1938, office for director Fritz Imhoff, black India ink on tracing paper

94
Sandoz headquarters in Basel, 1938, office for director Fritz Imhoff, pencil, watercolor, gouache. Bird's eye view, exuberant study in Spanish atmosphere

artists their plans for the future development of the company and its new administrative headquarters in Paris. On February 4, 1942 Tschumi gave Sandoz a preliminary study for a boardroom. The perspectives show two styles, on one hand a cameo effect, which sculpted the light, and on the other an almost tropical color range—red ochre, sienna, yellow-orange, turquoise, and jade green. This fever of projects recalled the ambiguous contemporary slogan for the "reconstruction of Europe" that stimulated the hopes and imaginations of architects in France as well as in the United States, as if the war could offer a clean slate on which a healthy modernity could be re-instated. Tschumi's whimsical impulses were channeled into a life-long project put up by Sandoz, his sculptor-partner: to become the sole architect for Sandoz France.

Here it is legitimate to reflect on the example presented in Basel by Otto Rudolf Salvisberg, a great orchestrator of corporate architecture for the firm Hoffmann-La Roche, a Sandoz rival. We know that before a career in Berlin, Zurich, Bern, and Basel the Bern native had spent three years at the Bienne *Technicum*. It would be impossible for Tschumi not to have seen Salvisberg's buildings for Hoffmann-La Roche during his stay in Basel in 1939, especially since these buildings represented the most recent architectural typologies of chemistry laboratories and offices.[29] Certainly the elegance that Salvisberg introduced into functionalism provided Tschumi with important references, such as the idea of a sculptural stairwell as a dynamic event. This theme had been addressed in Paris by Auguste Perret in his Museum of Public Works.

95
Sandoz headquarters in Basel, 1938, pencil, chalk, watercolor on tracing paper. Staircase and landing on second floor

96
Sandoz headquarters in Basel, 1938, pencil, chalk, watercolor on tracing paper. Third floor, perspective of gallery outside of boardroom

97
Sandoz headquarters in Basel, boardroom, 1938, pencil, chalk, watercolor on tracing paper. A flash drawing suggesting Pompeian atmosphere

98
Sandoz headquarters in Basel, boardroom, 1938, pencil, charcoal, chalk, watercolor on tracing paper. Use of a basilica configuration

99
Sandoz headquarters in Basel, anteroom of Fritz Imhoff office, 1938, pencil, charcoal, gouache on Canson paper. Entrance integrated in the wood-paneled apse

100
Sandoz headquarters in Basel, anteroom of Fritz Imhoff office, 1939, axis of the door in curved wood-paneling. Photograph by Simone Mengani, 2007

101
Sandoz headquarters in Basel, anteroom of Fritz Imhoff office, 1939, wall lamp in apse, opalescent glass and metal. Photograph by Simone Mengani, 2007

102
Sandoz headquarters in Basel, pedestal table in boardroom, 1939, late Art Deco taste. Photograph by Simone Mengani, 2007

103
Sandoz headquarters in Basel, boardroom, 1939, table, wall, and ceiling lamps. Photograph by Simone Mengani, 2007

1947–1950: The Sandoz Headquarters at Rue de Penthièvre

In 1943 Jean Tschumi was called on to teach in Lausanne. Crossing the border and settling in Switzerland presented logistical and administrative difficulties that had to be negotiated at the highest diplomatic level. The laboratories of Sandoz France continued to produce, despite the absence of their architect. In 1944 Tschumi chose an office and home on the Boulevard de Grancy, near the Central Station of Lausanne. In 1947 he obtained confirmation of his role as director of architecture. The war had strengthened the industrial presence of Sandoz France, so there was an urgent need to establish a headquarters that could accommodate the entire management division as well as executives. Seven individual offices were needed. A former mansion (*hôtel particulier*) was acquired on 6 Rue de Penthièvre, a street that led into the Faubourg Saint-Honoré in Paris. Work started up again in these new surroundings. The transformation was radical, both on its facade and in its interior floors, which quickly swallowed up 2,864 square meters. Construction lasted one year, and the office opened in 1950. The technical equipment was subject to extensive preliminary negotiations, and the architect actively sought competitive bids from contractors. Because the management's tendency was to favor Swiss companies with a base in France (this would also be the case with Nestlé), the firms were put under considerable pressure.[30] For heating, Sulzer was chosen over the supplier American Air Filter, whose advertising referred to the path of electrons (Plate 105). The firm TEPRINA received the commission for telephones (Plate 104). Tschumi modulated his furniture studies according to the individual tastes of directors (Plates 108–111). It wasn't a question of buying tables and chairs, lamps and ashtrays designed by others; he produced dozens of individual variants, first at the scale of a postage stamp, then followed by larger, spectacular perspectives. The plans were rendered at 1:10 scale. Finally, the work was put forward at full scale.

For the main entrance, Tschumi proposed to reformulate the factory's logo (which dated from 1916)[31] into a play of Sandoz "S" figures inscribed in a circle that recalled an elegant yin and yang (Plate 106). But the old logo was already on all the prod-

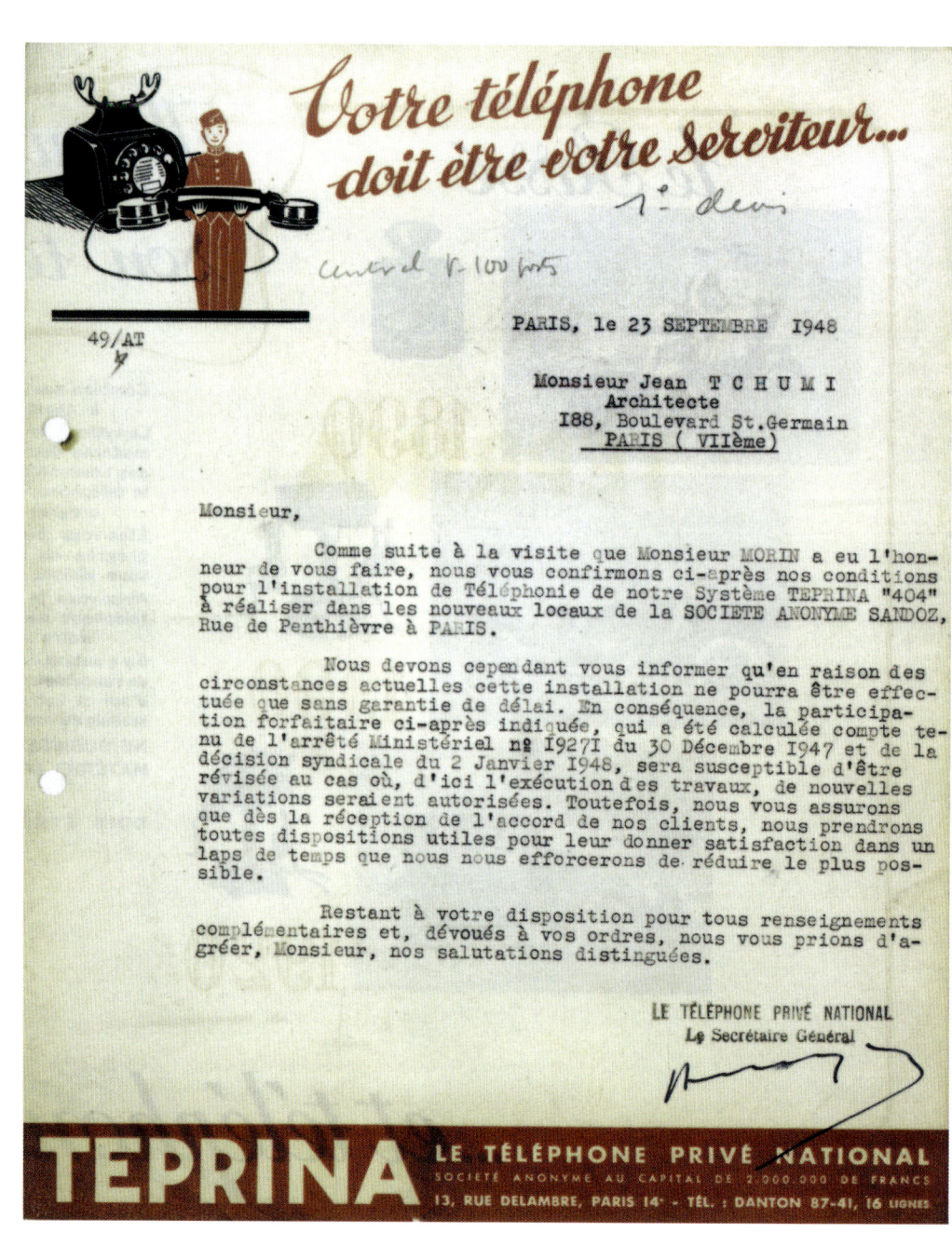

104
Letter to the architect from the telephone installation engineer, 23 September 1948

105
Bulletin of American Air Filter Company, Louisville, Kentucky, circa 1947. Document consulted by the architect when working on Sandoz headquarters in Paris

uct cartons traveling the New York streets as well as on the doors of the trucks for Sandoz Chemical Works. Alas, the new entrance would be left without a logo. The clients were satisfied with the carefully executed work done for their luxurious new offices in Paris. The commercial success of Sandoz products in the 1950s led them to look further. Seven years after its move, management calculated that it needed an additional 6,000 square meters of space for its offices. The architect was sent to seek out available sites. In November 1957 Tschumi began work on a schematic design for the Avenue Pierre 1er de Serbie, not far from Trocadero. For the next ten years he explored the beautiful areas of the northwest, the 16th *arrondissement*, and the affluent suburbs of Neuilly and Levallois-Perret, identifying opportunities. He studied six cases, for each of which he imagined a potential development model with square meters allocated and mixed-use programs. Tschumi's site sketches and small-scale perspectives, in addition to his real estate prospecting, also interested Nestlé, which was registered in Paris under the acronym "SOPAD" (Société de Produits Alimentaires et Diététiques). Sandoz and Nestlé assisted each other in expanding their businesses. At the time of his sudden death, the architect had received the commission for the new SOPAD headquarters on the Quai Paul Doumer in Courbevoie (Plates 185, 186), a project that would be continued and realized posthumously by André Aubert. For its part, Sandoz France, weary of looking for land in the 16th *arrondissement*, had acquired ownership of the Manoir Richelieu in Rueil-Malmaison in Hauts-de-Seine. Tschumi submitted a first draft for the project in July 1961. A few weeks after the architect's death, its final study and implementation would be divided between two protagonists, Bernard Zehrfuss, another Pontremoli disciple and a respected "comrade," and Basel's Martin Burckhardt, a skilled professional who had the confidence of central management.

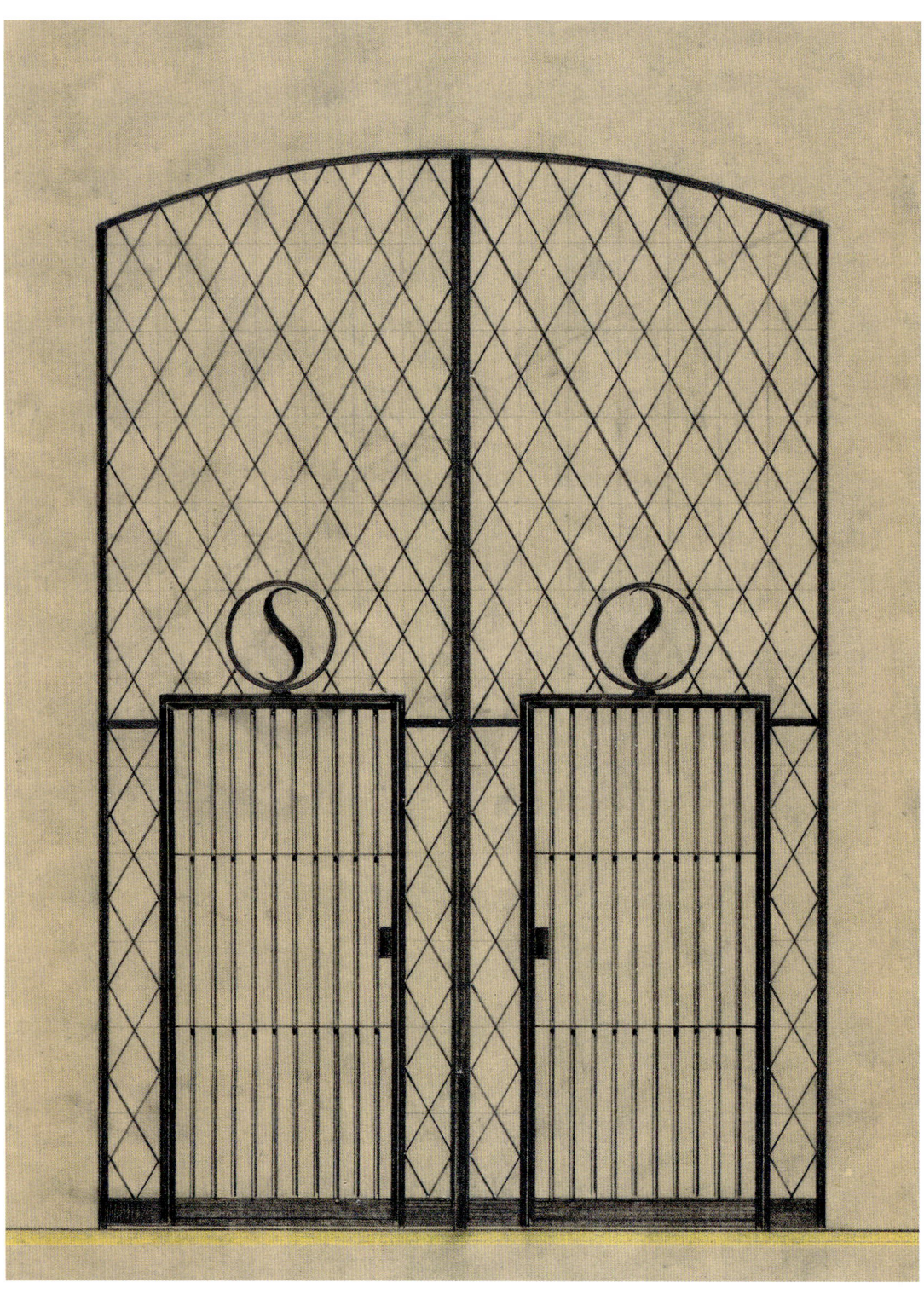

106
Entrance gate to Sandoz headquarters in Paris, circa 1948, pencil and India ink. Rejected proposal for a new logo

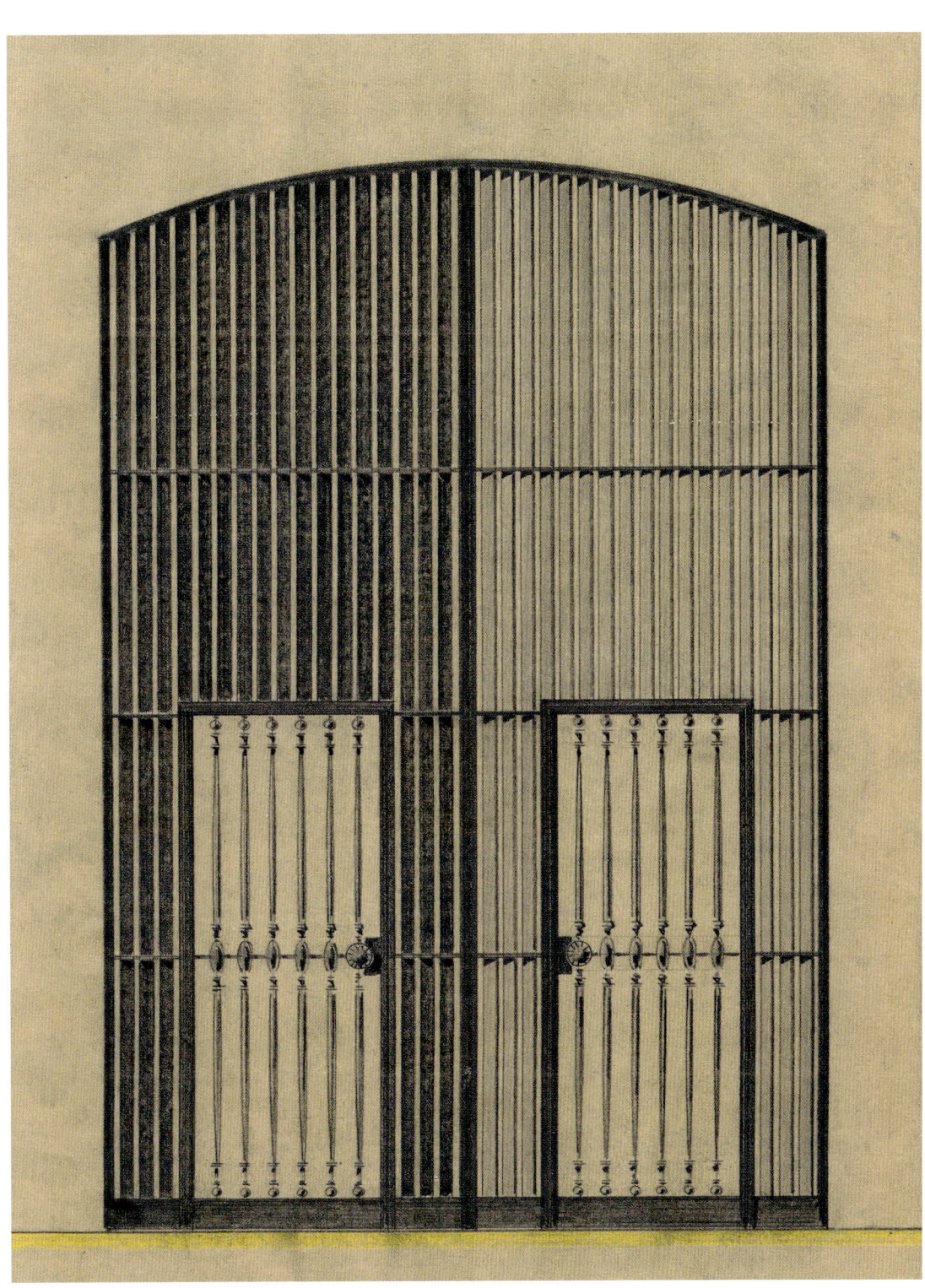

107
Entrance gate to Sandoz headquarters in Paris, circa 1948, pencil and India ink. New offices as part of extensive transformation of a former mansion

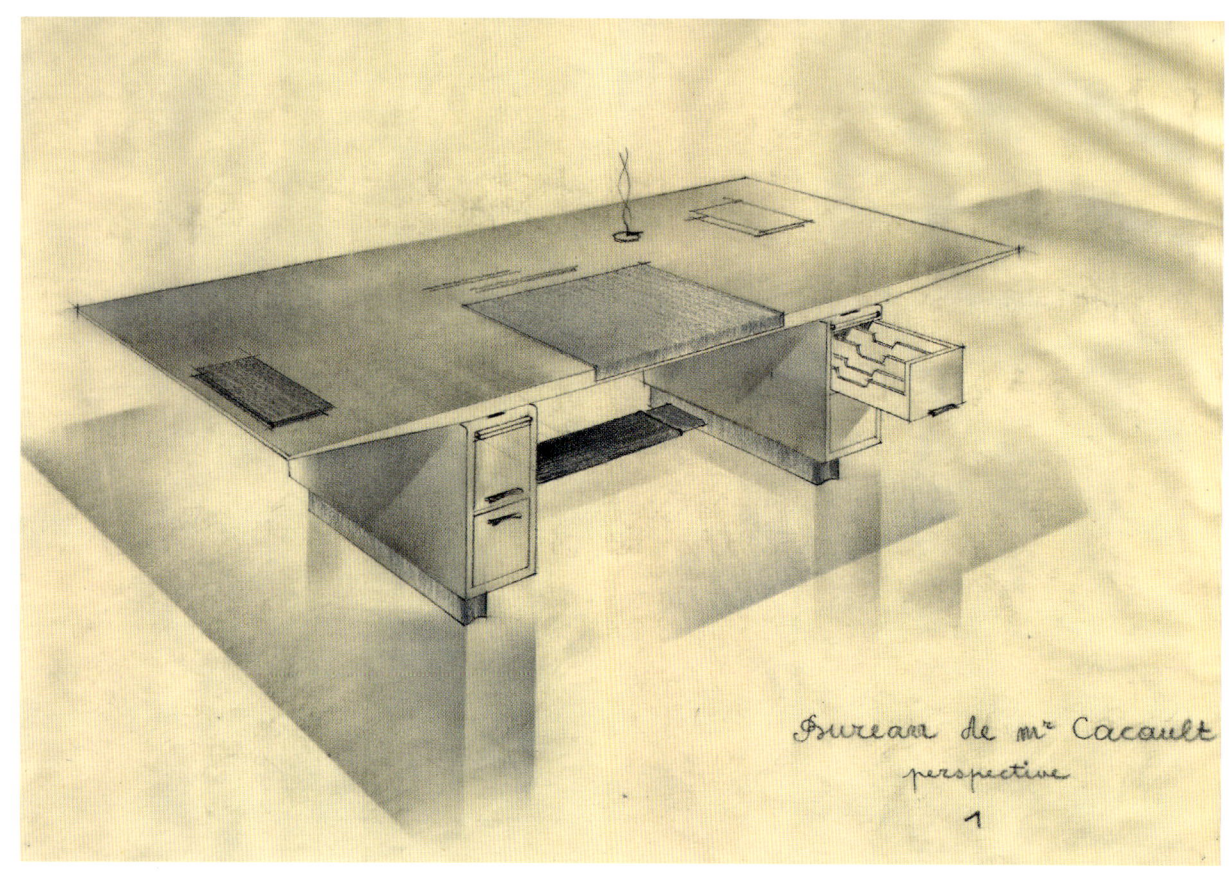

Bureau de mr Cacault
perspective
1

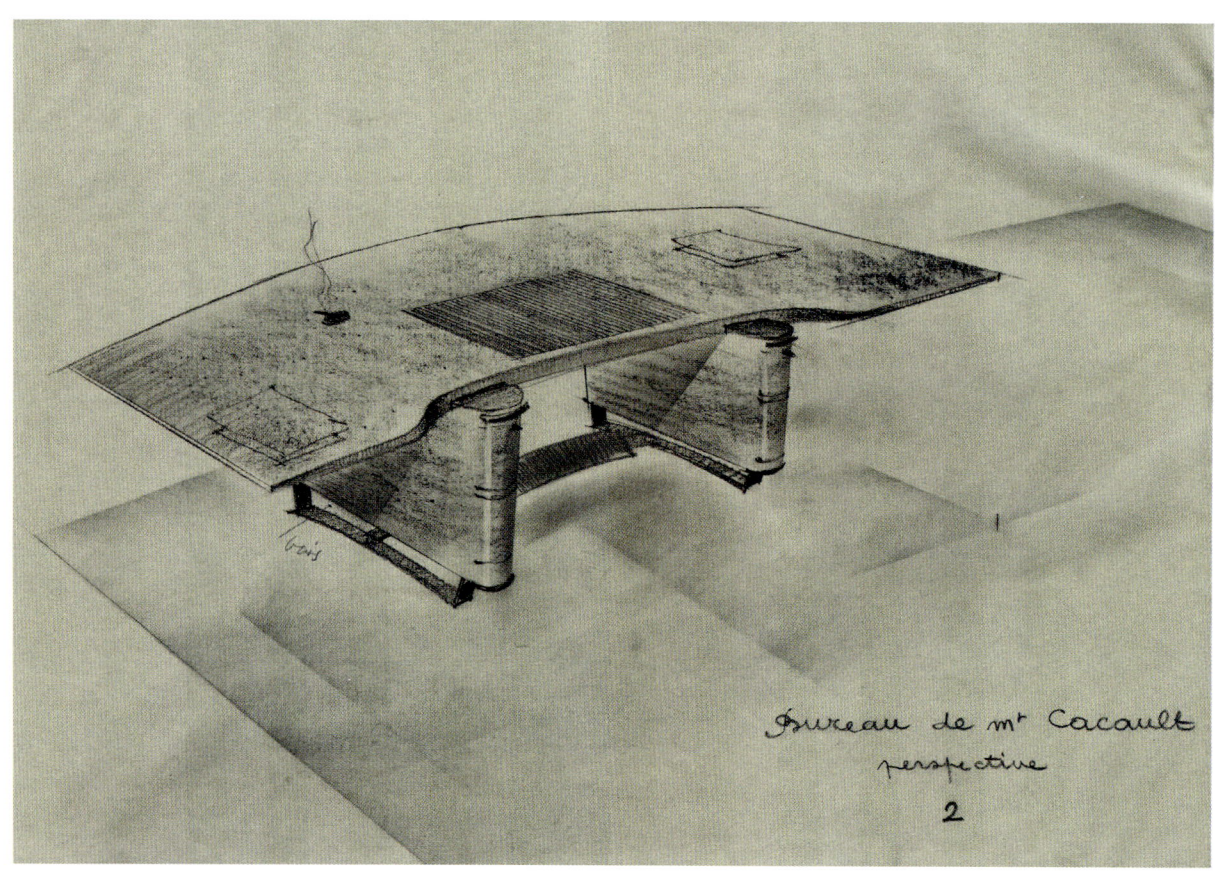

Bureau de mr Cacault
perspective
2

108
Sandoz headquarters in Paris, director's desk, 1949–1950, pencil and stump on tracing paper

109
Sandoz headquarters in Paris, director's desk, 1949–1950, pencil and stump on tracing paper

110
Sandoz headquarters in Paris, desk lamp, 1949–1950, pencil and stump on tracing paper

111
Sandoz headquarters in Paris, floor and wall lamps, 1949–1950, pencil and stump on tracing paper

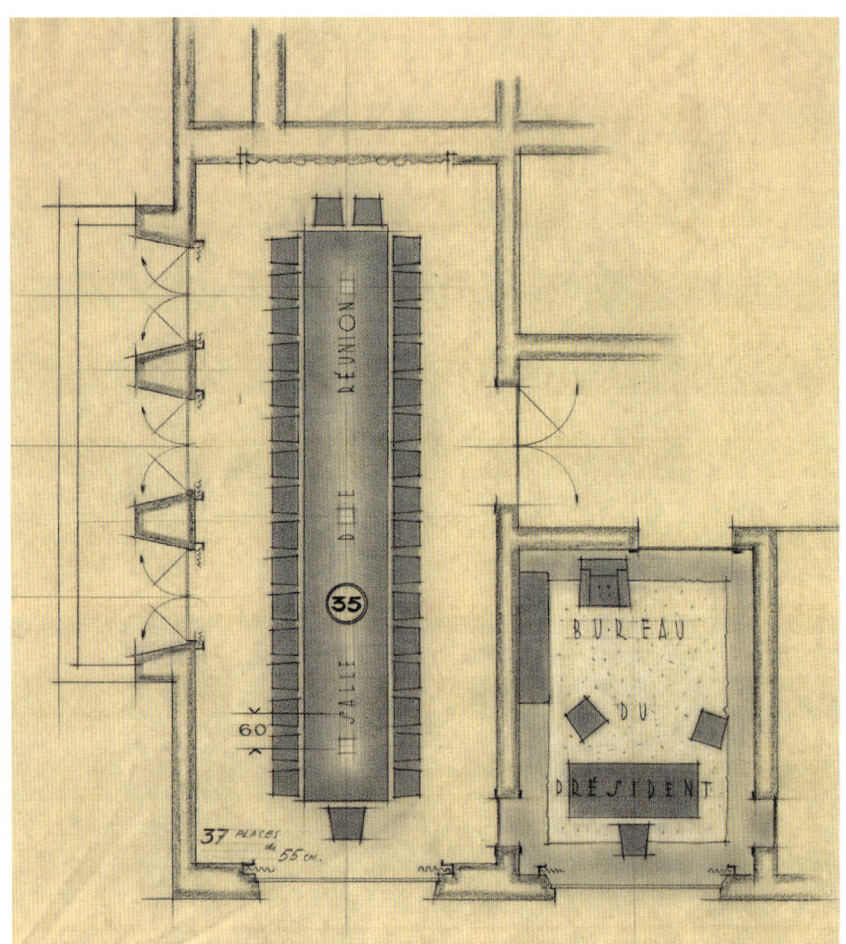

112
Sandoz headquarters in Paris, plan of assembly room and director's office, 1949, pencil and India ink on tracing paper

113
Sandoz headquarters in Paris, variant for table of board of directors, circa 1949, pencil, stump, charcoal, and gouache on tracing paper. Aerial perspective

114
Sandoz headquarters in Paris, perspective of boardroom, circa 1948, pencil, charcoal, India ink, and gouache on Canson paper. Two of Edouard-Marcel Sandoz' sculptures are seen backlit.

115
Sandoz headquarters in Paris, perspective of bar and social club under roof, 1949–1950, pencil, charcoal, pastel, and tempera on tracing paper

PLACE RODIN
Bureaux
Logement
3
Bureaux
15 . 70.
9 . 40.
360
Logement
12 . 60 720
180
Total
Terrain 6075 m²
364.

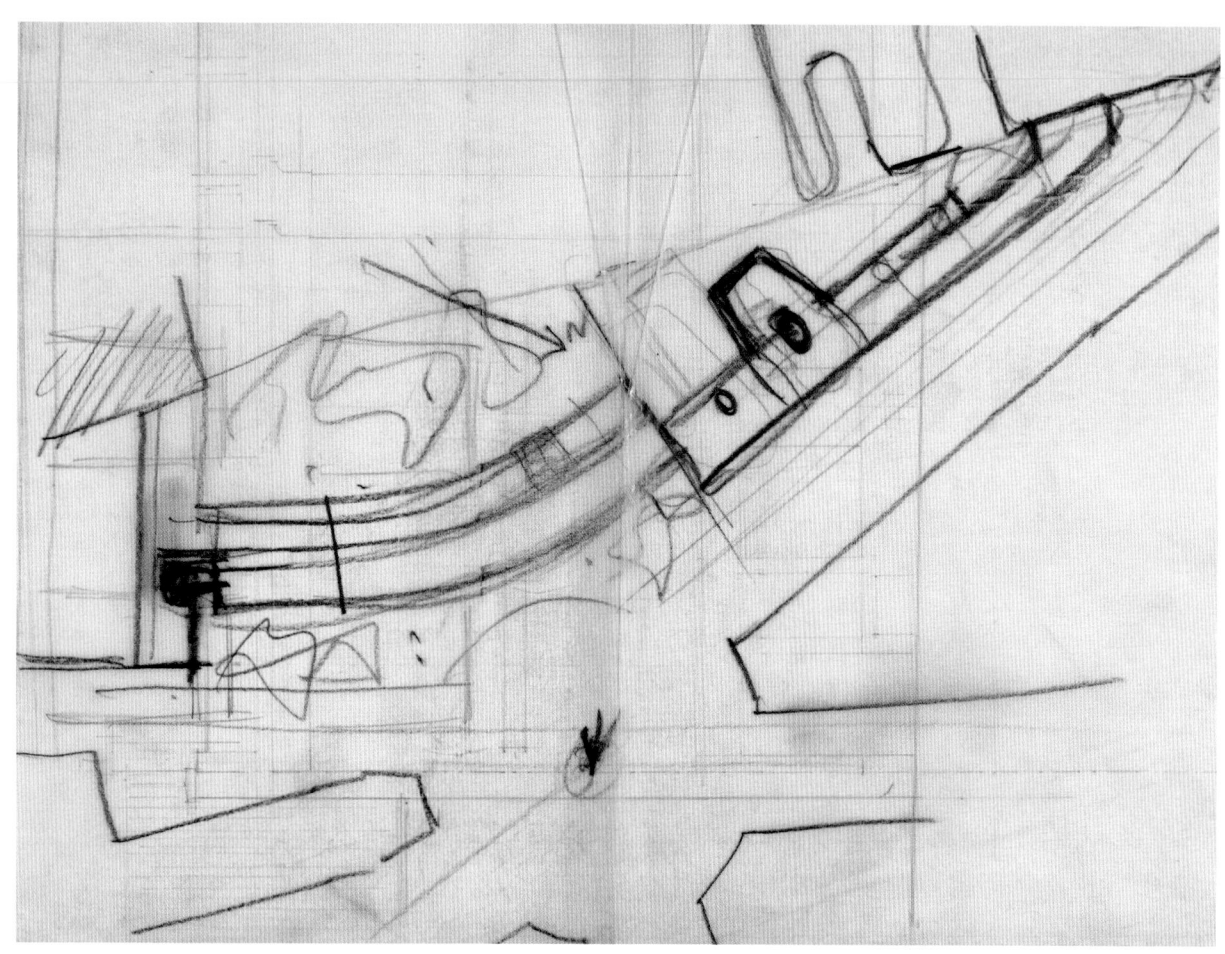

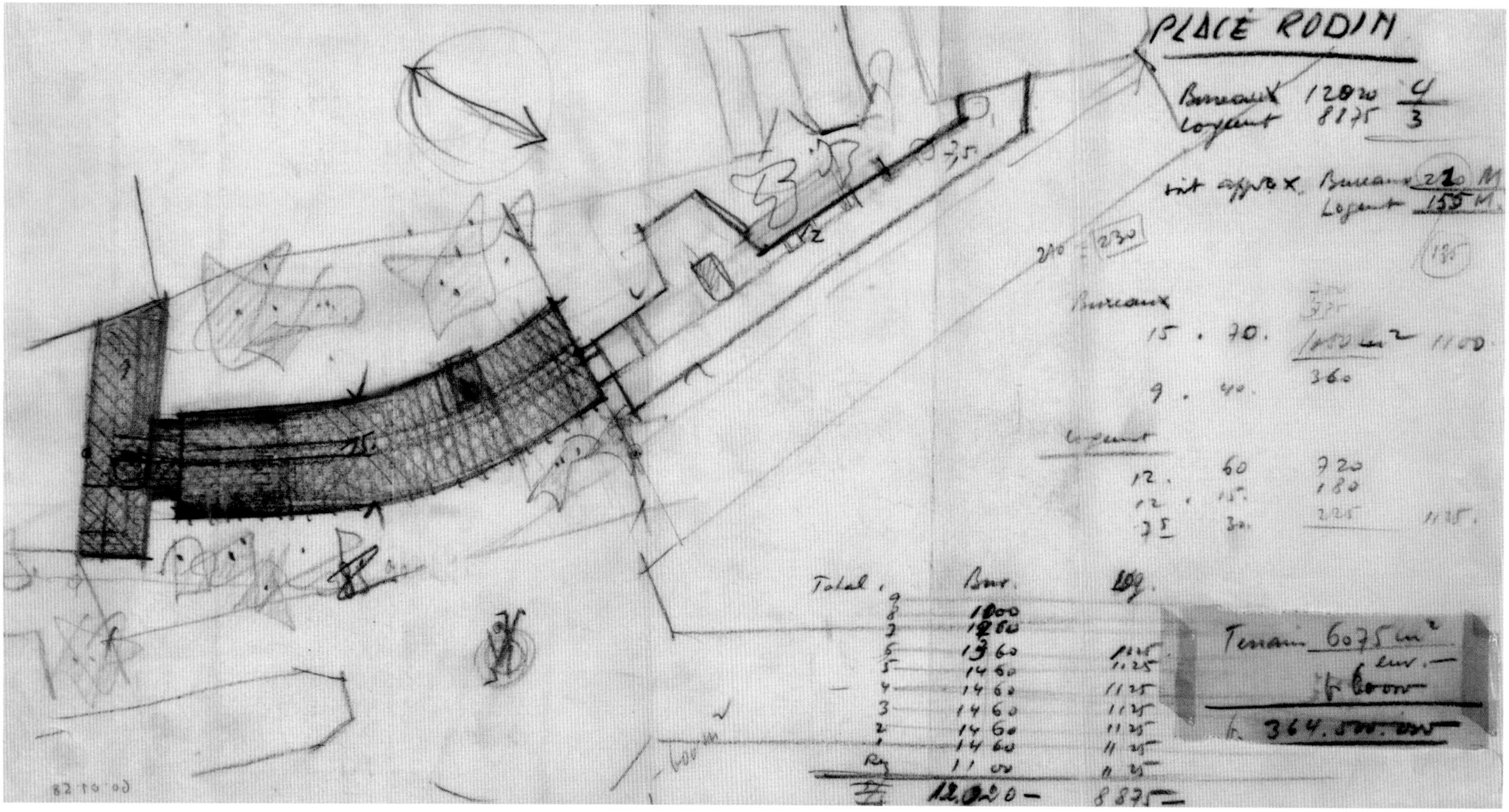

116
Prospecting study for new urban site for expansion of Nestlé headquarters in Paris, 1955, pencil on tracing paper

117
Prospecting study for new urban site for expansion of Nestlé headquarters in Paris, 1955, pencil on tracing paper. Assessment of surfaces required for an office building flanked by an apartment building on Place Rodin

118
Prospecting study for new urban site for expansion of Nestlé headquarters in Paris, 1956, ball-point pen on tracing paper. Location at Boulevard de Lannes

119
Prospecting study for new urban site for expansion of Nestlé headquarters in Paris, 1956, pen and blue pencil on tracing paper. Location at Boulevard de Lannes

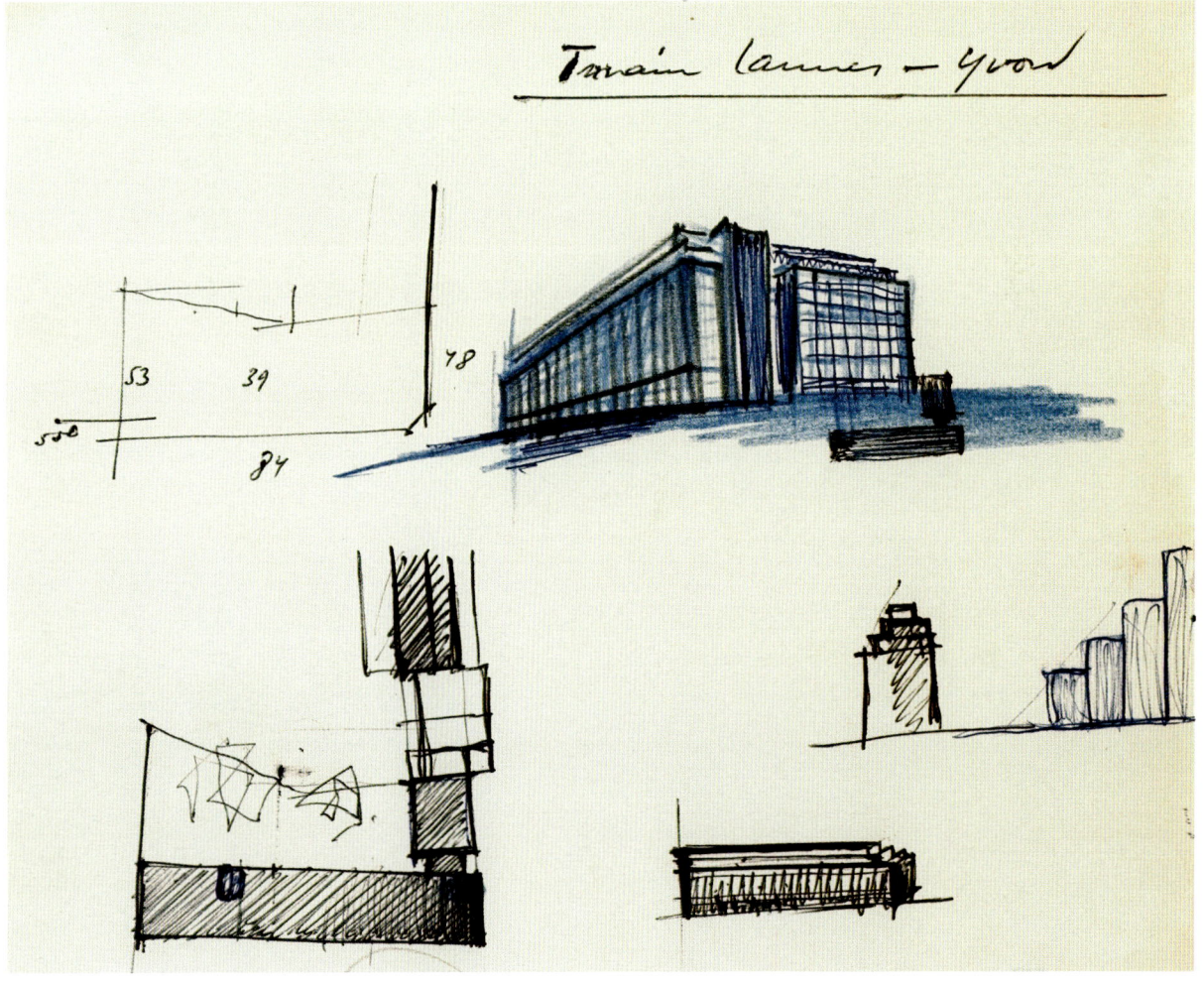

1947–1953: The New Sandoz Factory in Orléans

At the end of the war, Tschumi had finally found a project that would express his mature architecture. As he would confide to some of his students and employees, "After the diploma, it takes ten years to become an architect."[32] Tschumi was 43 years old when he received the commission for the Sandoz chemical manufacturing plant in Orléans. He would no longer have to play the role of *ensemblier* or "decorator." Now his architecture culture was vast. He followed journals and books in both French and German and chose his references from the highest level of the discipline, from Le Corbusier (whom he pretended to ignore) as well as Perret and Mies. As recounted in the 1950s by Peter Collins, an English architect familiar with the Parisian and Swiss milieus, Mies and Perret represented two expressive and synchronous versions of modern classicism as applied to reinforced concrete and steel.[33]

What is a chemical plant? Is it an industrial building, a loft behind large glass facades? Such examples existed in Basel, where Tschumi had seen the sites of Sandoz competitors like CIBA and Hoffmann-La Roche. In 1947 the Orléans proposal allowed him to express his own alternative vision. The laboratories of a chemical plant had to take on the form of an office building and veer more toward domestic architecture than toward the programmatic expressions of a specialized industry. Today, this idea may sound obvious, but who would have known then? Perhaps only Salvisberg in his signature "Building No. 27" for Hoffmann-La Roche, which dates from 1938 and, from a distance, resembles a blow-up of a Hans Schmidt house. In Orléans, Tschumi selected the rather Haussmanian model of the six-story building (*rez+5*) (Plates 121, 122), and yet we are far outside of any dense urban setting, but instead on sandy terrain on the left bank of the Loire near a bridge dynamited in 1940.

By 1942 the architect had foreseen the reconstruction of the bridge and the possibility for Sandoz France to install itself along the western edge of the road. He even proposed locating a new stadium across the street. The bridge was not yet rebuilt in

120
Sandoz Laboratories in Orléans, Edouard-Marcel Sandoz' group *Three Donkeys*, bronze, eastern facade and garden. Photograph by Jacques Boulas, circa 1962

1947 at the beginning of the project, but it would one day take on the name of Pont Joffre. Tschumi cherished the referential principle of the Parisian bulk *rez+5*, which could also be found in a tree-lined park beside the lake near the Nestlé site in Vevey.

The most urgent need for Sandoz in 1947 was a building to house pharmaceutical production. It appeared like an isolated parallelepiped as it emerged on the banks of the Loire during the first phase of construction. In a second move, the architect planned an extension in the form of a block located perpendicular to the original structure in an L-shape. For reasons unknown to this writer, the second stage would remain forever on paper (Plate 125). In its superb isolation behind the plane-trees on the embankment, the plant provided an image that both illustrated its name and inspired the productivity of its builders: Reinforced Concrete SA (*Le Béton Armé SA*). Let's first examine the logic of the plan (Plate 123). On the ground floor, a portico base open on three sides accommodated nine 7-meter longitudinal spans and three transverse spans—a module that corresponded either to the depth of laboratories along the facade (7.5 m) or to their distribution along a central corridor (2.5 m). On one hand, this basic rectangle could organize overlapping organizational models that were customized for pharmaceutical production. On the other, it permitted an autonomous plastic treatment of the

121
Sandoz Laboratories in Orléans, plaster model, 1948–1949, view from northeast

122
Sandoz Laboratories in Orléans, plaster model, 1948–1949, view from southwest

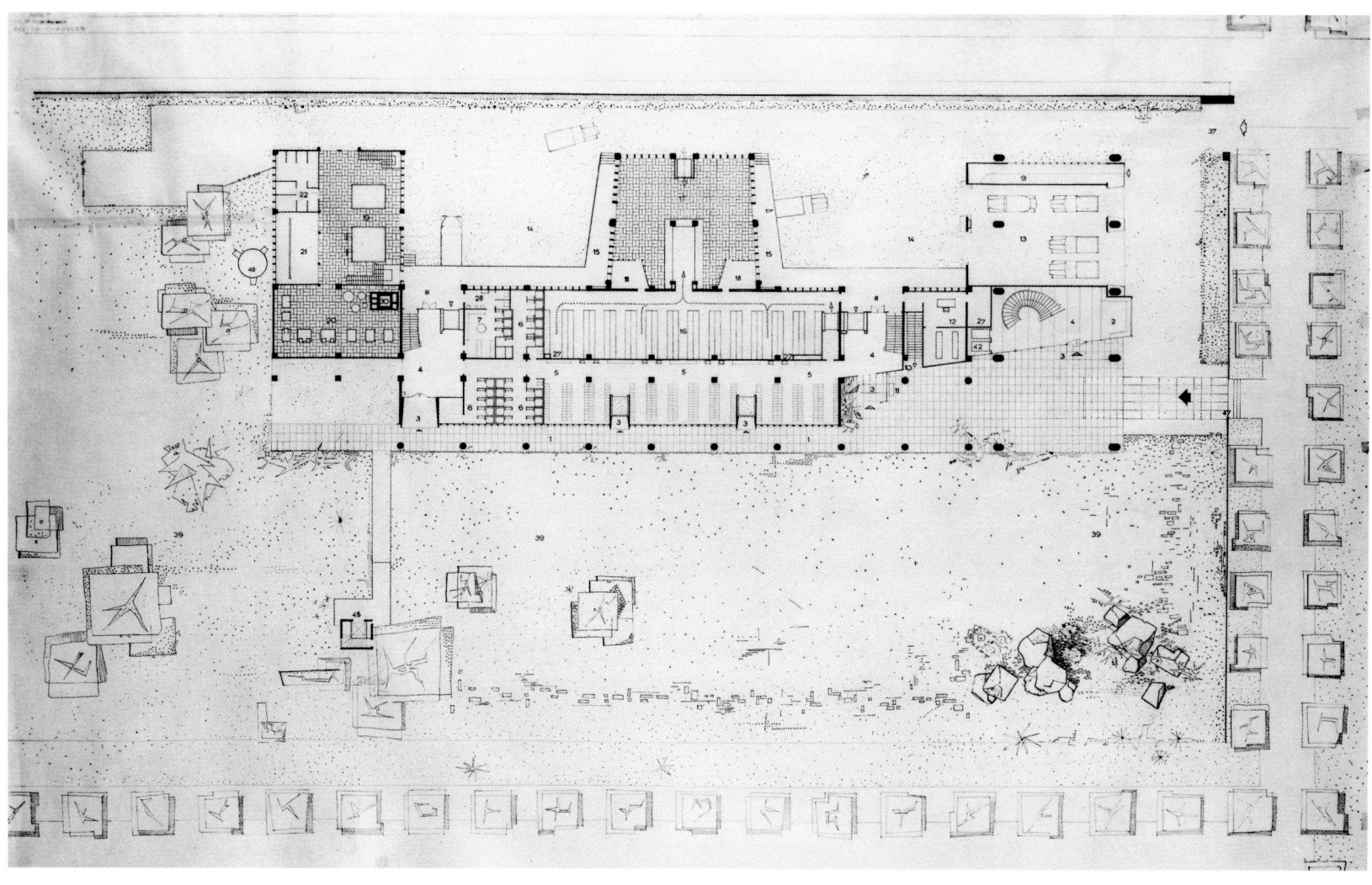

123
Sandoz Laboratories in Orléans, plan of ground floor, circa 1953, pencil and ink on tracing paper, drawing copied for publication in *L'Architecture d'Aujourd'hui*, portico running along eastern facade, sanitary equipment and showers enclosed behind the portico, storage and shipping organized in western platforms

124
Sandoz Laboratories in Orléans, cross section,
circa 1950, showing terrace, kitchen, and
canteen on the 6th floor

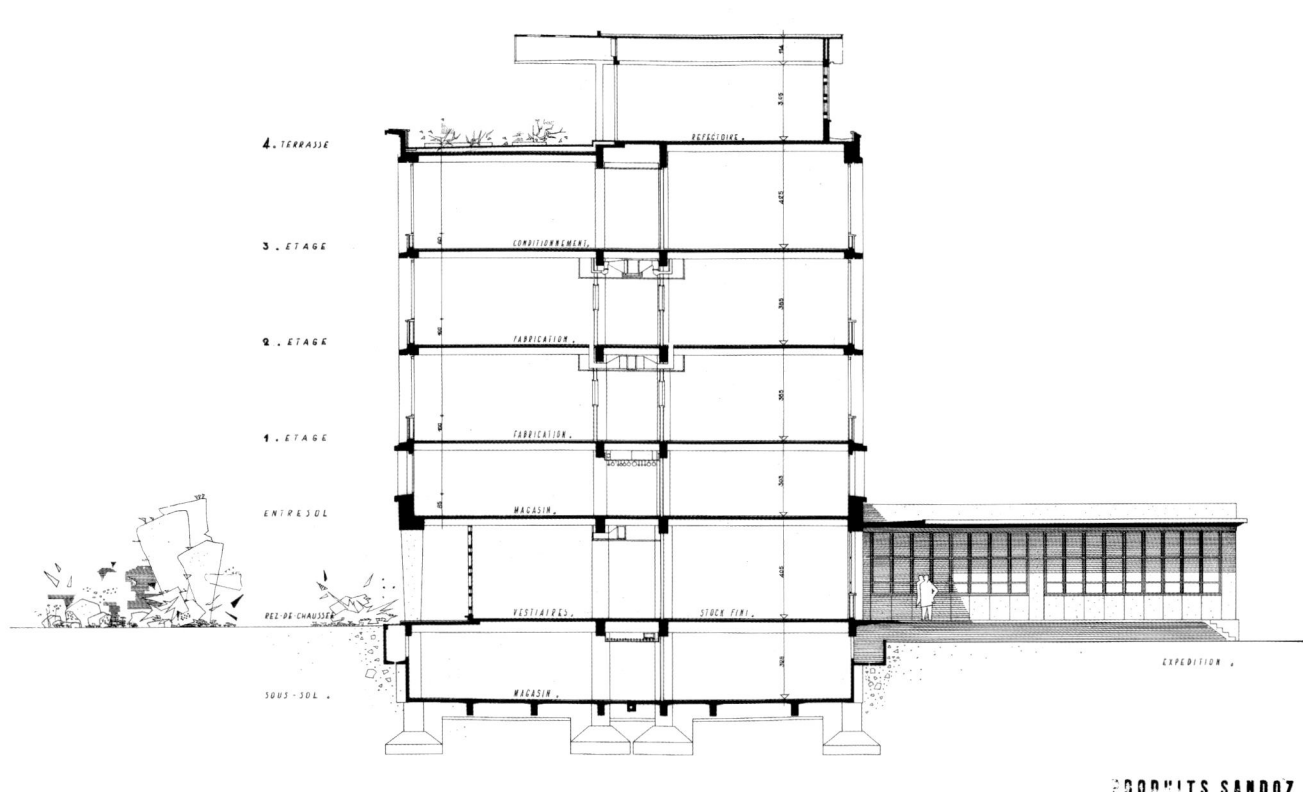

SANDOZ A ORLEANS

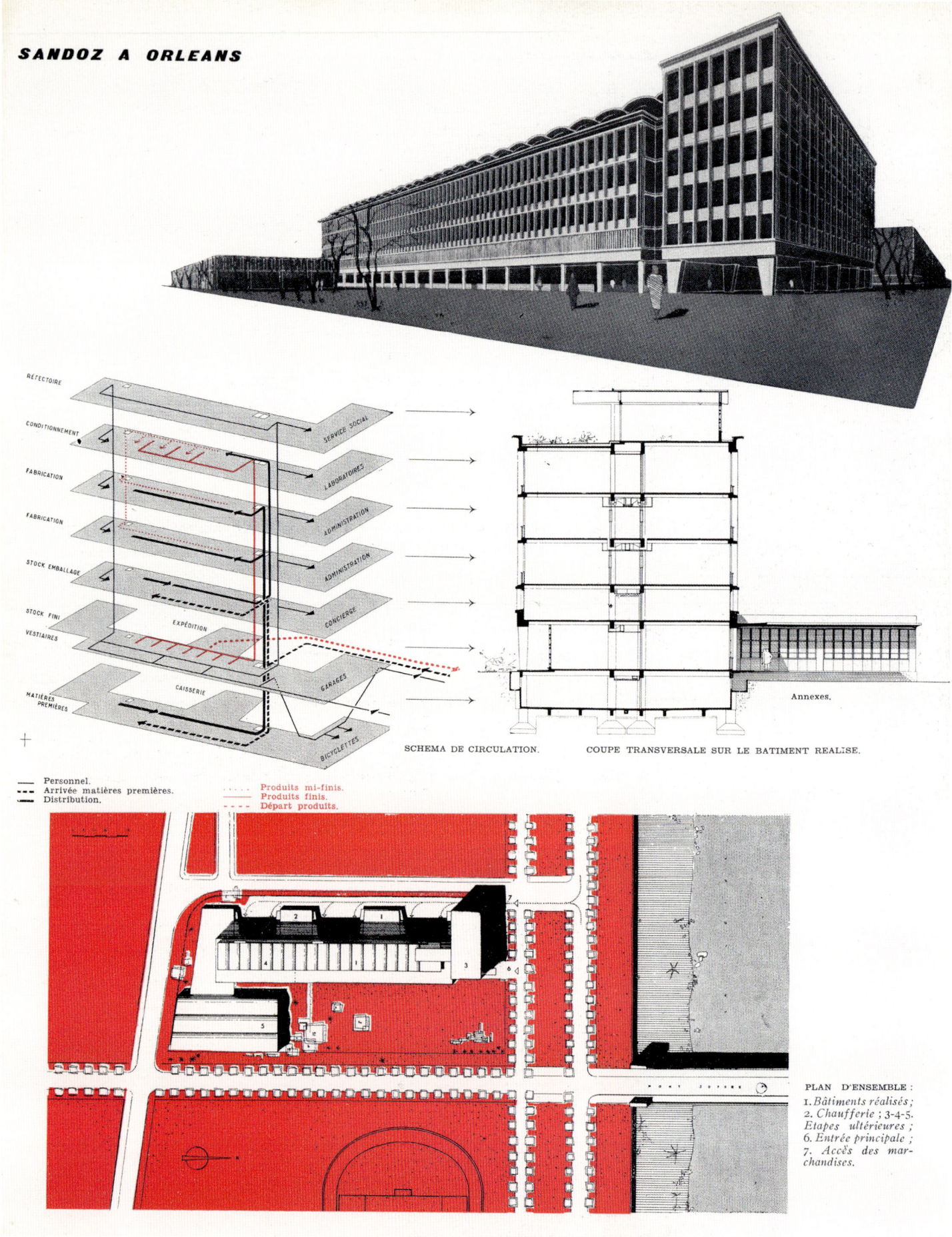

SCHEMA DE CIRCULATION. COUPE TRANSVERSALE SUR LE BATIMENT REALISE.

— Personnel.
--- Arrivée matières premières.
--- Distribution.
.... Produits mi-finis.
.... Produits finis.
--- Départ produits.

PLAN D'ENSEMBLE :
1. *Bâtiments réalisés* ;
2. *Chaufferie* ; 3-4-5. *Etapes ultérieures* ;
6. *Entrée principale* ;
7. *Accès des marchandises.*

building envelope. Such monumental isolation allowed the architect to look for precedents in classical architecture, as Perret would have wanted.

What was the organizational flow chart in Orléans? The basement was allocated to the storage of raw materials and to a garage for workers' bicycles. The ground-floor portico accommodated an entry for personnel, including the female workers—then the majority—who had to be separated from the men. Working in a laboratory meant taking bacterial precautions in the form of showers and scrupulously clean clothing.[34] Hence the presence, beyond the portico, of changing rooms. To contain the phenomenon of voyeurism while also allowing the filtration of light, the architect deployed robust claustra screening walls. These walls were prefabricated and consisted of reinforced-concrete modules. The same level contained hidden housing for technical and infrastructural elements, including the heating. Finished products were shipped from a platform reserved for trucks that was built out on the west side. Tschumi designed a first-floor mezzanine (even though he considered it a rather obsolete urban typology inherited from the nineteenth century). The mezzanine included secure storage areas for products and technical infrastructure for laboratories that required fluid control. The architecture of this opaque intermediary level contrasted markedly with the lower level of the portico. The mezzanine provided a strong horizontal base on which the three floors of laboratories were stacked. The height between slabs in this zone measured almost 4 meters. These three stories supported a roof terrace that was designated for the kitchen and the staff canteen.

As tedious as this description may be, it nevertheless helps highlight how the practice of academic rationalism[35] that Tschumi acquired from his professional training at the Beaux-Arts enabled him to reconcile the program (in this case, the organizational structure of pharmaceutical production) with the choice of a *parti* (a distinct parallelepiped in a unified plastic form (*unité*), a key theme during the French reconstruction). But the overall unity of the work is also indebted to its furniture and decoration. A clear stylistic evolution is evident if we compare the work for Sandoz in Basel with that of Sandoz in Orléans. The range of products designed in the 1950s exalted streamlined profiles. Hence-

forth, mobility would overtake the solemn permanence of seating; armchairs began to swivel. The speed of sketching was mirrored in its results—dynamism and structural expressionism. In the blink of an eye, the same chassis profile could become a typewriter stand, a chair, or a lamp (Plate 43). The American invention of Be-bop in the post-war period supplanted Dixieland. The concept of elegance developed by William Lescaze during the days of "middle jazz" had been assimilated.

As for Tschumi's expressive treatment of reinforced concrete, I refer to his description that modestly references "architects" in the plural, crediting the team of his collaborators. Tschumi sided with Corbusian brute-ness when it came to concrete. He stayed away from the hammering and chiseling that Perret and François Lecoeur practiced so well, noting that "Since concrete is a poured material, the architects were keen on avoiding trying to imitate stone."[36] This recalls Robert Maillart's metaphor and lesson: that reinforced concrete is the sculptor's fount, not the imitation of wood or metal or stone.[37] Sculptural effects are the result of the imprint of the formwork, as was the case with the Unité d'habitation in Marseilles. This reference encouraged the architect to show something else, to enclose the structure with subtle profiles, to develop the prefabrication of elements for use as infills, window sills, and claustra. He varied aggregate sizes and introduced color effects. Under the windows, the sills were tinted with an aggregate of red-ochre porphyry. The treatment of angles resulted in a refined solution. Straight off the formwork, the portico columns combined Corbusian *pilotis* and Perret's slender profiles, and were terminated by a beam whose interior right angle outlined a slightly cantilevered abacus. Vertically, this abacus theme was repeated in two different ways: first on the mezzanine, where the exterior frame turned the corner inward, and finally under the cornice, where the same return angle is surmounted by a cubic pendant (Plates 127–129). These details, first worked out in sketches, were made possible by a mastery of concrete formwork that resulted in individual solutions, as distinct from the work of Perret and Le Corbusier. The construction of Tschumi's angles was determined by the meeting of two pilasters crossed at 90 degrees; this would have been a rare choice for Perret and his staff in Le Havre. At the risk of

125
Sandoz Laboratories in Orléans, unrealized proposal for extension of a perpendicular building toward west, diagram of functions and fluxes as published in *L'Architecture d'Aujourd'hui*, no. 47, April 1953

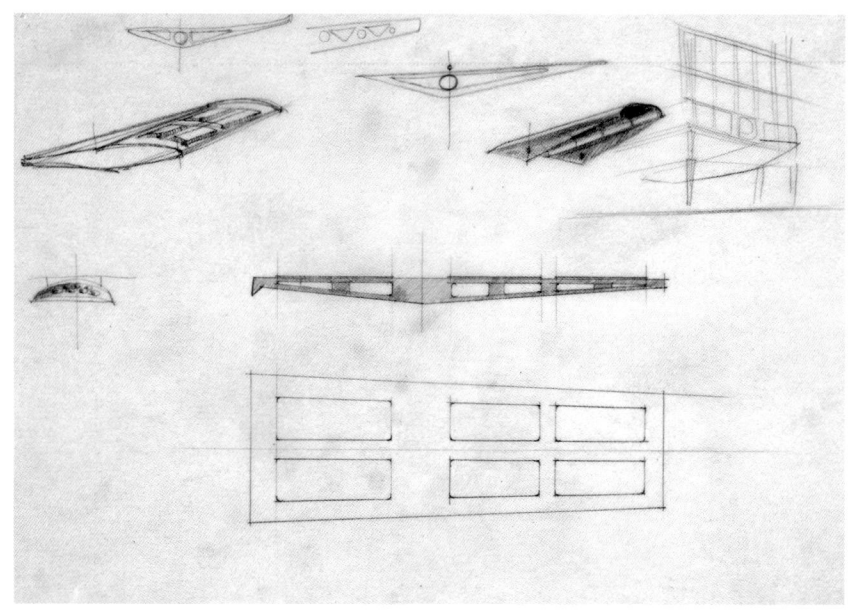
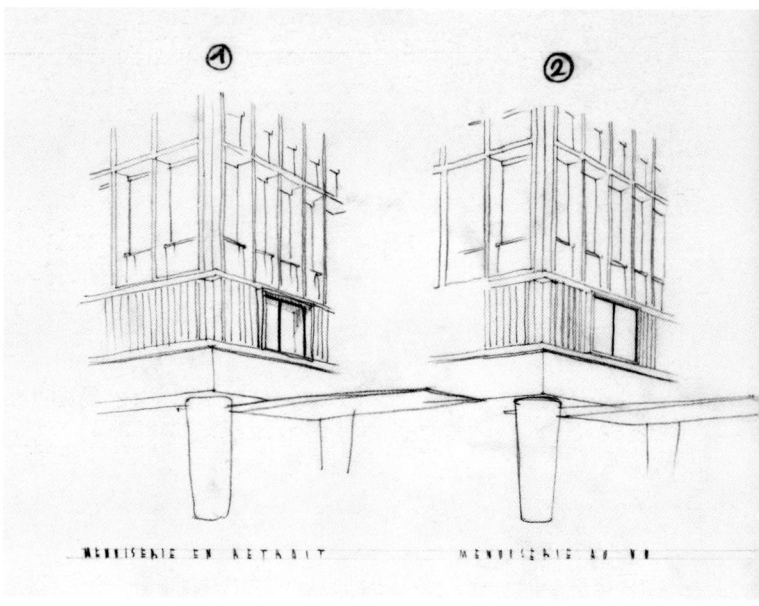

126
Sandoz Laboratories in Orléans, sketch for the marquee, circa 1950, pencil on tracing paper showing aerodynamic profile

127
Sandoz Laboratories in Orléans, variant sketches for window in the mezzanine, circa 1950, pencil on tracing paper

128
Sandoz Laboratories in Orléans, marquee at the northeast corner, steel-grid portico with fluted "Doric" columns. Photograph by Jean Tschumi, winter 1952–1953

129
Sandoz Laboratories in Orléans as completed in June 1953, view from the northwest

130
Sandoz Laboratories in Orléans, formwork for column, winter 1949–1950. Photograph by Jean Tschumi

131
Sandoz Laboratories in Orléans, 6th floor, arched canopy in front of canteen, November 1951. Photograph by Jean Tschumi

132
Sandoz Laboratories in Orléans, reinforced-concrete framework, November 1951. Photograph by Jean Tschumi

bordering on the absurd, can we ask ourselves if this *topos* of the angle in set back doesn't summon up the Miesien inclination toward the dynamic expression of the vertical and the eloquence of the frame?

Behind the massive cornice ridge whose profile was worked out at 1:1 scale lies the roof terrace. Its features offer another example of the performance capabilities of reinforced concrete: the thin-skinned, round, self-supporting vaults of the refectory allude to Perret but have the distinction of punctuation by circular holes (Plate 131). The technical complexity of this example contrasts with the simplicity of its plastic effect, by which it functions as a canopy whose ripples direct our vision toward the "Gothic" panorama of Orléans, with its churches and towers. The staff canteen was the ornament that illustrated the owner's corporate identity. But why all this technical effort? In *L'Architecture d'Aujourd'hui* Tschumi stated that he wanted the building to be "a crowning *(couronnement)* designed to avoid a brutal cut into the sky."[38] It seems that the word "brutal" was a nod to Le Corbusier, as if elegance had to replace austerity.

Tackling the important Orléans commission was not without difficulties for the architect. Design work began in the Lausanne office in spring 1947 and continued until summer of the following year. The architect wanted the client to pay him in Swiss francs, but the work was the responsibility of Sandoz France (Plate 133); hence his fees would have to be paid in French francs. After the building permit was obtained in 1949 Tschumi moved the entire project over to his Paris apartment on the Boulevard Saint-Germain, which served as a second office. His draftsmen, chosen from among his Lausanne students, accompanied him to Paris.[39] According to the testimony of Max Richter, who was in charge of construction administration for the building and assisted Tschumi in Lausanne, the construction documents included some 1,310 plans.[40] All of the furniture was rendered at 1:1 scale. In 1951, two years before construction was completed, Tschumi informed the client that the initial budget estimate of 570 million French francs had risen to 644 million. This cost overrun (quite economical for private architecture) was absorbed without difficulty. On June 2, 1953 a banquet served under the vaulted arches on the terrace brought together the owner, the staff, and the team of builders to celebrate the end of construction.[41]

It bears repetition that the construction of the Sandoz laboratories on the Avenue du Champ de Mars in Orléans represents a mature work, distant from the abrupt if often astonishing assertions of an *opera prima*. It embodies deep reflection, reflecting the opportunity to design a building that is personalized down to its furnishings. We must distinguish those Tschumian idiosyncrasies that are particular to Orléans from the obsessive themes that emerged in subsequent buildings. Among the former are his didactic presentations of prefabricated claustra, thin-shelled vaults, and creative solutions to the corner. Among the latter fall the porticoed ground floor and the dramatic entrance, topped by a long aerodynamic metal awning (Plate 128). In Orléans, the corporate architecture of Sandoz France endorsed the most important German *Werkbund* axiom: "Architectural quality equals the quality of industrial production."[42]

133
Sandoz Laboratories in Orléans, the architect (left) with the two directors, Gosselin and Chauffour, under the plane trees on the left bank of the Loire, 25 May 1950

134
Sandoz Laboratories in Orléans, women at work in the suppository production unit, circa 1953

135
Sandoz Laboratories in Orléans, reinforced-concrete modules for the claustra, western wall of canteen on the 6th floor, circa 1953

1951–1956: The MVA Headquarters in the Le Cèdre Landscape of Lausanne

The building for the insurance company Mutuelle Vaudoise Accidents (MVA) in Lausanne was a testing ground and official *carte de visite* for Tschumi, a building that would legitimize the architect's mandate for the Nestlé headquarters in Vevey. It was also a signal expression of corporate architecture. The competition for the commission was limited to four local architectural firms.[43] To the extent that the client enjoyed the political and financial support of the Canton of Vaud, the competition itself was responding to an issue of public morality. Press attention focused on the project because of trees. Located in the countryside near Lausanne, Le Cèdre was well known for its four specimens of the coniferous species called "evergreen."[44] The trees appeared as if the ancient of days, the source of the regional *genius loci*: everything happened first and foremost as if they were the principal judges of the project's success or failure. The site is a glacial moraine overlooking the lake, backlit toward the south. To achieve his goals, the architect described his project as a reverential bow to the importance of the landscape. He and his team of young designers developed an execution technique that allowed for bold formal strokes, foregrounding the cedars' silhouettes without hiding the architecture of the facade (Plate 137). Tschumi's composition could be broken down into four different parts. The first is the park, the natural context to be elevated. On the north side, facing the city, three cedar trees framed the main facade for the management area, set on an axis with the Avenue de Milan. To the south, lakeside, two romantic relics consisting of a cedar tree and an octagonal gazebo focalized the composition. The first two program components for the management and the secretariat took the shape of an "open T-square," in the architect's words.[45] The secretariat followed the diagonal of the Rue des Bains. The *parti* is both urban and landscape. The last part of the program, namely the dining and concierge facilities, occupied the lower slope, invisible from the reception hall.

The competition jury delivered its verdict early in February 1952. The conclusion, influenced by the Geneva architect Marc Saugey, was postponed,[46] but the owner could not wait. Elective affinities emerged between the client and the architect.[47] Despite the jurors' comments, Tschumi refused to alter his project at all. The schematic design was approved in June and the contract signed in September. The architect's sentiment seemed to capture and elucidate the desire of the MVA executives: to adopt a modern corporate identity in line with the group's economic importance in 1950. This rather romantic attitude provoked a unique response; the two directors, Roger Bobillier and Marcel Delarageaz, invited Tschumi on a study tour of the United States[48] (Plate 136). But what could this trio of boys see on America's East Coast? Delarageaz chaired the steering committee of the Théâtre du Jorat, so they went to a Broadway musical—the colorful Polynesian folklore of "South Pacific" by Richard Rodgers and Oscar Hammerstein. For his part, the architect made sure to see two things that would have an impact on his work. First, the blade of aluminum, glass, and reinforced concrete otherwise known as Lever House that had sprung up not far from Fifth Avenue. At the time the U.S. headquarters of the British multinational Lever Brothers, it had been designed by Gordon Bunshaft of the firm Skidmore, Owings and Merrill. Then, the office furniture by Harry Bertoia and Charles and Ray Eames. The justification for the trip was a need to obtain information on corporate architecture. Several preliminary contacts were made. But with whom?[49] The agenda was planned with time for another stop in Stamford, Connecticut, where Nestlé had offices. What can we conclude from this escapade *in medias res*? That the visitors from Lausanne wanted to bring back impressions, lessons, and questions. Their first priority was to look at the sizes of offices. Should there be large common areas where dozens worked side by side? The second priority concerned the electrical equipment, telephones, and air-conditioning, in short, the infrastructural conduits. How could the offices be ventilated and heated to accommodate extreme temperature changes from summer to winter? Would windows need to stay closed for other seasons besides winter? Tschumi observed the new double-glazed Thermopane systems. The third focus was on "socialization" areas like restaurants. Without changing the *parti* of the "open T-square," these three points of interest encouraged the development of the project in order to reach compromise solutions between America and Lausanne.[50]

136
Jaak De Koning, *Coming in 1958*, 2003, watercolor at postcard size, nostalgic portrait of the Lockheed Constellation

137
Competition for MVA insurance building in Lausanne, north facade, November–December 1951, testing the *variante* of a 15-bay facade with expressive use of a Chinese brush. Tschumi's winning project will have 9 bays.

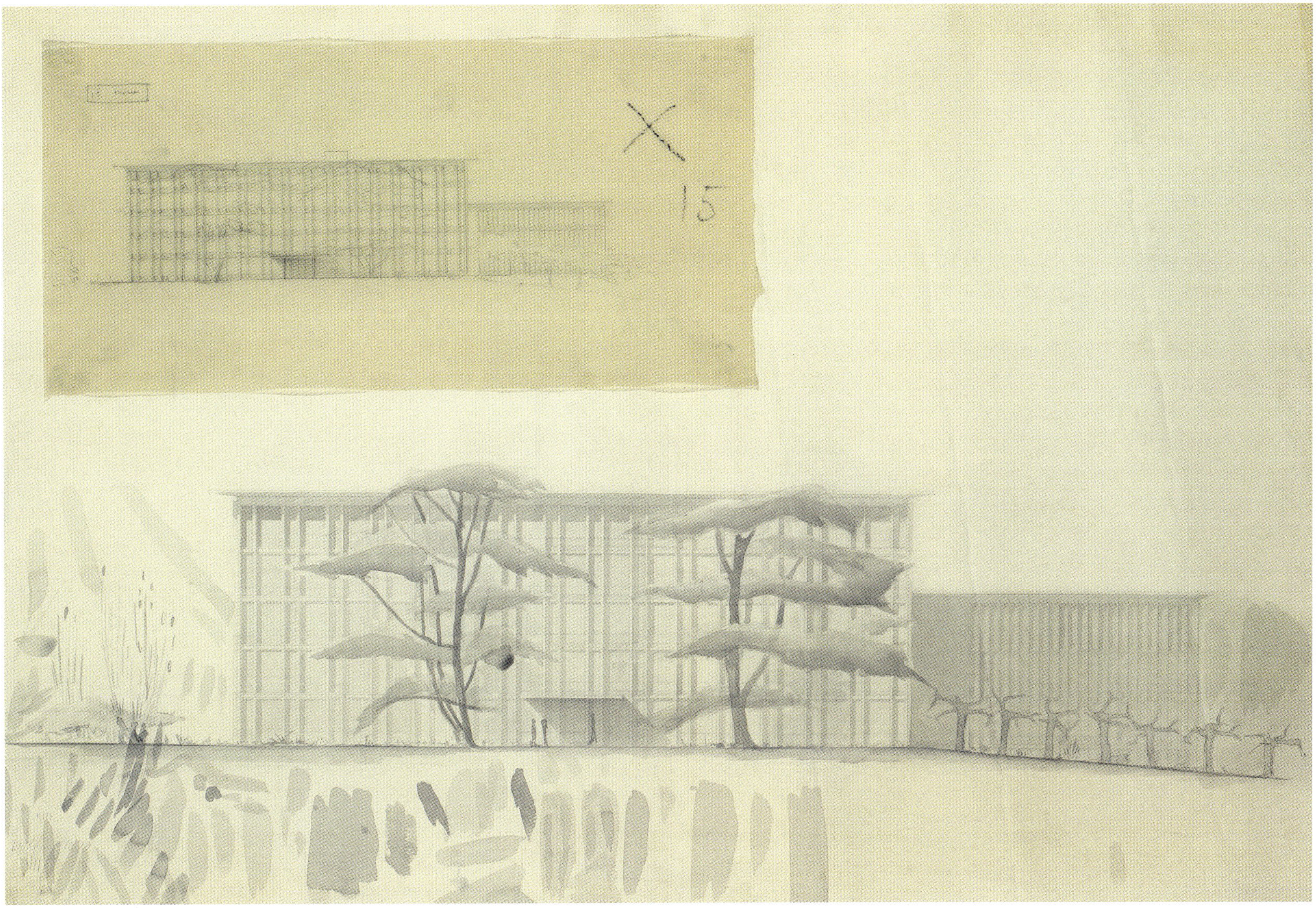

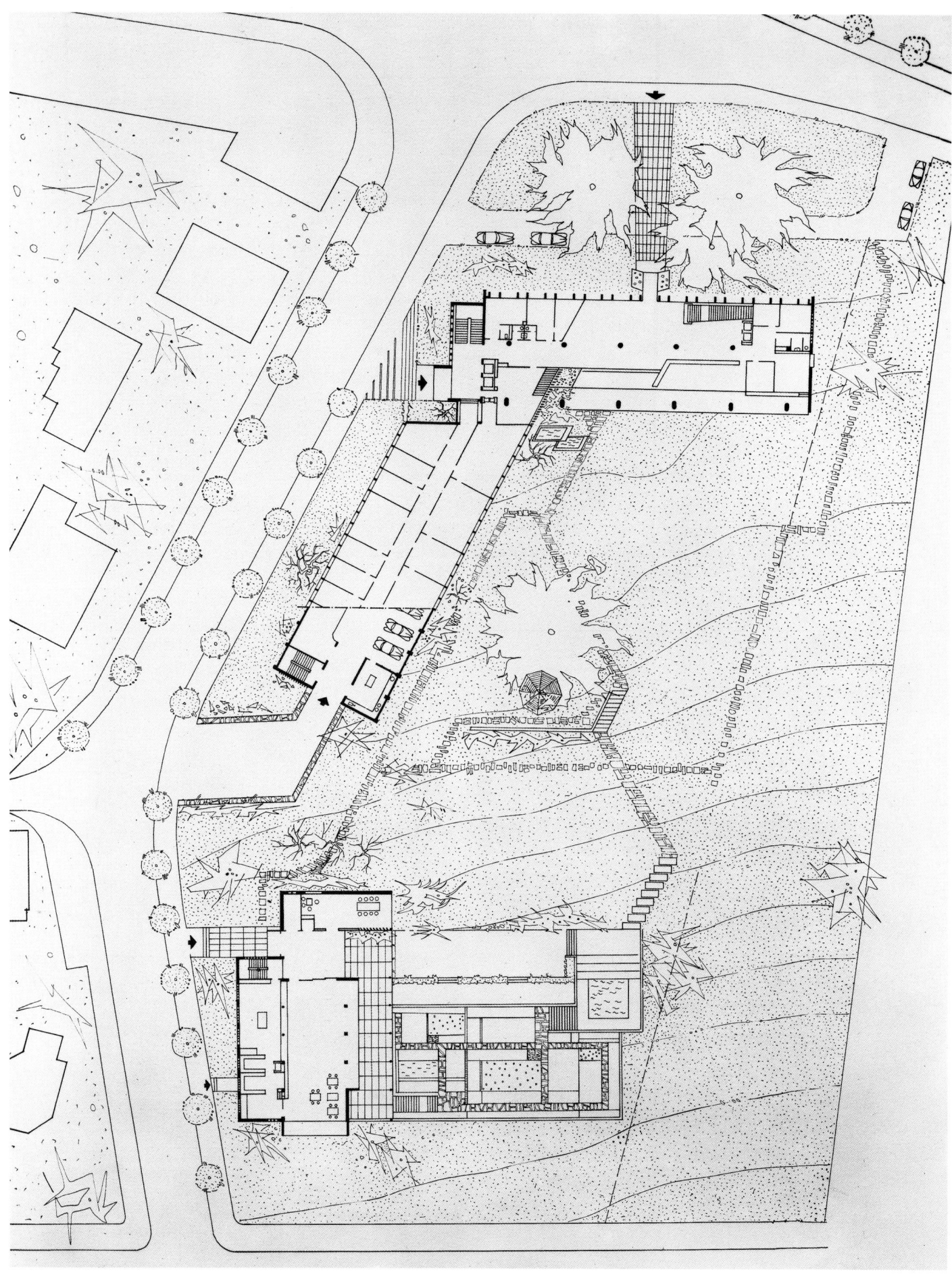

138
MVA insurance building, Lausanne, 1956, redrawn for publication, "open T-square" with four components: rectangular quarter of reception and directors' offices, oblique wing of secretariat, canteen building to south, central garden

139
MVA insurance building, Lausanne, 1953, pencil on tracing paper. Western facade with two elements, vertical with employees' entrance, secretariat wing

The architect interpreted the hierarchical principle of the company. Using a cabinet maker, the MVA executed a series of models for each floor at 1:50 scale in order to study the programmatic distributions.[51] At the core of the management area Tschumi placed a central aisle that distributed the offices along the facade. The owner expected customized solutions. The boardroom was moved to the fourth floor, just below the roof garden, which allowed for the organization of receptions that could take advantage of the view. In the diagonal core of the secretariat building, the passageways complied with another principle, one that posited the need to shape offices according to changing uses. What dominated this area was the *enfilade*, or compartmentalization of units more or less the length of a pullman rail car. A costly system of mobile metal partitions could allow for these adjustments. The electrical and telephone connections were provided by ground boxes embedded in the concrete slabs. The idea of this system, as well the notion of a self-service dining hall, came from the United States.

The successive phases of construction were documented in photography and film, two black-and-white mediums that exalt contrasts between the dark tonality of steel and the lightness of concrete.[52] This documentation was used as much for advertising the masonry industry as it was for publicizing the MVA.[53] Construction began in spring 1953 and lasted three years. It was organized in two simultaneous stages, the wing open to the square and the central core. Detached and placed below the park, the dining hall and the concierge apartment were built last.[54] The architect and the concrete contractor secured the land to consolidate the total footprint of the building. This was the first time that Tschumi had been commissioned to design an underground parking lot. He used the opportunity to pursue his passion for underground urbanism. Thus, the secretariat wing lay over a long-span automobile entrance that was accessible by a road connecting down the hill to the Avenue des Bains. The oblique profiles of the frame embodied a kind of aerodynamic elegance[55] (Plates 142,

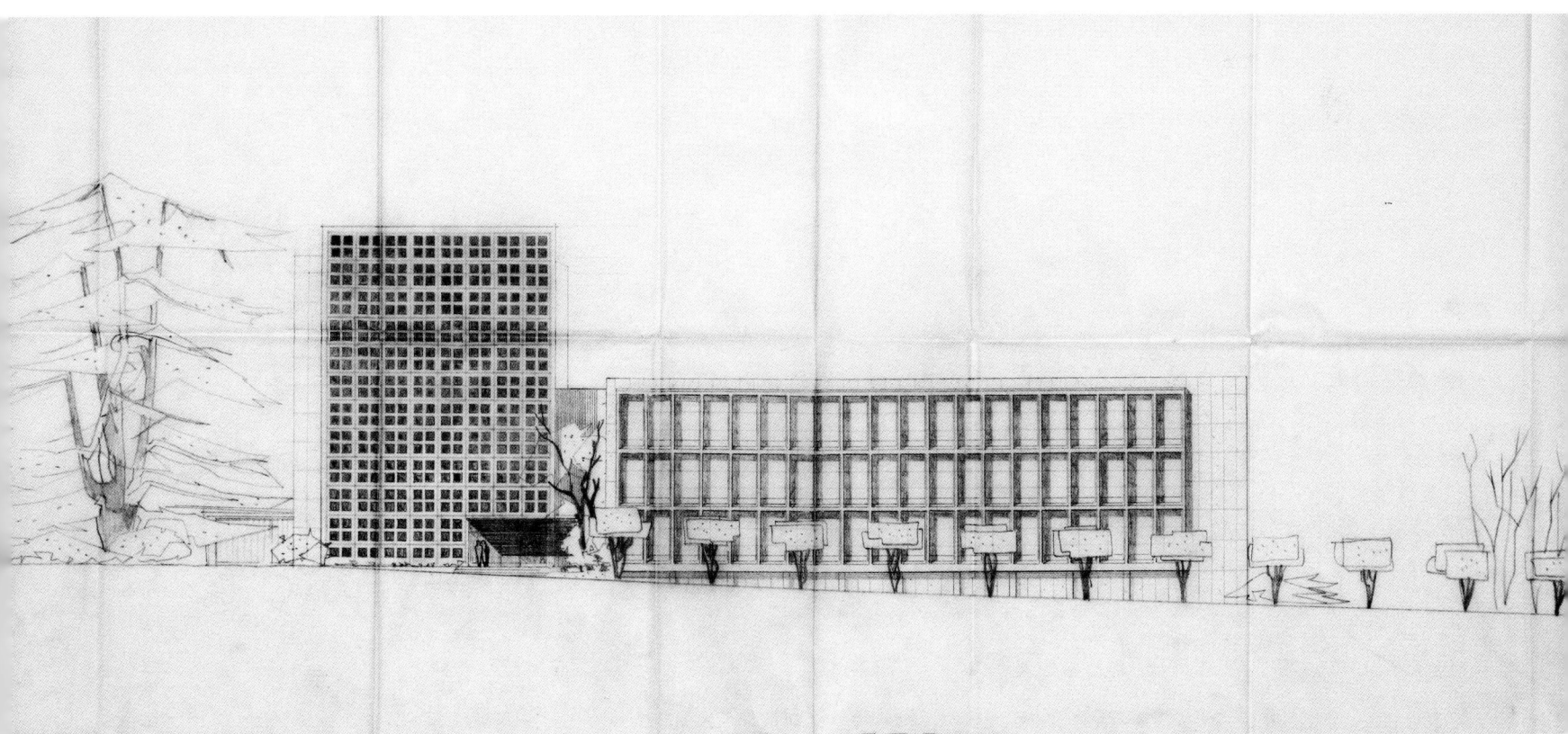

143). The construction typology of the long-span portico (no pillars)[56] and the double lane of the central driveway, as well as the parking perpendicular to the facades, facilitated movement and reduced the risk of accidents. The architect also designed with the driver in mind—he proposed that underground spaces also had a right to daylight. The nobility of this space comes from the side windows, coupled with the vertical planes of the wall. The floor was sheathed in an impermeable cement surface dyed red. Once transmuted into pedestrians, motorists would find a glass box located at the end of the portico, providing access to a vestibule with two elevators.[57] Excavated into the slope, the garage elevated the secretariat wing onto a pedestal whose level corresponded to the ground floor of the management area. The architect used the mechanical metaphor of the hinge to describe the meeting of both sides on the "open T-square." In fact, the main entrance of the MVA was located on the west side, a large, punctured, screen-like facade or claustra. This is where the whole staff would arrive each morning, whether by car or on foot from the bus stop. The claustra, made out of prefabricated reinforced-concrete panels, filtered the light that fell into the hallway (Plates 139, 146). The monumental entrance overlooking the city was primarily a symbolic sign reserved for visiting guests. The elegant *tour de force* of the 10-meter-long aluminum marquee outlined a gesture of urban greeting.[58]

If the wing situated on the Avenue des Bains was structured by roads and traffic, the management wing responded to two landscape rules: to foreground the spray of cedars and to open a transparent perspective across the ground floor in the direction of the Lake Geneva panorama. Faced with public opinion, this argumentation was repeated like a refrain as much by the employer as by the architect: "At the northern edge of the site, the remarkable decorative effect of the hundred-year-old trees has been preserved, thanks to the understanding of the MVA management, which did not hesitate in granting the architect the ten-meter set-back he needed in order to save them."[59] The central core unified a number of unique elements. This unity-in-diversity would be unequaled outside of the EPUL auditorium, as if the architect were trying to increase the technical situations, subtlety of detail, and variety of his materials in order to form a

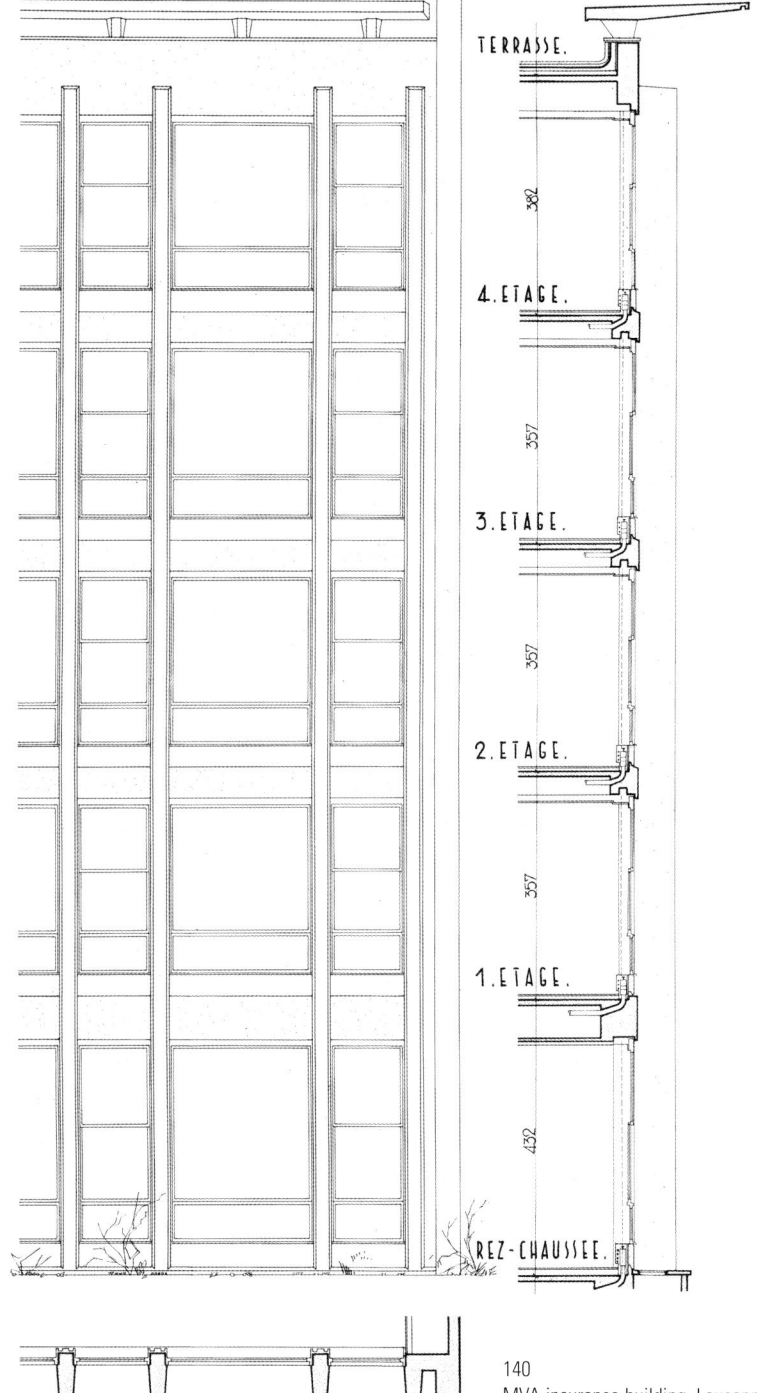

140
MVA insurance building, Lausanne, elevation and sections of northern facade toward the city, 1956, redrawn for publication. The cornice and bay proportions follow a classical ternary palazzo rhythm, B-A-B.

141
MVA insurance building, Lausanne, northern facade toward the city, photograph by M. Vuillemin, 1956, showing the reflection of the cedars and the transparency of the reception hall

kind of didactic anthology. By wielding luxury and restraint, shadows and blinding light at the MVA, Tschumi introduced constructive *tours de force* into the mysterious and hushed atmosphere of a *Stimmung*, like an aquarium emptied of its water.

In rare and probably unique circumstances, Tschumi here encountered clients who were willing to invest in technologies, equipment, furniture, and decoration of the highest possible caliber.[60] The architect entered their game, proposing to follow difficult and sometimes complicated rules. The masonry company was prepared to follow him into terrain that required tolerances of one millimeter.[61] But designing the rules of the game meant mastering solutions. A sense of composure emerged. A first model of complication (in the watchmaker's sense of the term) emerged in the ceiling of the reception hall. "Tschumi arrived one morning at the Paris office with a sketch subdividing the entry-hall ceiling into triangles."[62] We know that this majestic space had to build up the transparency of the building and frame the alpine lake, much like a postcard.[63] The perverse visitor who dared to focus on the ceiling would have been rendered breathless by the spectacle evolving above his head. The projection plane of isosceles triangles was expanded into a three-dimensional network forming diamond-beveled sides. In plan, this play achieved the "open T-square" effect at 124 degrees. Here was an exquisite geometry whose combinatorial logic of triangles and rhombuses seemed to defy any rational explanation. Were the polished facets put there for seduction? Modeled in three dimensions, the ceiling was made of triangular planes of cement or gypsum that echoed each other in monochrome. Can one imagine the difficulty of this construction site, involving the three-dimensional meeting place of oblique reinforcement bars and orthogonal framing? At the MVA, the re-bars combined grids, curves, and oblique lines. Is this a lesson drawn from the *Wire Mesh Chair* designed by Charles and Ray Eames? Can a chair inspire an armature? Could the presence of Eames chairs in some of the offices be a clue? Our head spins, particularly because the technical prowess doesn't end there. It continues in the flight of stairs, formed out of a single pour, that flows toward the east, in the direction of the directors' suites. "The steps and the intermediary landings were made from slabs of serpentine cut 15 cm thick; we thought about hollowing out the said landing, as in a shell."[64] As one stands under the staircase, everything seems to move according to a series of trapezoids differing in plan and section. Where does this urge to surprise, to find virtuoso sculptural solutions, to aim for the never-before-seen, come from? My mouth is still gaping. It isn't simply a problem of distinguishing oneself from Perret or Le Corbusier. It is impossible to make even the slightest assumption about the sources of this poetic subtlety. In the end, the only plausible assumption might be found in Tschumi's discovery of Bertoia's fascinating chairs. Is it possible that the ceiling of the MVA lobby was a commentary on the Bertoia *Diamond Chair*? Is the fact that Tschumi mixed his own chairs with Bertoia's furniture sufficient indication? (Plate 148) If there is a poetics of the diamond, it does not originate in a few unique facades observed in Ferrara or Lisbon.[65]

Does the MVA engage in a theoretical "discourse"? It may be possible to read one in between the lines of the project. That discourse would be an ironic rejection of Le Corbusier's "Five Points" (1927). My remarks should be interpreted in the context of one country, Switzerland, extending from

142
MVA insurance building, Lausanne, western wing, wooden forms of the underground garage portico. Photograph by M. Vuillemin, 2 October 1953

143
MVA insurance building, Lausanne, underground garage, photograph by M. Vuillemin, 1956, showing lateral penetration of daylight

144
MVA insurance building, Lausanne, concrete frame of western wing and ceiling of reception hall, photograph by M. Vuillemin, 20 May 1954

Geneva to Romanshorn, where the Five Points and the more recent *Modulor* (1948) were received by the young as both a recipe for and a guarantee of modernity. Tschumi liked to distort the system of five points. The rules of composition, proportion, and the subtlety of geometry have no need for the *Modulor*. As president of the UIA, he knew that the industrialization of reinforced concrete called for modular coordination rather than the Corbusian effort to patent the Golden Section. What did Tschumi make at the MVA? No *pilotis*, but instead a variegated range of pillars, columns, pilasters, and bearing walls. For him, the free plan (*plan libre*) was not the direct result of the pin-point structure but equally of the bearing wall. His framing system introduced flexibility. In the secretariat wing, the second purpose of the standardized panels was to modulate the opening and partitioning of the offices. Through a supreme irony, the gables act as the wind-bracing. Do the facades of the central body imitate Janus? Cityside, we see that the monumental cornice stops high pilasters that run from the ground up. A pair of pilasters generates the framing of bays according to a B-A-B sequence. This studied harmony shows an eye to the Italian Renaissance *palazzo*.[66] Facing the park, the same pilasters are transformed into *brise-soleils*. They have been inserted into a frame without a cornice, supported on pillars. The gable wall of the west entrance creates a nesting square within the square. In another *tour de force*, the homogeneity of the facade has been achieved by using prefabricated panels perforated with four-square holes.

"Make hay with the Five Points" is what this building erected just a stone's throw away from the architecture school seems to proclaim.[67] Tschumi agreed with Le Corbusier only on the importance of the roof terrace, which at Le Cèdre had additional value as a Belvedere reserved for the management's receptions. The Tschumian use of reinforced concrete raised the problem of color—not the washable wallpaper colors that Corb laid out in his famous *Clavier de Couleurs*, produced for Salubra,[68] but rather the real color of cement. The testing was carried out on-site. Danish Aalborg White cement was used for the hammered east gable and the prefabricated ceiling panels in the central hall. Furthermore, using green, yellow sand, and crushed Jura limestone aggregates, the architect modulated the local greenish tones of the exposed concrete frames facing the city and the park.[69] Such polychrome turned up in plaster and stonework. As Tschumi put it, "A muted range of yellow, gray, and purple is the foundation on which to play with vivid accent colors (blue, red, yellow, or black) used on certain walls, panels, doors, stairs, and furniture components."[70]

Two issues related to corporate architecture remain to be addressed. The first concerns the company's dining hall, while the second refers to the individual artworks that the client wished to add. Following a trip to London the MVA directors introduced what became known as "*la semaine anglaise*."[71] We know that the invention of the weekend, as far as paid holidays were concerned, disrupted urban culture and increased the use of automobiles. At the MVA, the issue of working hours was as follows: "The five-day week was introduced without reducing working hours. Indeed, the shorter lunchtime break compensated for a lost Saturday without any loss of time…. Since the days became longer, two breaks of ten minutes each were interspersed in the morning and afternoon, during which coffee or tea was served to everyone on rolling carts."[72] At a time when it was still customary to "return for dining at noon," some 235 people learned about the American model of "self-service."

145
MVA insurance building, Lausanne, serpentine tubes for heating system introduced in reception hall ceiling. Photograph by M. Vuillemin, 30 April 1954

146
MVA insurance building, Lausanne, introduction of prefabricated reinforced concrete panels into the frame of the western facade showing geometrical play of the square within the square. Photograph by M. Vuillemin, 4 April 1955

147
MVA insurance building, Lausanne, 1956, staircase in the reception hall. Photograph by M. Vuillemin

148
MVA insurance building, Lausanne, 1956, second-floor landing and spiraling eastern staircase, one Diamond and two Large Diamond chairs by Harry Bertoia. Photograph by De Jongh

The lunch break lasted 45 minutes, while spaces for play (ping-pong, table football) and rest, a terrace, and a garden were placed alongside the restaurant. The menu was lavish. The meal began with soup, followed by two vegetables with meat or fish on Friday, and dessert. The MVA subsidized food and offered a graduated fee rate for fathers according to the number of children they had. Wine, beer, ice cream, and coffee were available at no extra cost.[73] This politics of familial subsidy responded to the ideology of a "mutual society." The directors enjoyed the same cuisine in a separate room. They relied on the friendliness of their staff. They did not want a canteen, so they offered a *"foyer"* instead. To reach it, you had to leave the building and walk out into the street.[74] This option was important because it established an interlude between work and recreation as well as a change of landscape. The construction of the dining hall took place during the last phase of the building site. However, the program and its implementation were instated from the outset.

Rumors spread that Tschumi was not interested and had even distanced himself from building a dining hall for the MVA.[75] This view always seemed strange to me, rather like those rumors that often color the tenacious and enduring "collective memory" of local firms. As *Patron*, Tschumi headed up his two offices in Lausanne and Paris. He divided the work and delegated responsibilities, as we saw in Orléans. But he also knew to be present when key decisions had to be made. Hence it seems impossible that the architect would leave the design of the dining area to someone else. In his brief and unassuming speech on the day of the inauguration he said that 970 plans had been drawn.[76] We know that the MVA design unified a multitude of unique elements. The dining hall expanded the range of unusual solutions, with reinforced concrete finding in it another design opportunity. Its program was articulated through three components: the restaurant, concierge housing, and the garden. The configuration of its parts illustrated three themes: the pavilion, the house, and the rock garden. The latter was the antithesis of the park to the north. Situated along the north slope facing Bellerive-Plage, the building longitudinally superimposed and combined two functional layers that opened up along its eastern face. A subtle play with the terraces extended toward the garden. From the garden one could see the articulation of the roof areas as a delicate sculptural animation placed atop a pedestal (Plate 151). From below, one saw a view quite different from the "brutalist" meeting of enclosed forms. The lakeside fenestration in the dining hall is a large, 6-meter-tall rectangular frame that seems to make an ironic allusion to Le Corbusier's duplex atelier, even if it expresses the restaurant interior through a literal transparency. The concierge's apartment was embedded in the massive plinth and had a sense of second-class comfort about it, if one were to make comparisons with the three classes of rail travel.[77] Grafted onto the pavilion-like dining area, the garden to the east was planted in an orthogonal geometry. The constraint was that one needed to rake the shrubs and paths. In this way, it functioned like a French garden, a sort of summer dining annex. To be sure, the MVA foyer was more fragile than the main building, which was built above the park. The insulation materials were lightweight, and the thickness of the cement was minimal. Perhaps this fragility corresponded to the poetics of the pavilion type. Its long-term maintenance would prove difficult, and the debate on its restoration would be re-sparked 40 years later.[78]

To complete the adventure of the MVA in all its beauty, the building owners sponsored a competition for "pictorial decoration" and sculpture.[79] The notion of decoration has evolved over time to refer to a more ecumenical, thus fluid, concept of an "integration of the arts," which could be viewed as either friend or foe of a "synthesis of the arts." In French-speaking Switzerland the slogan of integration was echoed in the annual volumes of *Architecture Forms + Functions*. If painting, after Fernand Léger's cry of "Give us our walls!" hoped for creative opportunities, sculpture proclaimed its autonomy in space; this was a reflection of old corporate tensions among painters, sculptors, and architects. In the same period, American jazz singers such as Sarah Vaughan were better paid than the pianists who accompanied them. But why did the MVA leadership finance a painting and sculpture competition? Perhaps it was due to a desire to garner more publicity. While the competition was restricted to Swiss artists (many of whom were nevertheless known on the international scene), the jury panel was made up of French and Italian practitioners.[80] The media

149
MVA insurance building, Lausanne, 1956, eastern facade under morning light. Photograph by M. Vuillemin

150
MVA insurance building, Lausanne, 1956, eastern facade at night. Photograph by M. Vuillemin

was anticipated, and would serve its purpose.⁸¹ It was Tschumi who defined the competition's program and sat on the jury. Five decorative proposals were accepted, offering the MVA its crowning achievement of modernity.⁸²

Let's leave the details of the building's commission and formal description in order to rejoin the issue of symbolic production. The directors of the MVA and its architect were acclaimed in Lausanne's liberal press.⁸³ The *Gazette de Lausanne* provided an exceptional record of the event—seven columns spread out over eight pages. Today this presentation still offers a remarkable document by virtue of the quantity and quality of information. Fifty-five companies were credited for their participation in the first and second phases of work, providing an accurate mosaic of a construction site in the 1950s. Tribute was paid to the workers who had nonetheless continued to work during the freezing "Siberian" winter of 1955. The editor set the tone of the reporting by titling his column "A City that Runs Well."⁸⁴ This title put into question a persistent misconception: that Lausanne was a city that had gone wrong, according to a play on words by the poet Charles Ferdinand Ramuz.⁸⁵ In 1930 Ramuz had written that Lausanne had taken a bad urban turn, regretting the absence of a café with a lakeview terrace on the Place Saint-François as well as the lack of an enlightened chef. The *Gazette* also erased earlier denunciations of concrete as evidence of "Communist" banality,⁸⁶ observing that "Concrete, this noble material, posed difficult problems at Le Cèdre."⁸⁷ Again, the headline seemed to reverse its common connotation as a destroyer of landscape. The MVA's corporate architecture took on the value of a status symbol on the shores of Lake Geneva, a competitive assertion of pride that demonstrated excellence and efficiency. The numerous requests for visits were celebrated by management. Three thousand copies of an elegant catalog, rich in its use of photography, were printed.⁸⁸

151
MVA insurance building, Lausanne, canteen pavilion and mineral garden. Photograph by M. Vuillemin, 28 January 1957, showing sharp winter sun and melting snow

1956–1960: Nestlé Vevey, the Pinnacle of Corporate Architecture

The Nestlé headquarters in Vevey was the most publicized project of an architect whose international reputation came late.[89] We know that the commission was given to him following the success of the MVA in Lausanne. In Vevey, the center of a global empire devoted to the industrial processing of milk, cereals, chocolate, and coffee—a kind of empirical nineteenth-century pharmacy—would give way to a more scientific version that left indelible traces in millions of hungry mouths. The name of the German founding father of the Swiss business was translated into a logo. In the German Black Forest from whence he descended to Lake Geneva, his name meant "little nest." "Nestle" would then be renamed "Nestlé." The logo on the milky breakfast-meal box depicted a nest built on an oak tree, where the mother was feeding something that looks like a succulent worm to three competing chicks. Thus, one of the major chapters in Swiss industrial history was written around its logo.[90]

In 1956 Tschumi met with the dual heads of the company, the Vaudois Jean Constant Corthésy (1907–1976) and the Swiss-Italian Enrico Bignami (1905–1993), both managing directors.[91] The architect and his clients were the same age. Corthésy's rather corpulent body seemed identical to Tschumi's. They agreed to discuss the project during their lunch breaks, skipping a meal in the hope of losing some weight.[92] Bignami, who was taller, was a force of nature. The stature of this trio impressed visitors. These details seem anecdotal, but they helped to write the international saga of "Nestlé Alimentana," as told in 1962 by *Time* magazine under the Groucho Marx-like title, "From Soup to Nuts." The title of the article alluded to the acquisition of the British manufacturers Crosse & Blackwell, which preceded the acquisition of Findus and other Swiss, Austrian, and German brands. As the *Time* reporter noted, "Nestlé likes to hire butcher's sons, train them, send them out in the world steeped in arduous jobs before bringing them back to headquarters." He continued on to say that the building was "a visionary achievement of glass and aluminum on the shores of Lake Geneva."[93] Indeed, Corthésy had worked in South Africa, the Philippines, Venezuela, and the United States before returning to Vevey. Bignami was born in Lugano, where his father, a Garibaldian freemason, socialist, and pacifist, had taken refuge in the late nineteenth century. The son inherited his father's name and surname and went to Berlin where he met his teacher, Werner Sombart. Hired by Nestlé in 1926, he worked in its London and Milan offices. Needless to say, the two managing directors had mastered the English language, its nuances, and its technical vocabulary. The company expected a lifetime of loyalty from its managers and staff, according to the model Nestlé family in the bird's nest. Corthésy and Bignami practiced "innovative sales and caution,"[94] and worked through their mutual agreement and complementary effectiveness.[95]

A few laconic letters housed in the company archives illuminate the relationship of the three protagonists. The architect was dealing with two managers who had the habit of questioning the compatibility of financial plans. Tschumi had decided on the Y-shaped *parti*. He proposed different options as variants. Where were the management areas best placed? What type of window should be used? Decisions were made by Bignami, who then wrote to Corthésy. When Tschumi and Corthésy argued that air-conditioning the total building would cost an estimated 800,000 francs, Bignami countered that the inability to open windows in Vevey would induce a "psychological problem."[96] Hence an additional cost: the offices would have to be air-conditioned, but the curtain wall would also open with pivoting windows. A conduit linked to central ventilation would pump lake water with a temperature of about nine degrees, taken from a depth of 70 meters. The reinforced-concrete engineer was asked to reduce his fees. It was none other than Alexandre Sarrasin,[97] an illustrious protagonist of reinforced concrete known in Europe for his arch systems and formally economical vaults and bridges, who would be asked to do only two floors—basement and portico (Plate 164). The situation was rather comical if one considers that the bracing of the building was achieved by gables of reinforced concrete going up six floors. Regarding the gable design variants, Bignami selected a vertical aluminum *pare-soleil*[98] (Plate 157). It is true that the north gable, logically, would have made an exception. Here the floor surface created horizontal lines that signaled the uniqueness of this wing whose penthouse had a hanging garden (Plate 180). It was Bignami who chose to put management on the third floor, halfway up the building, rather than on the second floor or in the penthouse. He also decided on the choice of the glass. When two companies competed for the bid, it was still Bignami who decided where preference would be given. As at Sandoz, Tschumi practiced the controlled game of the variant. In other words, he organized a range of options without changing their basic principle. The owner would choose one of the options and identify with the outcome.

Bignami was inspired by Adriano Olivetti, for whom architecture and design were integral to contemporary culture. Bignami and Olivetti advocated the scientific organization of work. Adriano had taken refuge in Switzerland during World War II, and had participated with an Italian team of antifascist professors who (through contact with the University of Lausanne) had opened their school in a vacant hotel in Chexbres, not far from Lausanne and Vevey. During Italy's post-fascist reconstruction, Olivetti surrounded himself in Ivrea with architects, designers, economists, poets, and intellectuals to create journals (including one titled *Tecnica & Organizzazione*) as well as factories, workers' housing, and office machinery.[99]

Nestlé sought the services of an "in-house" architect, Willy Bühlmann, to supervise the project's completion as a permanent on-site presence. Tschumi conducted the work from his Lausanne office. Nonetheless, the responsibilities rested fully on his shoulders. Listening to management, Bühlmann quantified the program components, the size of offices, the range of furnishings. He visited the Aluminium AG headquarters in Zurich, a building that Hans Hofmann had just completed. He found useful references there—the lakeshore site, as well as the ultimate performance of Swiss aluminum. In the four-story central hall, the staircase reinterpreted the *topos* of the propeller, a sculptural move much in vogue in the 1950s (Plate 172). Aluminium AG introduced the practice of the secretary pool that Nestlé managers wanted to apply in their Vevey offices.[100] Bühlmann operated in Tschumi's shadow, but their confidence in each other's abilities was mutual. In spring 1956 management sent them both to the U.S., accompanied by their wives, in order to document office buildings and facilities. What were the systems for combining glass and aluminum in curtain-wall construction? With Ektachrome film rolling in his Alpa reflex, Tschumi photographed everything everywhere: clouds and landscapes through the window, highways and bridges seen from the taxi approaching Manhattan. His personal collection of slides has been conserved.[101] What did he look at when he went back to New York in 1956? The United Nations and Lever House (which he had already visited in 1952); The Museum of Modern Art was also a must. The trip continued to Boston and Cambridge, where Eero Saarinen had completed the large MIT auditorium, donated by the retail magnet Sebastian Kresge. Its skin consisted of a thin shell of reinforced concrete anchored in three points, resulting in a photogenic and widely disseminated work. Tschumi was thinking about providing a bold auditorium for EPUL. The following year his observation of the Saarinen project inspired him to design a thin-shelled structure whose geometric complexity exceeded what he had seen at MIT. Another leg of the trip entailed driving through Pittsburgh to see Harrison and Abramovitz's Alcoa Building, which offered a firsthand look at aluminum in action. Finally, the Washington Mall's wide-open spaces and monuments proudly displayed their gritty, gargantuan perspectives.

To return to our starting point: in January 1956 Nestlé bought the land of the Grand Hotel in Vevey (known locally as En-Bergère). Over the course of a decade, it became clear that the poten-

152
Dynamiting of the former Grand Hotel in Vevey by the Swiss Army, October 1956

153
Nestlé headquarters in Vevey, perspective of south facade toward the lake, detail, 1956–1957, tempera and collage on cardboard. Rendering technique developed by the draftsman Henri Curchod

154
Nestlé headquarters in Vevey, perspective of south facade toward the lake, detail, 1956–1957, tempera and collage on cardboard

155
Nestlé headquarters in Vevey, perspective of south facade toward the lake, 1956–1957, tempera and collage on cardboard

156
Nestlé headquarters in Vevey, perspective of south facade, 1956–1957, graphite, color pencils, India ink, and gouache on tracing paper. Variant of suspended veranda for the director's office, rendering by the draftsman Hubert Curchod

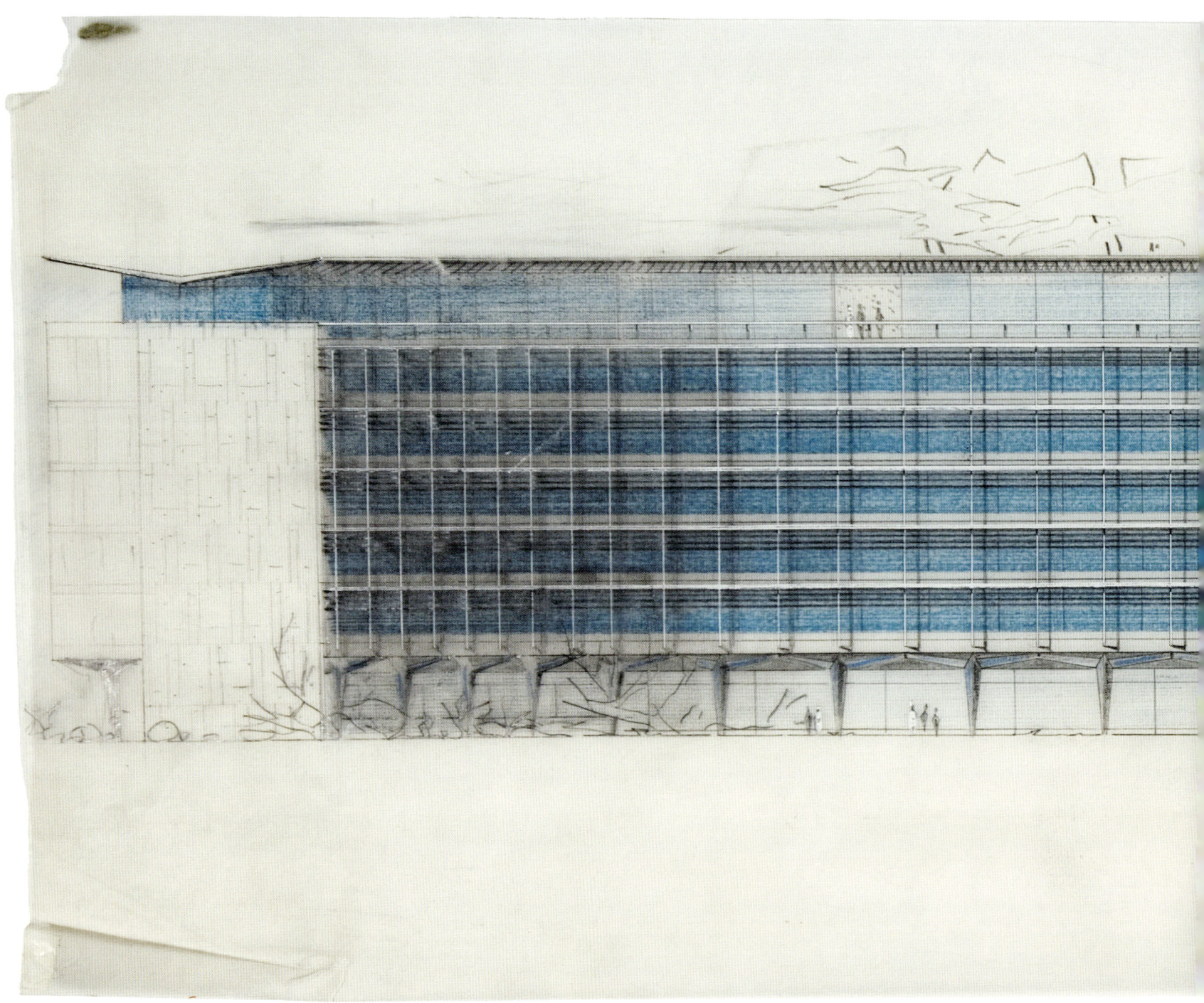

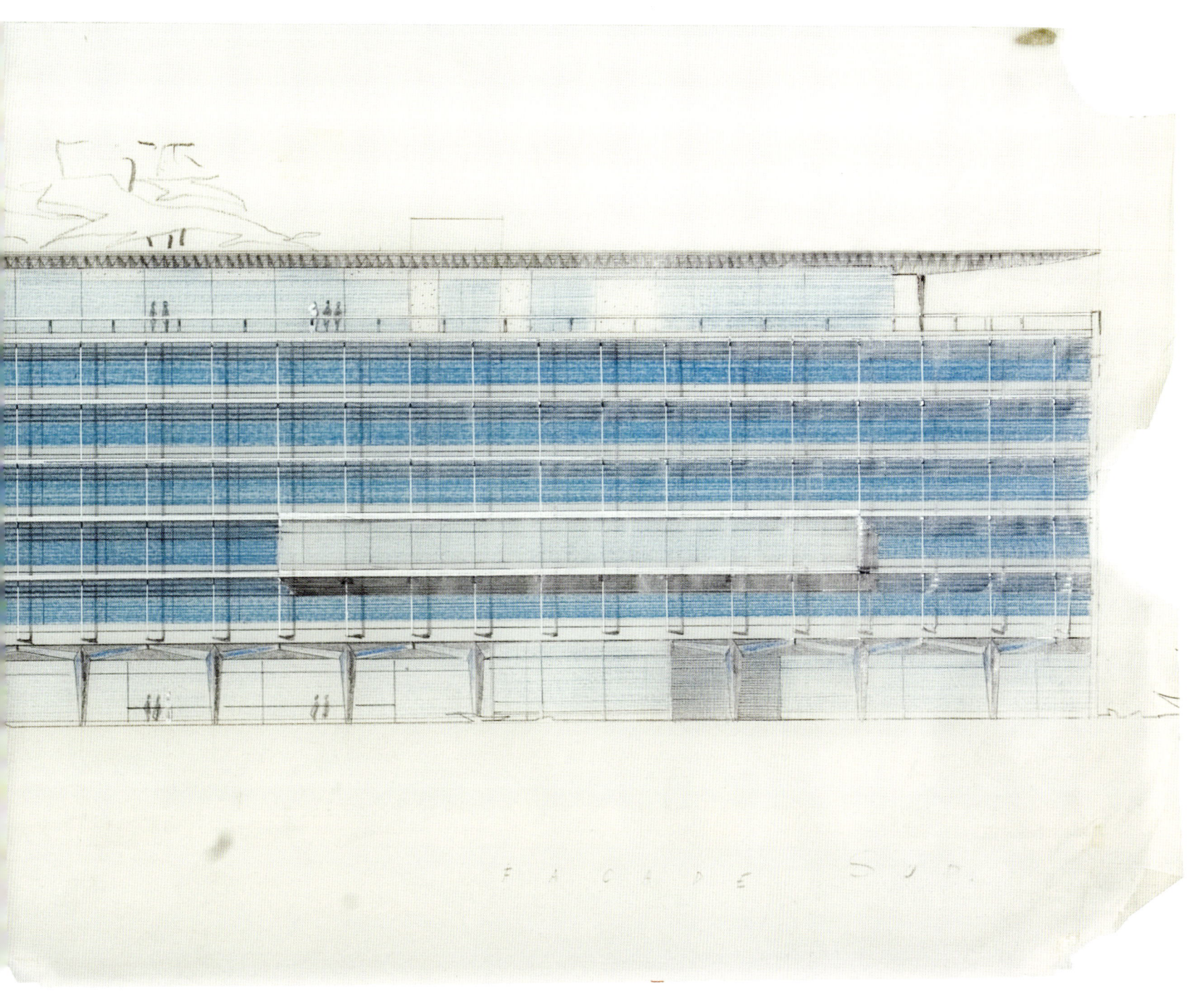

tial value of the land was beyond its hotel yield. The municipality took the lead and, in 1955, codified an extension plan according to the following scenario: the demolition of the hotel, followed by the division of the property into three lots, and the authorization for construction of three residential buildings.[102] The political situation changed when Nestlé acquired all of the land. To save time, the architect took into account the municipality's imposed guidelines. The previous year, a 12-story building had been proposed by another architect on behalf of another client on another site. A press campaign was launched in Lausanne to denounce the gigantism and the Americanization of "Vevey buildings."[103] The expansion plan set a height limitation variable from five to six floors. Under this constraint, the architect chose a Y *parti* that ensconced itself amid local idiosyncrasies. Trees that were relics of the Grand Hotel once again became the arbiters of the situation. On the Lake Geneva shore, the variety of trees qualified it as a tourist hot spot: old-growth cedars, cypresses, pines, catalpa, and chestnuts. The land offered good soil, consisting of layers of alluvial gravel and sand that were located above the water table. The rubble from the demolition of the Grand Hotel was used to rebuild the bank and to create a public path planted with hedges that effectively blocked the view into the private property.

In 1956 the architectural press brought up the Y *parti* for the UNESCO headquarters in Paris. Indeed, this example drew Tschumi's attention.[104] After much controversy,[105] the UNESCO project had been given to the firm BNZ. B stood for the former Bauhaus member Marcel Breuer, N for the Turin engineer Pierluigi Nervi, and Z for the French architect and former Pontremoli student Bernard Zehrfuss.[106] The Ys in Paris and Vevey occurred in the context of a friendly challenge. The project by the masterful threesome would be written about by Bruno Zevi.[107] If we examine the two buildings, the differences appear more numerous than the simple analogy of the Y *parti*. In Paris the UNESCO curve consolidated an ensemble of buildings that organized the structure of the Place de Fontenoy, which curved in relation to the axis of the Ecole Militaire. The pre-existing block of the Merchant Marine Ministry[108] (Plate 175) bends along a piazza that terminates at the UNESCO building. Here the Y was

157
Nestlé headquarters in Vevey, perspective of the eastern gable in dovetail, 1956–1957, tempera and collage on cardboard. Rendering technique developed by the draftsman Henri Curchod

158
Nestlé headquarters in Vevey, perspective of the northern gable in dovetail, 1956–1957, tempera and collage on cardboard, showing cornice as pergola above the roof terrace

a response to the urban context, while in Vevey it resulted from a clever interpretation of a quirky neighborhood. Like a sculpture isolated in a tree-lined park, the building offered a palatial event (Plate 181). In Paris, due to orthogonal outgrowths, the three wings terminate in right angles. In Vevey, the east-west wing is orthogonal and the northern and southern wings connect in a kind of boomerang, creating an asymmetrical composition. In Paris, the axial symmetry is reinforced by the arrangement of elevators to form an orthogonal core isolated in the center of a triangle (Plate 175). In Vevey, this kernel welcomes the cylinder of a double-helix staircase, and the elevators are chased down into the orthogonal wing (Plates 169, 170). These geometric differences were the logical result of two different building systems. Raised up on a portico made out of reinforced concrete, the corpus of offices suggests an analogy, but with a different structural principle. In Paris, the portico stood out over ribbed supporting beams made from reinforced concrete (Plate 176). In Vevey, Sarrasin's portico concrete masterpiece established a base for another contractor's steel framework. The floors were mixed slabs of reinforced concrete. The work fell to the engineer Maurice Cosandey, who used a process known in the United States as the Robertson Process.[109] A steel plate with deep corrugated waves was mounted on beams welded into the steel framework. A horizontal metal trellis provided the armature. Cement flowed out of small tractors that were placed as mobile reservoirs on the different floors. The tests were done in the materials laboratory of EPUL. On site, the economy of the system translated into time savings. The deadline for finishing the concrete was set for the end of December 1957; this was the time when the company would lay off its "seasonal" masonry workers, who then returned to their Italian provinces. Their possible reappointment depended on the goodwill of the contractor, who was given recommendations by his supervisors of Italian origin. In the film documenting the building's construction, the speaker talks admiringly of their "acrobatic and dangerous work." The pressure, then, was put on immigrant workers.

Nestlé managers were committed to documenting the progress of the building on film. It all began with the demolition of the Grand Hotel, a blasting

159
Nestlé headquarters in Vevey, proposal for Enrico Bignami's office, 16 February 1959, graphite, color pencils, India ink, and gouache. Perspective by Hubert Curchod, lake-blue armchairs by Tschumi

160
Nestlé headquarters in Vevey, second proposal for Enrico Bignami's office, February 1959, graphite, color pencils, India ink, and gouache. Perspective by Hubert Curchod, yellow leather armchairs and red carpet

161
Nestlé headquarters in Vevey, the bar in the attic floor, circa 1958, graphite, color pencils, India ink, and gouache showing dramatically lit entrance and double-spiral stairwell. Perspective drawn by Hubert Curchod

162
Nestlé headquarters in Vevey, boardroom, circa 1958, graphite, stump, and wash on paper. Proposal for a red and blue atmospheric evocation of Vevey's wine-growing *genius loci*

163
Nestlé headquarters in Vevey, boardroom, circa 1958, graphite, stump, and wash on paper. Proposal for a black-and-gold atmosphere, evocative of roast coffee

157

exercise that was entrusted to the Swiss army. Striking and unexpected images date from October 1956. In them, the collapsed structure disappears into dust. The sequence seems to anticipate the blasting filmed in St. Louis, Missouri at the Pruitt-Igoe project. This housing project never provided neighborhood facilities, but instead created a black ghetto and a federal slum[110] that would draw in poverty, gang violence, and the anger of private developers. The Pruitt-Igoe images traveled around the world. Afterwards, Charles Jencks proclaimed that the new "clean slate" dating from July 15, 1972 at 3:32 pm gave postmodern architecture its "primal scene" and, in effect, embodied a funeral oration for the Modern Movement.[111] In the same way, the civil engineering world remembers another cinematic sequence—the vibration and rupture of the suspension bridge over the Strait of Tacoma. The Tacoma images had found their didactic worth: Do not repeat the disaster. The Pruitt-Igoe images, however, were highly polemical. One beautiful evening in the late twentieth century, the Swiss Romande Television (TSR) exhumed the film that documented the demolition of the Grand Hotel in Vevey and showed it as an opening sequence for its nightly newscast. Courtesy of the TSR, millions of people thus saw, without knowing it, the October 1956 dynamiting that made way for the construction of the Nestlé headquarters.

Let's take another look at Sarrasin's portico. The pillars extend up diagonally from their foundation footings. They cross the underground car park (Plate 171). Then they join up in the hall, where they acquire subtle profiles made from beveled formwork. The pillars support a slab that is inscribed with a geometric pattern of triangles and diamonds that is executed in relief (Plate 170). The framework for the south wing has an underpinning of prestressed tension cables.[112] This variation is a three-dimensional replica of the UNESCO project, where the pillars in the hall emerge at right angles from a flat base that is more rustic than elegant. In Paris, the cement is gray and the horizontal imprint from the formwork seems to introduce a knife-cut profile; in Vevey, Tschumi demanded the Dansk cement that he had used for the MVA. The polyhedral facets were sanded after the formwork was removed, so that the work took on a sculptural quality. The geometry of the elevation is reflected in the floor paving, where a network of isosceles triangles inserts three different marble colors, moving from white through shades of gray, into the overall com-

164
Nestlé headquarters in Vevey, construction of the portico and "boomerang" western wing. Photograph by De Jongh, 11 December 1957

position. In plan, the five office floors adopted a longitudinal and compound subdivision.[113] The central span was reduced to two bays in the front, allowing for modulation. Reserved for management, the third floor had soundproof walls to enclose the customized offices and demarcate the waiting areas at the front. Daylight penetrates deep into the building. On the standard floor, the movable transverse aluminum partitions informed the use of space and introduced extreme situations. Behind the north facade, the design area occupied the full building depth of over 70 meters, following the example of American engineering firms. The central corridor, equally long, was left blank. Attached to the ceiling angles, two exceptionally long neon tubes were sure to provide adequate lighting.

On the sixth floor, the posts of the central span could obliquely hang two cantilevered steel beams, which emerged to form the cornice ridges. This Haussmanian attic sheltered a range of utilities: the kitchen, four restaurants (for staff, executives, management, and guests), two smoking rooms for executives and management, and a conference room that could double as a movie theater. If one were to lean against the cafeteria, whose curve responded to the double helix staircase, a surprise would be waiting: the attic floor was set level with the rock garden and the lawn planted over the north wing, intended for staff during their rotating breaks between noon and one pm. The expansion plan approved by the city of Vevey stipulated that, in this location, the building could be no higher than 4.50 meters (Plate 167). In order to respect the rules while also circumventing them, the architect used the ploy of the terrace to unify the volume. The waterproofing on the flat roof was assured by asphalt layers interspersed with aluminum sheets. A steel pergola sprang from the lawn. Its supports formed an upside-down V that, in turn, held up two cantilevered beams. Their profiles were tapered using a welding assembly that originated in the shipbuilding industry. They were braced by thin vertical tension rods. A niche of reinforced concrete was attached to the north gable to cut the north wind flowing down the Veveyse valley, creating a range of miniature-sized garden shrubs. This mastery of profiles returns us to the main point: does the concept of virtuosity have a meaning in architecture?

In developing the Nestlé project, Tschumi surrounded himself with a team of faithful designers

165
Nestlé headquarters in Vevey, view toward the lake, photograph by De Jongh, 6 January 1958. Construction of the ceiling above the reception floor of the portico according to prestressed reinforced-concrete design by Alexandre Sarrasin

largely chosen from among his students.[114] Drafting preceded construction, which took 24 months and would occupy him until spring 1960. There were weekly site meetings.[115] The engineer Maurice Cosandey remembers the architect proposing "on-site solutions."[116] Without disrupting the schedule or the constructive principles of the general structure, the architect relied on what he had learned from the MVA building to guide the technical organization of the finishes and furniture. Drawings served several purposes: to monitor the installation of standardized components, and to submit new proposals to the owner. The graphics were adapted to the task at hand. The ink lines drawn on tracing paper were on the level of "technical drawings" and intended for contractors; the colored perspectives were for the owner. The latter depicted the architecture amidst the landscape (Plates 154, 155). Overlapping paper cutouts designed to simulate the silhouettes of trees (or even the relief of aluminum sun-screens) were set over gouache laid down onto Bristol paper. What was the origin of this curious and unique technique? Did it convey the two clients' taste, or their architect's desire to seduce them? It is difficult to know.[117] It should be noted that this rendering technique, so distant from the highly perfected boards prepared for Pontremoli at the Beaux-Arts by means of chalk, washes, and gouache, combined the notions of "beautiful" and "picturesque" beauty, to use Edmund Burke's categories.

Particular care was taken in the choice of furnishings for the third floor, where the company leadership worked. Two individual offices, waiting rooms, and a boardroom were drawn and re-drawn in perspectives. The changes related to the chromatic range of the carpets, walls, doors, and mural panels. All of this work began in spring 1959, a year before the opening of the building. Choosing pencils that lent themselves to a pastel effect, the draftsmen sought to create an "atmosphere." Dominant yellows, blues, and garnet were contrasted. A similar treatment was accorded to the curved bar in the attic, the company's social gathering space (Plate 161). Tschumi left his designers to dream in color while criticizing their results on a weekly basis. He piloted the team and monitored it closely—as much for the technical fittings[118] as for the full range of furniture, chairs, tables, desks, ashtrays, and lamps.

In contrast to the MVA, where he juxtaposed his own work with work by Bertoia and Charles and Ray Eames, in Vevey he reserved his efforts for the higher-end furnishings for the management and reception areas. Responding to the two directors' taste for wood, he revisited the chassis of the chairs, introducing a comfortable touch of aerodynamics. Besides wood, his expressive efforts were mostly focused on aluminum, a material that embodied the architectural modernity of the years between 1950 and 1960 that Tschumi had observed in the United States.

Two pieces of bravura await us in Vevey, the staircase and the canopy. The qualities of the latter are evoked in a description supplied by the architect:
The entrance canopy has been developed in the spirit of the overall building, and the size and thickness of its profiles constitutes a real tour de force of extruded aluminum construction. Built using 3 mm horizontal members and 5 mm plates to form the oblique planes of the "V," it is 14 meters long with an 11-meter cantilever. This achievement is a witness to a pure expression of its material, executed by the metal fabricators Ramelet Frères and the engineer Matter in Lausanne.[119]
The material came from the Alusuisse Chippis plant in Valais. In plan, the canopy outlines a trapeze that is enlarged as if following the thrust of the cantilever, like a fan. For Tschumi, this technical feat embodied an elegance that found inspiration in aircraft construction (Plate 182).

A more difficult *tour de force* was required to construct the double helix space of the central staircase. The problem of the staircase makes up a central chapter in the structural theories taught at EPUL. Here, the achievements of the Renaissance are confronted with twentieth-century examples. The staircase was a form dear to at least two Swiss architects. Tschumi liked to illustrate an example from Salvisberg's work, namely a suspended spiral in the hall of his *Collegienhaus* in Basel. An additional reference is in Zurich at the Aluminium AG headquarters, where Hans Hofmann installed a vertiginous, twisting staircase on four floors. The systematic use of a particular reference should not be confused with stylistic "quotation." The reference implies a confrontation, and perhaps ultimately a counter-proposal. We already know that

166
Nestlé headquarters in Vevey, portico by Alexandre Sarrasin and steel frame construction by Maurice Cosandey. Photograph by De Jongh, 1958, showing red rust-proofing paint on the steel structure

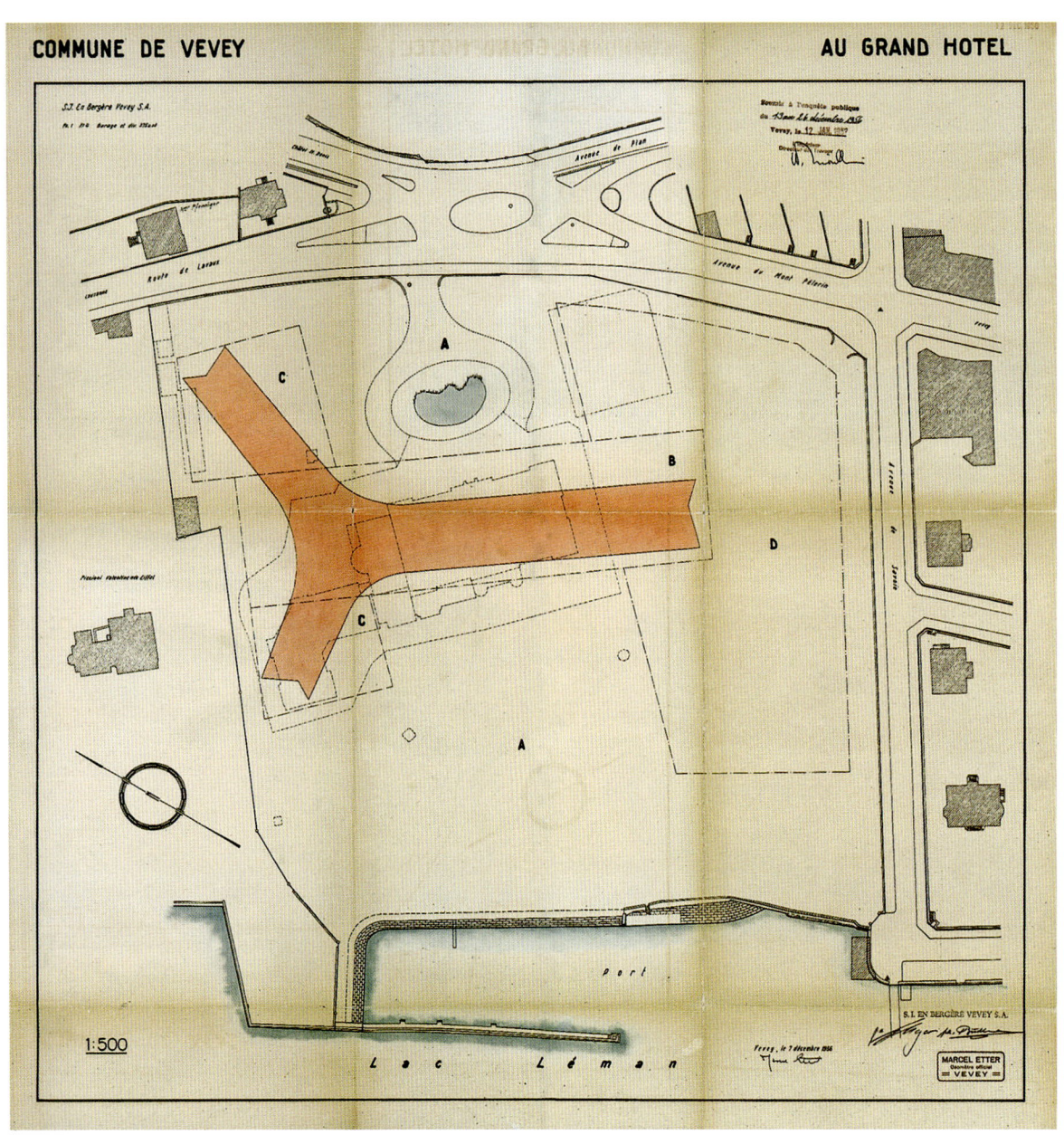

167
Nestlé headquarters in Vevey, plan submitted to the City of Vevey by Jean Tschumi and Willy Bühlman on 7 December 1956 and approved on 12 January 1957

168
Nestlé headquarters in Vevey, ground plan redrawn for publication, 1959. Rational inscription of the structure and schizophrenic evocation of trees in the park

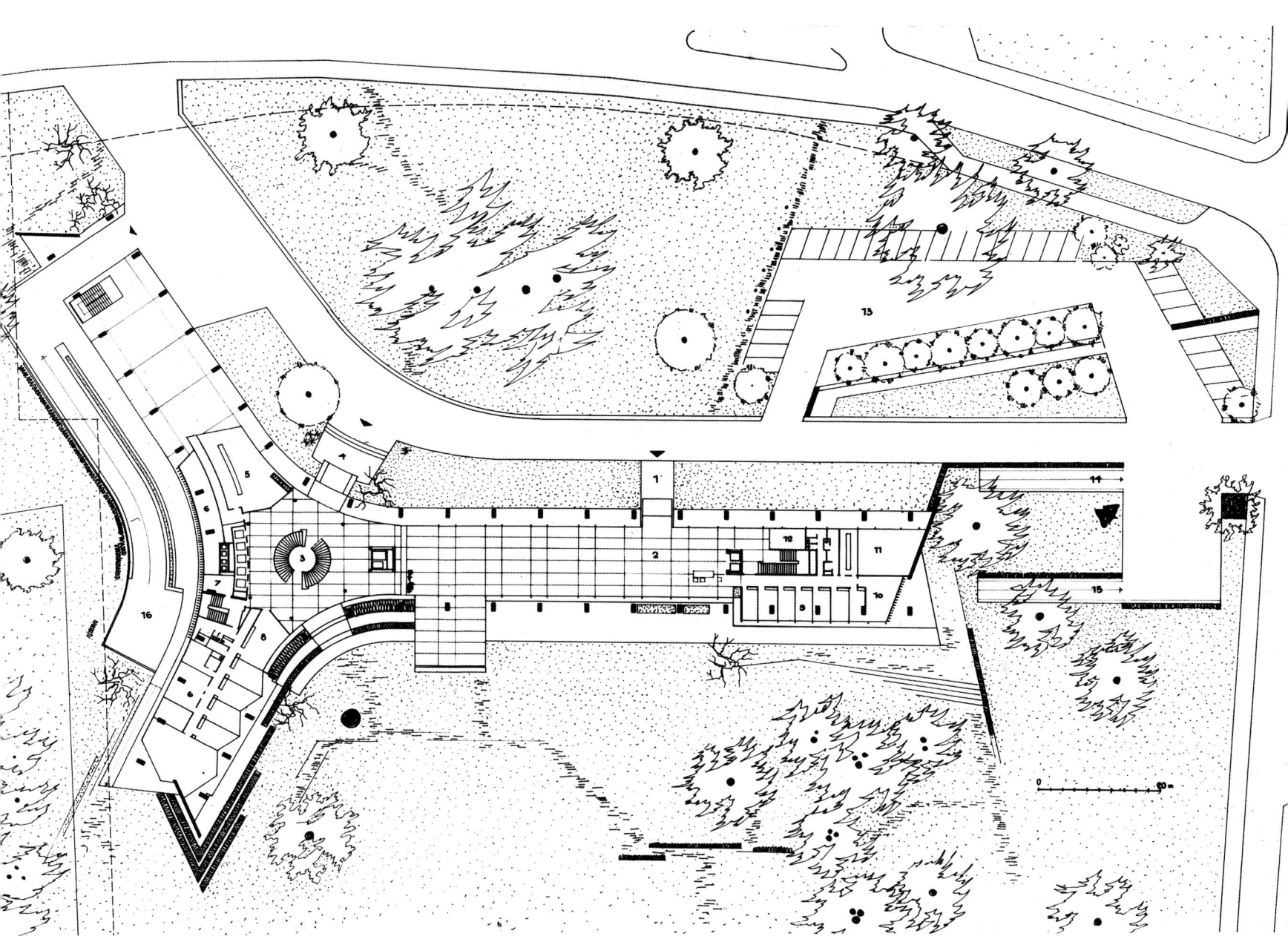

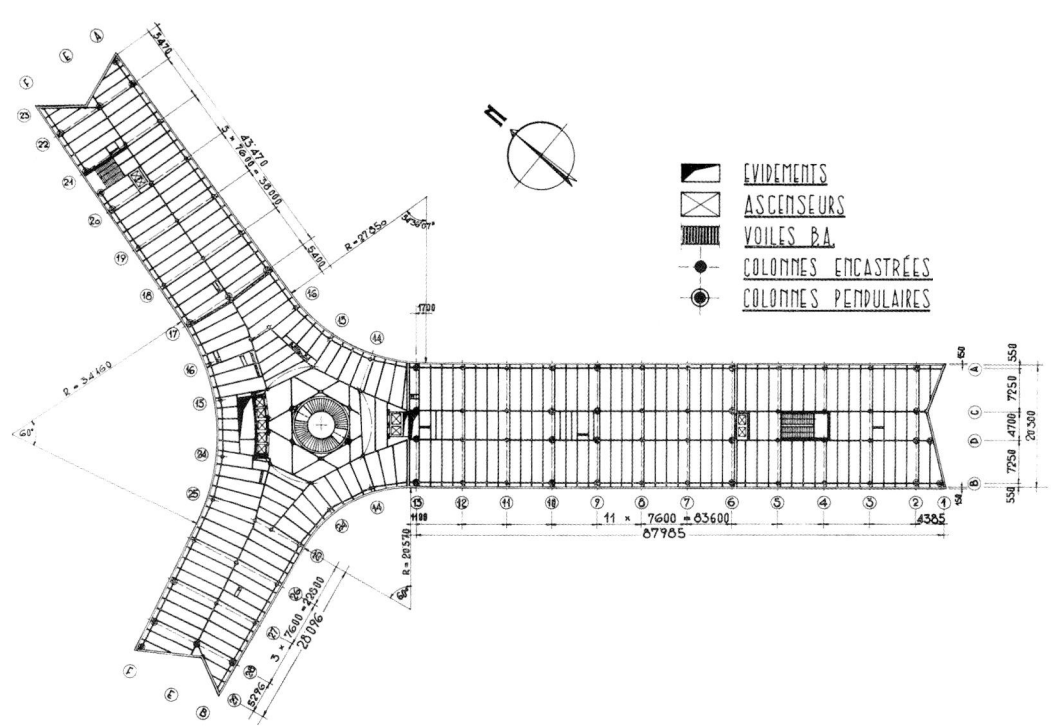

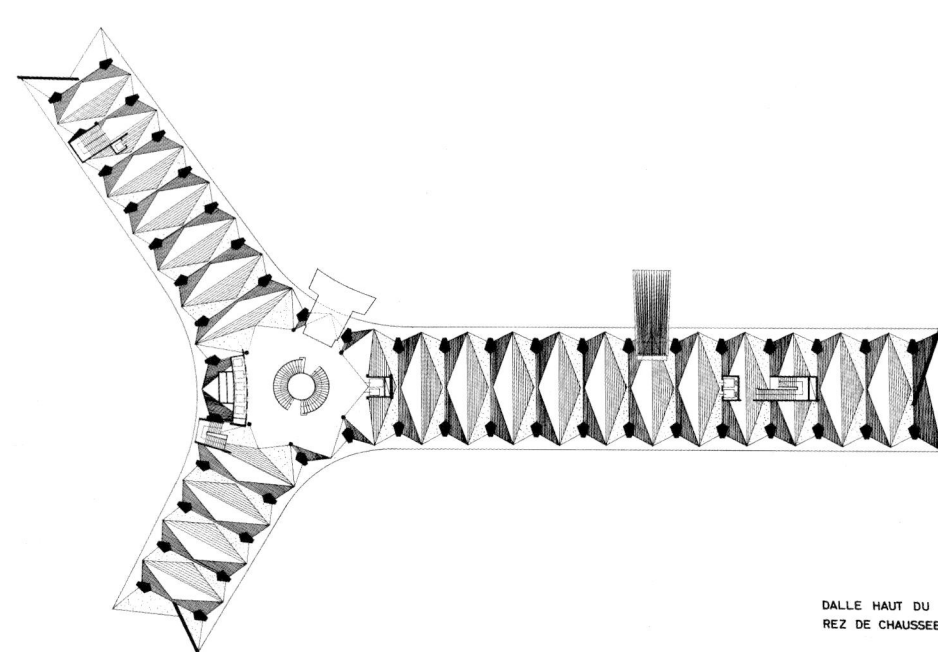

DALLE HAUT DU
REZ DE CHAUSSEE

169
Nestlé headquarters in Vevey, ground plan, as published by the engineer Maurice Cosandey, October 1959 with calculations of the curved and orthogonal bays

170
Nestlé headquarters in Vevey, ground plan, as published by the engineer Maurice Cosandey, October 1959, showing projection of the triangular and rhomboid ceiling

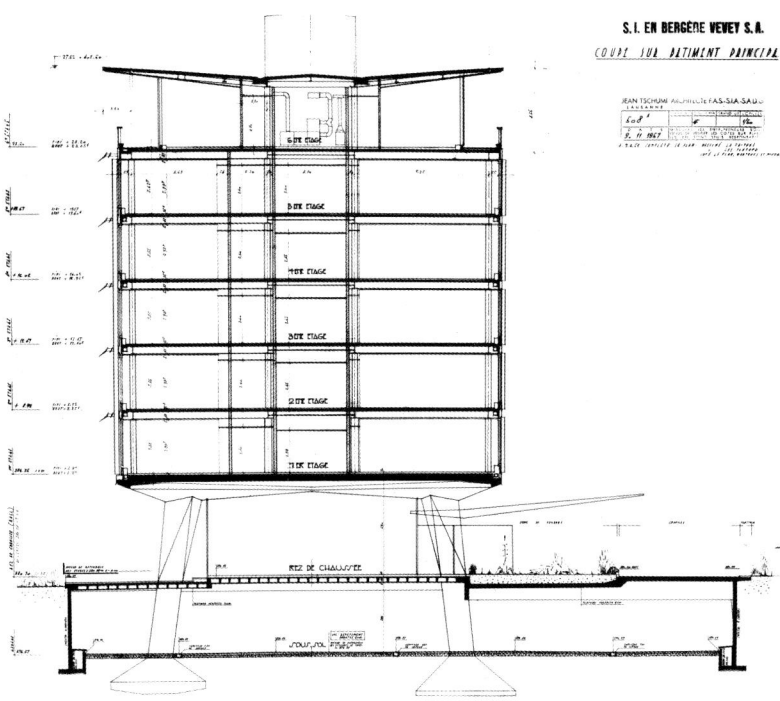

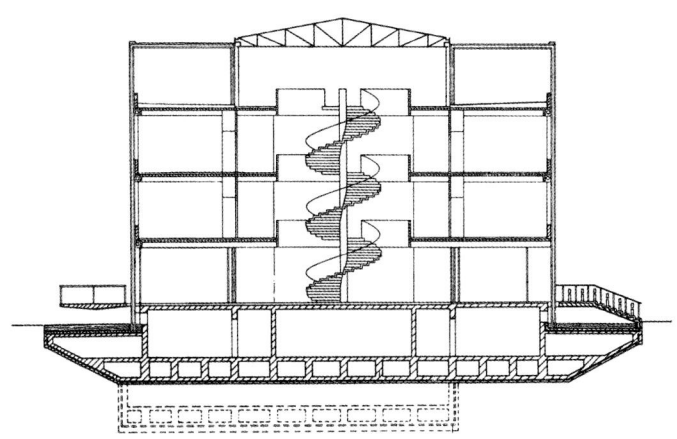

171
Nestlé headquarters in Vevey, cross section showing the underground garage and portico by the engineer Alaxandre Sarrasin, the steel skeleton by Maurice Cosandey, underground oblique structure, attic ceiling as monumental cornice

172
Hans Hofmann, architect, cross section through the headquarters of Aluminium AG in Zurich, built 1955–1956, as published in J. Joedicke, *Bürobauten*, 1959

in Vevey the main source of confrontation was the UNESCO project. At Nestlé, the double helix staircase was screwed and connected to the three wings of the Y, creating a kind of plunging perspective as well as a connection to the bar on the sixth floor. A sense of yearning is created under the conical rooflight. The breaks in the landings promote a whirling funnel effect. From the ground floor, the view toward the zenith opens up a curious spectacle, as if looking through a giant ammonite that had escaped from some millennial cataclysm. The eye sees only a single spiral (Plate 179), but we know that there are two. Is this an optical illusion? How does one master the technical *tour de force* of a double helix, especially one built out of metal? The timber formwork implemented by Perret or Lecoeur would be inoperative in this context. It is likely that Tschumi resorted to models, but information on this is missing. However, it is well known that the double helix at Nestlé was to be gallantly named *Chambord,* in reference to the castle of Francis I—a monument that personified its confluence of extravagance and rationality. The main and almost secret reference for Chambord was Bramante.

As an architectural "event," the Nestlé building was widely covered by the architectural press.[120] Mention has already been made of its distribution in four languages in six countries. This media success ran parallel to the commercial crescendo of Alimentana. The building served as a performative tool, as evidenced by the phenomenon of "postal sorting." This operation took place in an office located near the service entrance on the ground floor, and each floor had its own small freight elevator. Six months after the inauguration of the building in November 1960, Nestlé wrote to the Municipality of Vevey to submit a proposed extension. Tschumi suggested that the second stage take the form of a hexagonal tower on the northeast side of the building, isolated from the city. The Nestlé directors wanted to break ground on the project, but the architect's death postponed it. The subsequent extension was stuck onto the first building awkwardly and did not do justice to its functional organization.[121]

173
UNESCO headquarters in Paris, postcard, circa 1960

174
Place de Fontenoy in Paris, Ecole Militaire in the foreground, Merchant Marine Ministry to the left, and UNESCO headquarters by Breuer, Nervi, Zehrfuss. The Y *parti* as contextual response to Place de Fontenoy

175
Marcel Breuer, Pierluigi Nervi, Bernard Zehrfuss, UNESCO headquarters in Paris, ground plan showing three rectangular wings tied to a curved core in a symmetrical configuration

176
Marcel Breuer, Pierluigi Nervi, Bernard Zehrfuss, UNESCO headquarters in Paris, cross section showing orthogonal structure of the below-ground level and floor slabs built using reinforced-concrete beams

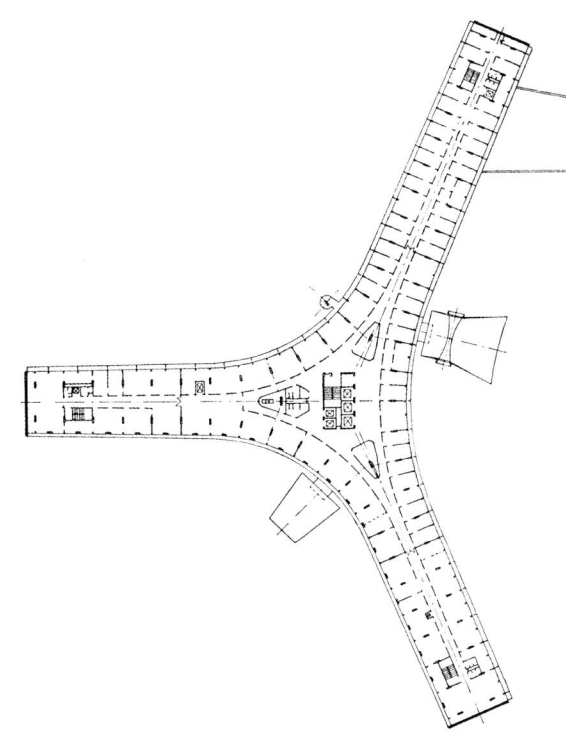
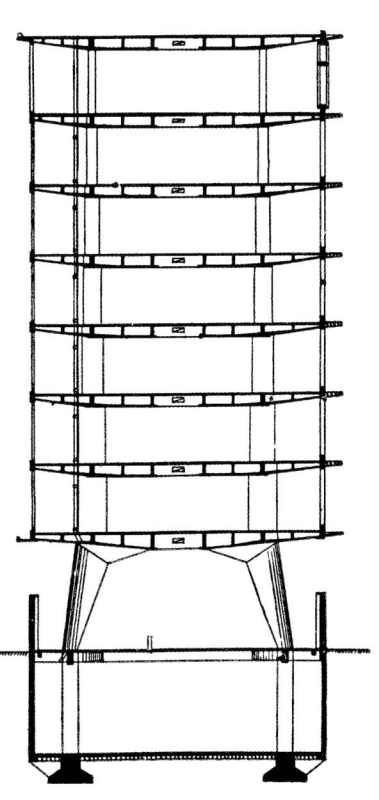

The critical reception of the Nestlé building is marked by two salient facts. The building received a prestigious prize from the Reynolds Metals Company. The jury was chaired by Walter Gropius, and its regulations were strict: Do not designate the presence of aluminum in construction,...but acknowledge an example where "the creative contribution of the architect [might exercise] a potential influence on contemporary architecture."[122] The jury had specific expertise on the topic; their report seemed more like a critique. We will see later that Zevi would adopt a contrary position. What were Gropius' comments? The *tours de force* of the canopy and the stairs were appreciated, but their performance was not enough to appeal to the jury. The report emphasized the expressive contrasts between metal and reinforced concrete, referring to "transparency," "sculptural stature," and "variable-depth" profiles. Its conclusion was controversial: "The jury assumes that the lack of imagination and 'sensitive' details in most projects [from] the United States is a consequence of the large quantity of prefabricated and standardized elements that are found in the United States, and the constraints imposed by the requirements of insurance companies." The European Tschumi was commended for his unbridled inventiveness as well as the "quality of sobriety and serenity" in his architecture.[123] In 1960 the Reynolds Prize meant that the winner was awarded a check for 25,000 dollars. The Lausanne press announced the news and referred to the award as the "Nobel Prize of architecture." In April of the same year the architect treated himself to a rich coast-to-coast study tour. He visited the architectural examples that would highlight the references for his future design work, the office expansions for Sandoz and Nestlé in Paris.

In the international reception of the Nestlé building, a second high point was provided by an article written by Bruno Zevi, one whose title could be translated as "A 'Y' that Pricks More than UNESCO"[124] and which appeared in the Roman weekly publication *L'Espresso*. Born in Rome, Zevi was 18 years old at the time of the Fascist proclamation of anti-Semitic "racial laws." He emigrated to London and then to the United States, where he obtained his

177
Nestlé headquarters in Vevey, double-spiral central staircase. Photographic print by Colorama Switzerland, 1960

178
Nestlé headquarters in Vevey, double-spiral central staircase with architectural reference to Bramante and Chambord. Photograph by De Jongh, 1960

179
Nestlé headquarters in Vevey, double-spiral central staircase seen from above, with *trompe-l'œil* effect of two staircases fused into one. Photograph by Eric Ed. Guignard, 1960

180
Nestlé headquarters in Vevey, terrace garden on north wing, view of subtle steel structure in form of a pergola

181
Nestlé headquarters in Vevey, south gable and north wing, view of cornice of the roof terrace in form of a pergola

182
Nestlé headquarters in Vevey, canopy made out of folded aluminum corrugated sheets.
Photograph by Eric Ed. Guignard, 1960

degree in architecture at Harvard under the guidance of Gropius. But it was Frank Lloyd Wright's "organic architecture" that he viewed as a priority. His political engagement with the antifascist resistance and the reconstruction of Italy relied on his faith in the radicalism of *l'architettura organica*, which was essentially democratic. While it is true that his review of the Nestlé building took place primarily within the controversy fueled by Italian magazines in Milan and Rome, the text also sought to revive international criticism of the Modern Movement. His first two books were translated into English, whereby the second, titled *Saper vedere l'architettura* (*Architecture as Space: How to Look at Architecture*), became a worldwide best seller. His humorous account of the Nestlé building aimed at the comparative rhetorical exercise of the *paragone*, according to a model that opposed Corneille to Racine, Voltaire to Rousseau, or Wright to Le Corbusier, with the latter being a kind of antihero because of his well-known Vichy-era associations. Zevi also condemned the principle of symmetry in modern architecture, even though the UNESCO "Y" form was a symmetrical composition. I have focused on the formal oscillations between the buildings in Vevey and Paris to show that Tschumi confronted his own work through the achievements of BNZ. Zevi's chronicle seemed based on a concept of style; it aligned Tschumi on the side of Le Corbusier in order to illustrate the point that the younger architect was better than his elder. The asymmetrical "Y" arrangement in Vevey piqued his curiosity, hence the pun of the title. But the compliment that Tschumi received was called *manierismo razionalista*. In 1950s France "Mannerism" meant artificiality, the mundane contortion of sacrificing art for fashion. In Italy *manierismo* referred to a neologism with a positive valence, a new stylistic category of art history that posited a willingness to put in crisis the language of the Renaissance. Paradoxically for Zevi, the Nestlé building, which served as a successful challenge to the teaching of Gropius as read through the work of Breuer, marked a moment of the Modern Movement that had since passed into oblivion. Tschumi had neither the time nor the desire to enter into this ideological quarrel. He continued his work in France for Sandoz and Nestlé. He resigned his teaching post at EPUL at the very moment when his presence in the international debate was sought after in Europe and in the United States.

183
Nestlé headquarters in Vevey, reception hall under the portico showing *Gesamtkunstwerk*: unity and overall design control

184
André & Co. building in Lausanne, 1960–1962, plan and model for a triangular building locally interpreted as illustrating the triangular logo for André. Tschumi's answer to Marcel Breuer

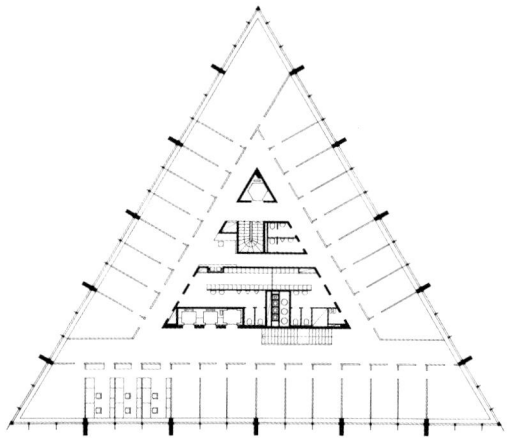

185
Headquarters of SOPAD (Nestlé) in Paris Courbevoie, south facade on the Seine, circa 1960, color pencil on tracing paper, proposal for a 5-bay facade as a blade on the waterfront

186
Headquarters of SOPAD (Nestlé) in Paris Courbevoie, circa 1960, photograph of the model, 15-floor proposal

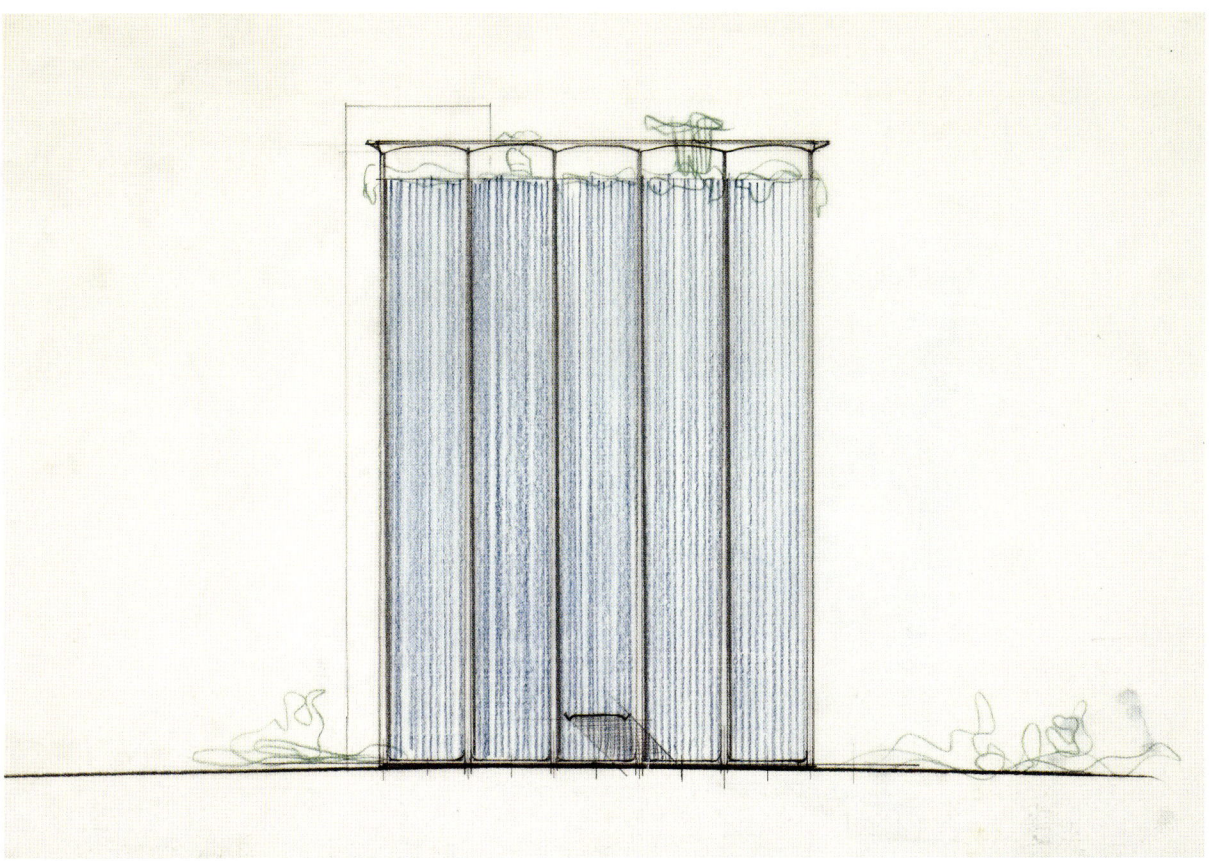

Notes

[1] Jons Messedat, *Corporate Architecture: Development, Concepts, Strategies*, Avedition, Ludwigsburg, 2005.

[2] The bibliography on this topic is vast. Among the many references, see Veronica Napoles, *Corporate Identity Design*, Wiley, New York, 1988; Wolff Olins, *Corporate Indentity: Making Business Strategy Visible through Design*, Thames & Hudson, London, 1989.

[3] A great deal has been written in Switzerland on the opposition between the culture of classical enterprise at the now-defunct Swissair and the more baroque culture of its former rival, Crossair.

[4] Built between 1873 and 1875, Richard Morris Hunt's headquarters for the New York *Tribune* rose to eight stories. Hunt was the first American architect trained at the Beaux-Arts.

[5] Among the ample number of studies, see Frederic J. Schwarz, *The Werkbund, Design Theory and Mass Culture before the First World War*, Yale University Press, New Haven, 1997.

[6] Tillmann Buddensieg, Hennig Rogge, *Industriekultur. Peter Behrens und die AEG, 1907-1914*, Gebrüder Mann, Berlin, 1993.

[7] Dario Matteoni, "De Koninck. La publicité et l'architecture d'exposition," in Maurice Culot, Caroline Mierop, Anne Van Loo et al., *Louis Herman De Koninck. Architecte des années modernes*, AAM, Brussels, 1989, pp. 164–185.

[8] Frederick Kiesler, *Contemporary Art Applied to the Store and its Display*, Brentano, New York, 1930; cited in Andrew Otwell, "Frederick Kiesler as a Commercial Designer," *Andrew Otwell's Art History Papers*, 1997. See also www.heyotwell.com/work/arthistory/KielserDesign.html.

[9] Enrico Castelnuovo, *Arte, industria, rivoluzioni. Temi di storia sociale dell'arte*, Edizioni della Normale, Pisa, 2007, p. 53.

[10] Laurent Sester, "L'entreprise chimique et pharmaceutique Sandoz SA," in Jean-Pierre Jelmini et al., *Les Sandoz, du Moyen Age au troisième millénaire. Une famille des Montagnes neuchâteloises à la conquête du monde*, Hauterive, Attinger, Hauterive, 2000, pp. 238–253.

[11] Letter to Dr. Baumgartner, Paris, 3 March 1951, Novartis Archives, Basel, A.283.1.

[12] The name of the Vaudoise school was Collège Henchoz de Château-d'Oex. See Félix Marcilhac, "Un artiste aux talents multiples, Edouard-Marcel Sandoz, 1881-1971," in Jelmini et al., op. cit., p. 254.

[13] See Bruno Foucart et al., *Edouard-Marcel Sandoz, 1881-1971*, Fondation Taylor, Paris, 1991; *Découvrir Sandoz, statuaire du regard*, Editions du Grand-Pont, Lausanne, 1991. See also www.sandozfondation.ch.

[14] Félix Marcilhac, op. cit., p. 260.

[15] Recollections by Edouard-Marcel Sandoz in *Sandorama*, April 1962, p. 16. Sandoz expressed admiration for Tschumi as an artist, but also for his character: "*Lorsque je l'ai rencontré en 1926, à la Galerie Malesherbes, chez Edgar Brandt, le grand ferronnier (il était un de ses tout jeunes conseils) je ne pensais pas que ce garçon excessivement naturel et simple me permettrait de le suivre dans une carrière merveilleuse qui s'interromprait brusquement, par un sommeil dont il ne s'est pas réveillé, dans l'express Paris-Lausanne.*"

[16] This idea was not really extravagent if one recalls that a section of the Himalaya Mountains, complete with its own "scenic railway," was built in the amusement park for the World Expo of 1935 in Brussels.

[17] As Edith Zweifel of the Swiss Tourism Board pronounced recently, "*Toblerone…est un concentré de Suisse… l'un des meilleurs ambassadeurs du tourisme helvétique*," *Le Temps*, 18 January 2008, p. 35.

[18] Le Corbusier & Jeanneret's Nestlé Pavilion featured a steel structure that could be disassembled easily. From Paris in 1928, it was moved a year later to Bordeaux and then to Marseilles. Arthur Rüegg, "Le Corbusier e Pierre Jeanneret, il padiglione Nestlé alla Fiera di Parigi 1928," *Progex*, Milan, no. 6, 1991, pp. 12–21.

[19] Two national pavilions remain unforgettable for their modernity: Sert's pavilion for the Spanish Republic and Aalto's Finnish contribution.

[20] One former student recalls that Tschumi once told him, "Le Corbusier has taken my ideas." As recounted by Robert Monnier, Neuchâtel, 6 July 2007.

[21] The first mention of a *Miro-Mirage* came up in October 1934, during the design of the Honfleur cabin for *Le Normandie*. ACM 0060.04.0078.

[22] The *Miro-Mirage* project occupied Tschumi and Sandoz from November 1937 to March 1938.

[23] Martin Steinmann, "Bedeutung als Funktion. Das Verwaltungsgebäude von Sandoz, der Bau 200 von Novartis, 1937-1939, 1946-1948," in Hans-Peter Wittwer et al., *Werke der Sammlung*, Novartis, Basel, 2004, pp. 244–253.

[24] The Sandoz brand is now part of Novartis. The current head offices at the center of the Novartis campus still reflect the original Sandoz designs.

[25] "Note to complete the application for authorization prior to commencement of work on the construction of a facility in Orléans for the manufacture of chemical products for pharmaceutical use by Sandoz SA Paris," 30 October 1947, ACM 0060.01.0091. This note summarizes the findings of the pharmaceutical company and the initial work by Tschumi in Noisy and Orléans.

[26] The biochemist Arthur Stolz played a decisive role in the politics of disseminating products within the medical profession. Personal contacts were made by letters. Practitioners were informed about the results. The scientific literature is printed in separate German and French newsletters. See "La publicité et ses images: Pharma," *Bulletin Sandoz*, no. 76, 1986, pp. 11–26.

[27] A new stage of work began in 1942. In 1945 the manufacturing of calcium vials was incorporated into a wooden hall. There were two successive stages of expansion, 1946–1948 and 1953–1955.

[28] Letter addressed to J. Häuselmann, 30 October 1940, Novartis Archives, M.320.14a.

[29] See the chapter titled "Industrielle Repräsentation und Eleganz zu den Bauten der Hoffmann-La Roche in Basel," in Claude Lichtenstein et al., *Otto Rudolf Salvisberg. Die andere Moderne*, gta, Zurich, 1995, pp. 180–185. See also Robert Spreng's photographic reportage in Alexander Bieri, *Robert Spreng und seine Fotodokumentation zu O. R. Salvisbergs Verwaltungsgebäude der F. Hoffmann-La Roche AG Basel*, Editiones Roche, Basel, 2001.

[30] Thus, the Schindler elevators, Sulzer heating, LUWA air conditioning, and Griesser awnings.

[31] Information relayed by Novartis archivist Carole Billod.

[32] As recounted by Alex Gerber in Bern, March 2003.

[33] Peter Collins, *Concrete: The Vision of a New Architecture. A Study of Auguste Perret and His Precursors*, Faber & Faber, London, 1959, p. 283. For more on Collins, who was an employee of Denis Honegger at the University of Geneva's Physics Institute, see Réjean Legault, "De la doctrine à l'histoire," *ARQ. Architecture-Québec*, no. 75, October 1993.

[34] François Neyroud states that the showers were an addition to the program and introduced by the architect himself: "This feature, executed in Sandoz France, piqued the jealousy of the heads of Sandoz in Basel and garnered the admiration of Ministry of Industry members." François Neyroud, "Jean Tschumi et les maîtres de l'ouvrage," *IAS*, no. 24, 16 November 1988, p. 9.

[35] Reyner Banham, "The Academic Tradition and the Concept of Elementary Composition," in *Theory and Design in the First Machine Age*, Architectural Press, London, 1960, p. 14.

[36] Jean Tschumi, "Laboratoire pharmaceutique Sandoz à Orléans," *AA*, no. 47, May 1953, p. 26.

37 Robert Maillart, "Le béton armé et son expression," in Max Bill, *Robert Maillart*, Girsberger (1949), Zurich, 1955, pp. 19–20.
38 Jean Tschumi, "Laboratoire pharmaceutique Sandoz," op. cit., p. 26.
39 Hubert Curchod, an architectural designer from Lausanne who had the *Patron*'s confidence, did most of his work in the apartment on Boulevard Saint-Germain, along with other students including Jean-Werner Huber, Charles Jeanneret, and Max Richter.
40 Figures submitted by Max Richter on 25 July 1996. In Orléans Richter monitored the site and dictated his reports via telephone to Madeleine Geneviève Bemelmans, according to Andrée, the secretary who oversaw the goings-on of the office. Richter remembers that Tschumi would drive to Orléans at high speed in his Ford Vedette, steering with his left hand, changing gears with his right hand, and with a cigarette in his mouth. His stops included enjoying award-winning gastronomy at the Auberge Saint-Jacques.
41 The famous banquet menu of 2 June 1953 read as follows: "*Les Pâtés d'Alouettes de Beauce Chauds en Croûte, Le Saumon de Loire Grillé Maître d'Hôtel, Petits Poulets Nouveaux du Gâtinais aux Primeurs, Les Fromages Assortis, Les Fraises d'Orléans Docteur Morère, Crème Fraîche, Sauvignon de Reuilly 1952, Château Houissant Saint Esthèphe 1949, Mumm Cordon Rouge, Café, Liqueurs.*"
42 Worked on from 1953 on, the second stage developed a perpendicular tower block for offices and laboratories as well as park annexes. This homogeneous expansion project would remain unbuilt. Necessary changes and additions were punctual. Work on the extension grouped at the south gable took place in 1961–1962. Then the sculptor Sandoz installed his bronze casts *Three Donkeys* on the eastern lawn. The buildings now belong to the pharmaceutical corporation FAMAR.
43 For more on the competition, see Patrick Devanthéry and Inès Lamunière, "Côté parc, côté jardin, le foyer du personnel de la MVA," *Faces*, no. 39, 1996, pp. 26–27.
44 For William Gilpin, the beauty of the cedar oscillated between a kind of Biblical sublimity and the British picturesque. William Gilpin, *Remarks on Forest Scenery*, vol. 1, Fraser & Co, Edinburgh, 1834, pp. 160–167.
45 *GdL*, 13 December 1956, p. 7.
46 Saugey was critical of Beaux-Arts formalism for its articulation of right angles, a motif that formed part of Eugène Baudoin's teaching in Geneva in 1950. Saugey saw in Tschumi a formidable competitor in the architectural programming of office buildings.

47 No document exists at this time to prove this conjecture. I am reasoning by analogy with the ulterior and documented situation of Nestlé Alimentana, where the architect and the two directors designed the new building in symbiosis.
48 In October 1952. According to François Neyroud, who met Roger Bobillier in 1988, this trip would have cost up to half a million francs. Cf. *IAS*, no. 24, 1988, p. 9.
49 We are in full conjecture here. Perhaps the directors of the MVA had written to General Life Insurance. Did the architect leave with his Alpa still camera? Likely so. However, I have found no prints or negatives. During his later travels to the US he used Kodachrome and Ektachrome film, slides of which are now housed at the ACM.
50 The fact of introducing both operable windows and a circulation system that allowed air to heat up but also to cool.
51 As recounted by Jacques Felber in a letter from 27 May 2008. Felber worked in the Paris office from September 1951 to December 1952, then in Lausanne from January 1953 to April 1954. "Mr. Tschumi brought us very explicit sketches from which we developed possible variations, which allowed him to make selections later on."
52 Remarkable photographs were taken by the *lausannois* M. Vulliemin. The film was made by an amateur filmmaker, Gustave Rochat, an employee of the MVA. Using this material, Roland Cosandey edited a VHS version that is available at the ACM.
53 A local firm run by the brothers Charles and Pierre Dentan.
54 Based on a public inquiry from December 1954, construction lasted 16 months until June 1956.
55 This elegance related to certain European cars: a picture taken in 1956 by Vuillemin compared the Peugeot 203 and the Renault 4CV, both French replicas of Volkswagen.
56 "The engineer designed the structural spans as two beams on individual supports when it would have been better to achieve them using framework." Letter from J. Felber, 27 May 2008.
57 The garage was designed for 20 cars and 50 motorcycles. By 1956 a third of the staff was "motorized."
58 Built by A. Félix Construction SA, the marquee was made of extruded aluminum beams folded in a "V" shape. Assembled in the hall of Comptoir Suisse, this piece would traverse Lausanne by truck convoy in September 1955. Tschumi watched with astonishment as it made its way through the Place Saint-François. According to his former student Robert Monnier, Tschumi feared that it would be too oversized, but the installation at Le Cèdres reassured him as to the accuracy of its proportions. Behind the trees, the canopy magnified the central axis of the facade.
59 Jean Tschumi, *GdL*, 13 December 1956, p. 7.
60 The work for Sandoz and Nestlé was managed by directors who wanted to save as much money as possible.
61 The contractor Charles Dentan stated this degree of tolerance for the reinforced concrete. His testimony, as transcribed in the *Gazette de Lausanne*, remains the fundamental source for this information. We also learn from the article that his firm was testing a span for the facade at full scale in order to determine the most appropriate choice of formwork. Cf., *GdL*, 13 December 1956, p. 9.
62 Letter from Jacques Felber, 27 May 2008.
63 On this transparency, see Gilles Barbey, "Signe des temps, le siège de la MVA à Lausanne (1954–1994)," *IAS*, no. 22, 1994, pp. 392–393.
64 Letter from Jacques Felber, 27 May 2008.
65 In 1953 Tschumi visited Lisbon on the occasion of a UIA conference.
66 In his theory courses at EPUL Tschumi, as a disciple of the notion of "pure visibility," referenced a succession of examples from the Renaissance (Bramante, Blois) and modernism (Unité d'habitation, *Gewerbeschule*).
67 On the construction system, see Hans Gutscher, "Rénovation du bâtiment Cèdre 1," *IAS* no. 22, 1994, pp. 402–405, and "L'immeuble administratif de la Vaudoise Assurances," *Faces*, no. 39, 1996, pp. 21–25.
68 Arthur Rüegg, *Le Corbusier Polychromie Architecturale. Farbenklaviaturen von 1931 und 1959*, Birkhäuser, Basel, 2006.
69 Gutscher, op. cit. For his part, Jacques Felber, in a letter from 27 May 2008, added that in order to choose the right green aggregate, "[Tschumi] went to La Chaux-de-Fonds with a cement fabricator."
70 Jean Tschumi, *Notice descriptive Mutuelle Vaudoise Accidents*, typescript housed at the ACM, p. 5.
71 According to Patrick Devanthéry and Inès Lamunière's research, this trip took place in May 1952, op. cit., p. 27.
72 "Lausanne, Le Cèdre," *L'Ordre professionnel*, 20 June 1959, p. 15.
73 See *GdL*, 13 December 1956.
74 The restaurant had a seating capacity for 100 people, so it seems that the architectural program envisioned two successive meal services.
75 30 March 1999. As Guido Cocci and I approached the Lausanne rail station, he

told me that the dining hall was the work of Jacques Felber. I have noted that the plans submitted for approval in December 1954 were overseen by Tschumi and bore the monogram of the designer Hubert Curchod, or "HC." An employee of Tschumi's during the design of the MVA, Cocci worked on the color schemes for the secretariat as well as for the management area. In a letter dated 27 May 2008, Felber stated, "I can say that Tschumi was not uninterested in the project for the dining hall. I had already received quite elaborate plans for the space from him, so I essentially just worked on the south and west facades." On 26 May 2008, Bernard Tschumi confirmed that on Sundays his father worked on color studies and details for the dining area. He even had his young son test the color pairings using gouache on black rubber or vinyl floor samples. Oh, those beautiful rainy Sundays!

[76] As noted by a reporter from the *Feuille d'Avis de Lausanne* (*FAL*), 29 June 1956, p. 15.

[77] The CFF suspended the third-class rail service in 1959 and the SNCF in 1956.

[78] Pascal Schmidt, "Est-il trop tôt pour parler de patrimoine?," *IAS*, no. 22, 1994, p. 400.

[79] The terms of the competition were set on 30 June 1956, ten days after the building's inauguration.

[80] André Bloc and Berto Lardera.

[81] For a special thematic issue titled "Architecture contemporaine, intégration des arts," *L'Architecture d'Aujourd'hui* devoted generous space to the competition. See *L'Architecture d'Aujourd'hui*, no. 11, 1957, pp. 14–17.

[82] For more details on the list of awards, see "Intégration des arts dans l'architecture, concours de Lausanne," op. cit.

[83] See *FAL*, 29 June 1956.

[84] Column written by Pierre Béguin, *GdL*, 13 December 1956, p. 7.

[85] Charles-Ferdinand Ramuz, "Sur une ville qui a mal tourné," *Aujourd'hui*, no. 55, 1930. See also Jean-Louis Kuffer, *Impressions d'un lecteur à Lausanne*, Bernard Campiche, Orbe, 2007.

[86] Charles-Ferdinand Landry, *Pour quatre coins de terre*, Paul Eynard, Rolle, 1948, p. 29. That Moscow's eyes were trained on reinforced concrete was a sign of a "Judeo-Bolshevik" conspiracy against the "homeland," a literary attitude inherited during the interwar years.

[87] The anonymous reporter attributed the words to the contractor Charles Dentan, *GdL*, 13 December 1956, p. 9.

[88] *Le Cèdre*, with text by Georges Caspari, photographs by M. Vuillemin, G. Rochat, and J. De Jongh. Three thousand numbered copies were printed. Lausanne, MVA, 10 March 1959.

[89] Publications on the Nestlé headquarters span six countries and were presented in four languages. In French-speaking Switzerland and France: *AFF*, no. 6, 1959, no. 7, 1960–1961; *AA*, no. 89, 1960; in German-speaking Switzerland and Germany: *Werk*, no. 3, 1960; *Bauen+Wohnen*, no. 5, 1960; *Baukunst und Werkform*, no. 10, 1960; in Italy: *L'architettura*, no. 6, 1960; in the U.K: *The Architect and Building News*, no. 37, 1960; and in the U.S.: *Architectural Record*, May 1960; *Architectural Design*, no. 9, 1960.

[90] In their 1992 account of their days at the EPFL, Francesco Della Casa and Eric Frei proposed the metaphor of "nid de coucou" ("cuckoo's nest") to designate the politics of buyouts and takeovers implemented by multinational companies in the years between 1960 and 1990.

[91] See *Dictionnaire historique de la Suisse* as well as consultable biographies on the internet: www.hls-dhs-dss.ch.

[92] As recounted by Enrico Bignami, 3 April 1990, in Lausanne.

[93] "Soup to Nuts," *Time Magazine*, 8 June 1962.

[94] Ibid.

[95] As recounted by the engineer Maurice Cosandey on 9 February 2008. Cosandey is with the specialist steel firm Zwahlen & Mayr.

[96] Letter from Bignami to Corthésy, 20 May 1957. Nestlé Archives, Gen. Mgt. File 9563.

[97] Eugen Brühwiler, Pierre A. Frey et al., *Alexandre Sarrasin. Structures en béton armé, audace et invention*, PPUR, Lausanne, 2002; Philippe Mivelaz, *Alexandre Sarrasin (1895-1976) et l'esthétique de l'ingénieur*, EPFL Thesis, no. 3865, 2007.

[98] I would contend that since Tschumi was opposed to the Corbusian vocabulary, he avoided using the term "*brise-soleil*" as much as possible.

[99] Carlo Olmo et al., *Costruire la città dell'uomo. Adriano Olivetti e l'urbanistica*, Edizioni di Comunità, Turin, 2001; Alberto Abriani, Evelina Calvi, "The Olivetti Advertising Dream," *Rassegna*, no. 43, September 1990, pp. 21–29.

[100] We do not know whether Tschumi visited the Aluminium AG in Zurich, built 1955–1956. For this structure the owners deployed a large-scale publicity venture through journals and manuals. See Jürgen Joedicke, *Bürobauten*, Gerd Hatje, Stuttgart, 1959, pp. 192–193.

[101] This collection covers three of the four trips Tschumi made to the U.S. They were as follows, in chronological order: the first trip was subsidized by the MVA but images remain missing; the second was sponsored by Nestlé in 1956; the third was with a committee from the UIA; finally, the fourth trip was made in order to receive the Reynolds Prize in October 1960. The photos are undated, and only roughly one out of 100 images contains a caption. There are known trips to Manhattan, MIT, Boston, Pittsburgh, Washington, Chicago, Detroit, and San Francisco. The picture-taking was feverish, and the results were often mediocre. Tschumi was especially fascinated by the landscapes of American cemeteries.

[102] Dominique Gilliard, "Estimation of the Value and Historical Legacy of the Nestlé Buildings in Vevey and Lausanne," 20 December 1995, pp. 2–6. Unedited memoir for use by the Service des Monuments Historiques in the Canton of Vaud and the management of Nestlé Alimentana.

[103] Ibid., p. 2.

[104] In Paris Tschumi was well situated to follow the polemics of the project. In 1957 he visited and photographed the sizeable *œuvre*.

[105] Carola Hein, *The Capital of Europe: Architecture and Urban Planning of the European Union*, Praeger, Westport, 2004, pp. 33–35.

[106] Shortly before his death in 1962, Tschumi was offered the commission to design the new headquarters of Sandoz France in Rueil-Malmaison in Hauts-de-Seine. Sandoz subsequently asked Bernard Zehrfuss and Basel native Martin Burckhart to take over the project.

[107] Bruno Zevi, "Un Y piccante più dell'Unesco," *L'Espresso*, 11 September 1960. Reprinted in *Cronache di architettura*, vol. IV, Laterza, Bari, p. 331.

[108] In a C.V. from 1927 given to Stucky, Tschumi cited that he had worked at André Ventre's office when the latter was building the Ministry of Merchant Marines.

[109] Maurice Cosandey, Etienne Rossetti, "L'ossature métallique du nouveau bâtiment administratif Nestlé à Vevey," *Bulletin de la construction métallique*, no. 22, October 1959. Rossetti worked alongside Cosandey in Lausanne for Zwahlen & Mayr. Cosandey knew about the Roberston process that had been experimented with for the first time in Geneva through the work of Marc Saugey for the city's central station. See Nicole Staehli-Canetta, "Le siège administratif de Nestlé à Vevey," *Faces*, no. 39, 1996, pp. 42–47.

[110] See Lee Rainwater, *Behind Ghetto Walls: Black Families in a Federal Slum*, Aldine Publisher, Chicago, 1970.

[111] Charles Jencks, *The Language of Post-Modern Architecture*, Rizzoli, New York, 1977, p. 9.

[112] Alexandre Sarrasin, *GdL*, 22 April 1960: "*Les trois portiques de l'aile sud,*

sur lesquels la charge de la colonne centrale atteint 385 tonnes, ont reçu une précontrainte auxiliaire."

[113] Joedicke describes this compartmentalization of *"dreibündige Anlage mit paralleler Flurentwicklung als Sonderform für Büro- und Laborgebäude."* He is referring to the CIBA building in Wehr, Germany, constructed in 1949 by Egon Eiermann, in Joedicke, op. cit., p. 34.

[114] The exception was Hubert Curchod, who lacked a university degree but was drilled by Tschumi in order to become his quick conceptual "tool." As recounted by Léopold Veuve, 28 February 2008. An employee from Tschumi's Lausanne office, Veuve recalls that the *Patron* arrived at the office one day with a 5 cm-long receipt on which he had outlined the Y section of the building.

[115] Peter Baer et al., *Building on Our Foundations*, Nestlé SA, Vevey, 2000, p. 82.

[116] Per a telephone conversation of 16 February 2008.

[117] At a meeting on 20 March 2008, Albert George, a former student and employee during the design phase of the project, recalled that the *"découpage"* perspectives came from Curchod's brush and scissors.

[118] According to George, Tschumi corrected plans sent by particular contractors as well as the shop drawings for the elevators and heating system.

[119] Jean Tschumi, "Bâtiment administratif Nestlé à Vevey," taken from a review in *Aluminium Suisse*, no. 6, 1960, p. 4.

[120] See note 89. In addition, the Nestlé building appeared in a metal contruction manual. See Max Fengler, *Skelettbauten mit Fassadenelementen*, Alexander Koch, Stuttgart, 1962.

[121] See Jacques Gubler, "Three Steps and a Bow," in *A Modern Move: Transforming Nestlé Headquarters in Vevey, Richter and Dahl Rocha Architects*, Birkhäuser, Basel, 2002, pp. 25–28.

[122] "For the creative value of the architect's contribution to the use of aluminum and its potential influence on the architecture of our time." This text appears on a plaque that was unveiled in Vevey.

Teaching at EPUL

Geneva and Lausanne from a Bipolar Perspective

The acronym EPUL stands for the Polytechnic School of the University of Lausanne.[1] Spoken aloud, the syllables resemble the high-pitched cry of a bird, a sound that remained with Lausanne's population long after the change in the school's initials from EPUL to EPFL.[2] The School of Architecture and City Planning at the University of Lausanne opened in fall 1943. The Allied armies had just led the military conquest of southern Italy. Debated by the cantonal parliament in 1942, the pedagogical plan was approved by only a weak majority; an amendment opposing the school was denied by a vote of 61 to 59.[3] Why the creation of this new institution? The school was proposed in response to a new employers' credo, defended by the Society of Swiss Engineers and Architects (SIA), to monitor and control professional skill sets. Beginning in 1939, a crisis had arisen in the construction industry whereby engineers and architects who held academic degrees were hit hard. Their competence was measured in the same hierarchic way as projects submitted by businessmen, draftsmen, and licensed technicians. In Switzerland the organization of higher education was within the province of the cantonal government. However, in Lausanne from 1941 on the reform of local laws regarding the policing of construction would impose the official title of "architect" or "engineer" as a prerequisite to public inquiries. Laws changed, but building opportunities were rare. Cement was reserved first and foremost for military and paramilitary projects.

In Switzerland there was only one school of architecture, the Federal Institute of Technology (ETH) in Zurich, the nation's scientific and intellectual capital. ETH enjoyed national status, and its budget and professors were favored over those of other institutions. I should add that for those happy few architects from francophone Switzerland, there was a second option, namely the Paris Beaux-Arts. A Beaux-Arts diploma allowed entry without administrative obstacles into the SIA, then the Swiss employers' labor union for construction. In Switzerland the "liberal professions" lived through World War II as a kind of unmerited hiatus, or forced unemployment. The discussion about competence provoked a new federal law concerning professional training, effective from 1941 on. Henceforth, architectural designers who had been awarded diplomas were, in principle, no longer allowed to take on the title of "architect." It was left to individual cantons to clear the way for this professional reform. Plans for architecture schools were hatched in Fribourg, Geneva, and Lausanne. It was in Geneva (at the instigation of a prominent official who was anxious to pre-empt Lausanne) that the mission was achieved first, with an architecture school inaugurated in fall 1942.[4] In Lausanne the situation was overseen by the director of the School of Engineering, Alfred Stucky, an internationally known hydraulic engineer and a specialist in reinforced concrete. Stucky consulted with local architects, drafted a program, and defended it to the political authorities. He proposed that architectural education be integrated into his school. A letter from Stucky to Tschumi mentioned the resistance on the part "of Lausanne architects...opposed to the creation of the school...."[5] It is true that Alphonse Laverrière, DPLG, and a prominent personality in the Lausanne scene, had wanted the teaching of architecture to develop within the Cantonal School of Design, which he directed.[6]

In Geneva and in Lausanne the scenario that governed the creation of architecture schools re-

187
Portrait of the architect by anonymous photographer, circa 1960

sembled a kind of *mise en abyme*. Leaders were sought who could represent the fledgling institutions in the eyes of the local press. In Geneva a group formed of local architects studied the curriculum and offered improbable candidates. The choices emanated as much from dreams as from polemical debates. Finally Eugène Beaudoin, who worked on urban renewal projects in Marseilles during the Occupation, accepted the post.[7] In Lausanne Alfred Stucky did not hesitate over who he felt personified the discipline of architecture; it was he who invited Jean Tschumi, but through which channels of recommendation? Sources on this subject are scant. In order to shorten administrative procedures during the war, Stucky presumably sought out a native Swiss who was familiar with local industrial and artistic circles. Probably the recommendation came from Edouard-Marcel Sandoz, who was well known in Lausanne. He animated the scene with his polyedric personality: he was a manager at the highest multinational level, an artist, a patriot, and a personal friend of General Guisan. The degree of this conjecture is proportional to the evolving political and military situation.

The simultaneous choice of Beaudoin and Tschumi introduced a prickly symmetry. Beaudoin's pedigree was star-studded and transparent. He had received the prestigious Rome Prize, participated in some of the major projects of modern France, and served in an official capacity as town planner for Marseilles. Tschumi, on the other hand, presented a versatile background.[8] He cited his experience with Brandt's industrial concerns (including his wartime efforts) as well as his technical work for GECUS, his knowledge of underground town planning as well as his proposal (formulated with Utudjian) for a tunnel under the English Channel. His cited projects included furnishing the "luxury apartments" for *Le Normandie* as well as decorative work for the Sandoz headquarters in Basel. Focus was placed on his architectural projects for Nestlé and Sandoz France, for whom Tschumi designed and built laboratories on two different sites.

The Beaudoin and Tschumi tandem was unusual. The two were fond of recalling their initial meeting at the Beaux-Arts, where both were Pontremoli students. Tschumi had lent a hand in com-

188
Exhibition of EPUL students' projects coincident with the UIA founding congress in Lausanne, 1948

pleting the final presentation boards that earned Beaudoin a ticket to Rome in 1928. In the 1930s Tschumi admired, and probably envied, the achievements of the firm Beaudoin and Lods. The fact that in the 1940s the two would meet in Switzerland within a 60-kilometer radius reinforced their competitive reflex. Since both were called on to assume the role of *Patron*, they observed each other from a distance. What pedagogical program could they invent other than an adaptation of what they had experienced under Pontremoli in Paris? Indeed, the exercises they proposed in Geneva and in Lausanne were founded on the Beaux-Arts tradition. The division of students into two rankings (*classes*),[9] analytical studies, quick drafts, and a curricular organization that adopted three temporal degrees of increasing complexity—all were elements that stemmed from their Paris lineage. The pedagogical vehicle for both schools would be the "*atelier*," a term that Tschumi referred to with a capital "A." How could the studio system help to develop student skills? Tschumi observed that "the *Atelier* [would] be the crucible for crystallization of their young talent."[10] Capable of persuading political authorities, the magical metaphor of the crucible or melting pot would have to contend with the resistance of facts. Could the individual studio become identified with the school itself? Wasn't the success of the Parisian model due to an eclectic confrontation of tendencies, a rivalry of "schools within a school"? Even though they shared an institutional memory inherited from Pontremoli, Beaudoin and Tschumi distrusted each other.[11] This atmosphere of mutual competition and emulation took on a canonical status, and proved to be productive. Tschumi wanted to show that the results of his teaching methods in Lausanne would be superior to Beaudoin's in Geneva, and vice versa.

If one were to examine the rare published results today,[12] one would have to conclude that the quality of the student work from Geneva and Lausanne, as presented in magazines, represented a comparable level of skills and intrinsic difficulty. Faced with public opinion, Geneva stressed the cosmopolitanism of the city and the international nature of its student population. In the canton of Vaud the same argument unnerved politicians. Nevertheless, in 1950, when EPUL awarded 23 certificates of architecture, 25 percent were given to students from Turkey, Asia, and the Middle East. The proof lay in the resultant commissions for graduates: a luxury hotel in Istanbul, a national library for the city of Ankara[13] (Plate 189), a private club in Tehran, an engineering school in Damascus, and a movie theater in Bangkok. It was understood that foreign students, who were supported by well-to-do families, chose Switzerland because of its proclaimed "neutrality" and its willingness to engage in armed resistance, as broadcast by the press.

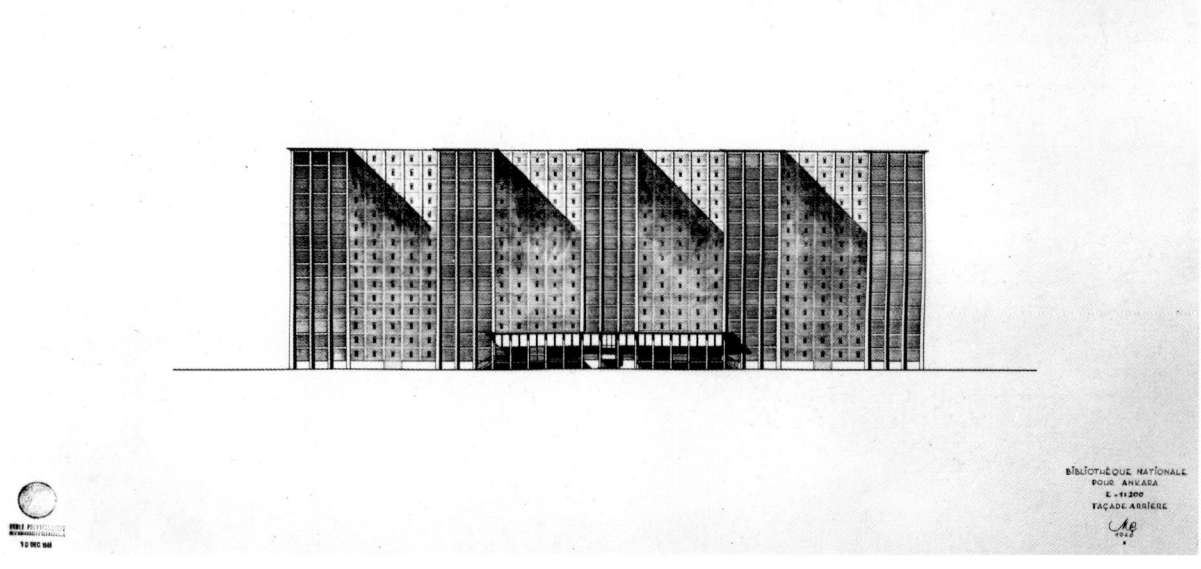

189
Thesis project by Mukadder Çiser for a "National Library of Ankara," rear facade, December 1946. First diploma awarded by EPUL

The Exercises at EPUL

For Beaudoin as well as for Tschumi, the first practical contradiction stemmed from the fact that the studios that they wanted to open severed ties with previous graduates. In the Beaux-Arts *ateliers*, "the elders" (*les anciens*) played a crucial role. It was they who represented the *Patron*, conveying the basics, the know-how and idiosyncrasies. They acted according to the principle of mutual instruction as theorized and implemented by Pestalozzi during the Enlightenment. In Paris Tschumi spotted two Swiss, Jean Zumbrunnen and Jean-Louis Ruche, who had begun their studies at the Beaux-Arts. He immediately repatriated and installed them at his Lausanne drawing boards to finish their studies while functioning as "*les anciens*" (Plate 194). In spring 1948 the former designed a fruit-packing center in the Erieux Valley, while the latter proposed a new international institute for advanced studies in psychology. Their work, among other work chosen to illustrate the projects and accomplishments of the second and first *classes*, was exhibited in the Salle David of the Palais de Rumine. The exhibition took place during the inaugural congress of the UIA in Lausanne in June 1948 (Plate 188). Tschumi and his pupils wanted to furnish proof that their school could compete at the level of the Beaux-Arts.

The academic program established a set of learning thresholds with the obligatory passage of benchmarks. The first pedagogical forays were utterly neoclassical, renewing Durand's method as outlined in his *Précis*. Students were required to draw on the same sheet and at the same scale the plans, sections, and elevations of a symmetrical building. The "house with three openings" or "five openings" (Plate 190) instilled the power of the orthogonal axis in the composition of plans and apertures, in the correlation between the three canonical operations of plan, section, and elevation, and in the use of ink washes and poché. The first year of study entailed documentation of local examples, among them the doors of the Hôtel de Ville[14] and the "Hôtel Empire de Monrepos," along with the neo-Florentine Palais de Rumine. Over the years, the exercises maintained tension between two poles of representation, drawing with drafting rulers and freehand drawing. Perspectives developed by building up characteristics as much as by the free hand.

The quick sketch, perfected (*chiadée*) in ten hours, was opposed to the analytical study, referred to as "*analo*." The large format of the *analo* referenced the publication of buildings culled from the reservoir of ancient, medieval, renaissance, and twentieth-century architecture. The ensemble and the detail would begin to collide, with the scales corresponding to each other in a binary way (Plates 191, 192). The students pursued a restricted number of canonical examples that were passed down, year after year, as a sign of camaraderie. What was the meaning of the *analo*? There were two. The first invoked the crafting of drawings, focusing on the proper construction of lines as well as training in the use of ink washes, poché, and shadow projections at a 45-degree angle. The second was conceptual. What would students learn if they drew the facades of the Parthenon, the Museum of Public Works, the Unité d'habitation in Marseilles, and the propylene of the Knossos palace, all at the same scale? They would learn that the power of a building is relative to its monumental presence in the city. Paradoxically, the *analo* operated outside of any urban context; students copied and recopied graphic information found in the studio's library. In spring 1943 Stucky allocated 3,000 francs to Tschumi so he would return from Paris with a first-rate collection of works.[15] In Geneva the same year a 3,500-franc credit was invested in starting an architectural library.[16] The purpose was identical: to nourish the notations and visual material for the *analo* exercises.

The Geneva-Lausanne model of excellence renewed the tradition of the quick sketch or "sketch-sketch" (*esquisse-esquisse*), to use Beaux-Arts terminology. The exercise consisted of developing a program that was not identified in advance on a single sheet of paper in large (75 × 106 cm) or medium (52.5 × 75 cm) format in a restricted amount of time. The program would be submitted in the morning, with the drawings returned in the evening; according to the city and season, the time would vary from eight to ten or twelve hours. Contrary to the quick sketch, the sketch-sketch needed to deliver fireworks. The simple sketch marked the first stage of a plan that would evolve over the course of one or more weeks after drafting-table corrections. No architectural program was simple, easy, or basic in itself, but the sketch-sketch aimed

190
Pierre Foretay, first-year exercise, House with Five Bays, 1951, derived from J. N. L. Durand's 150-year-old method of composition

191
Analytical study, circa 1950, confronting the Palace of Knossos with Auguste Perret's Museum of Public Works in Paris and Le Corbusier's Unité d'habitation in Marseilles, all at the same scale

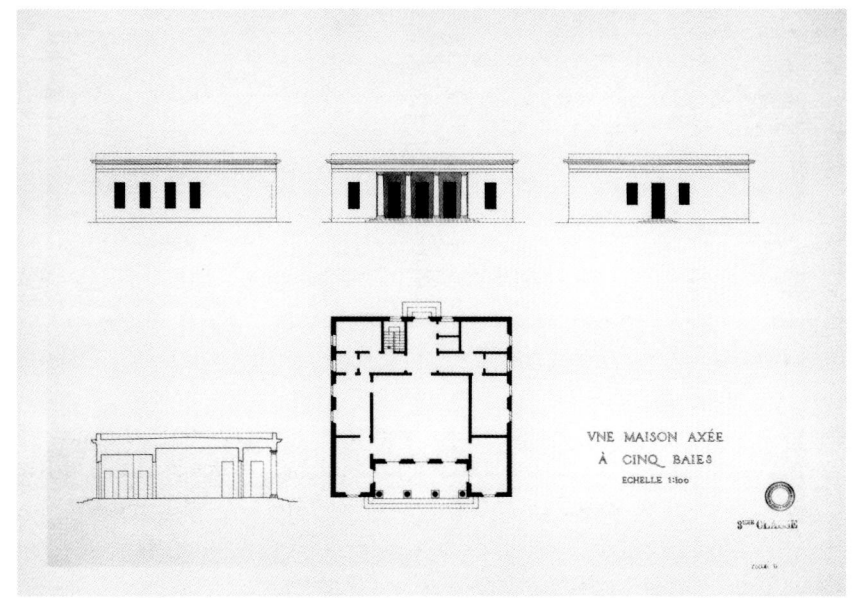

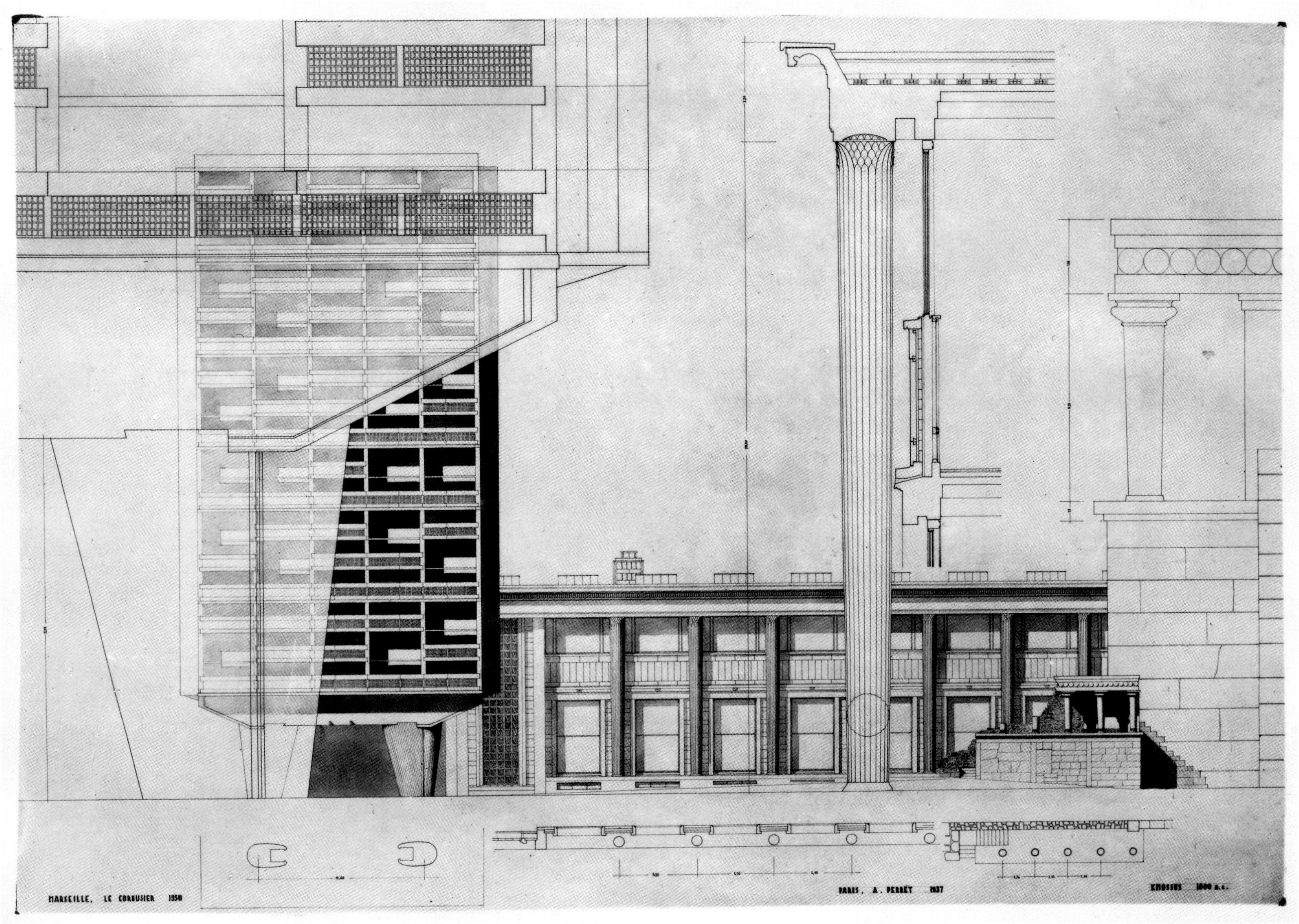

192
Georges Van Bogaert, analytical study, 1947–1948, juxaposition at the same scale of the Parthenon, Sanmicheli's Palazzo Pompei in Verona, and Auguste Perret's Museum of Public Works

193
Analytical study, 1955, juxaposition at the same scale of two medieval towns, Romont, Switzerland and San Gimignano, Italy, and metropolitan Manhattan

194
Jean-Louis Ruche, Cinema-Theater, 1947, "sketch-sketch" exercise with a 10-hour time limit

195
Gérard Küpfer, Observation Tower, circa 1950, "sketch-sketch" exercise

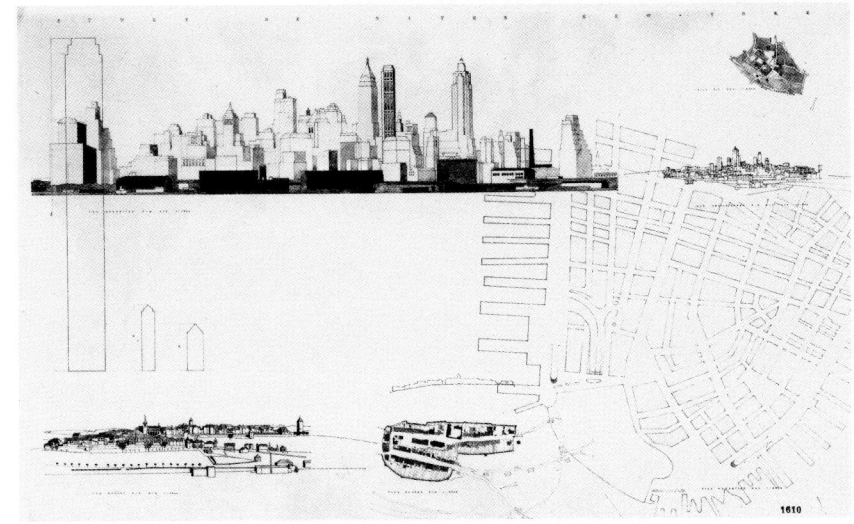

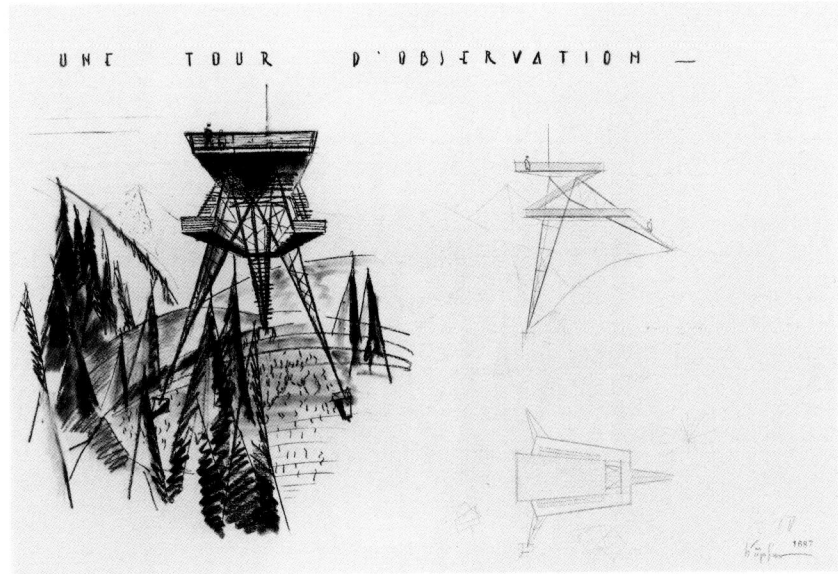

to discourage rapidity (which, in practice, would be demanded by impatient clients). The resultant impeccable "perfected" perspective embodied a project synthesis, providing an exercise in direct communication with a hypothetical client who expected a quick illustration (Plate 196). Tschumi relied on Zumbrunnen's assistance to oversee the sketch-sketch exercises. Archives show that the professor offered his pupils programs that coincided with the schedule of his own private commissions.[17] For example, at the end of the war Tschumi built a plant for Sandoz in Noisy-le-Sec; in January 1946 he offered his pupils a sketch-sketch program titled "a plant for pharmaceutical glass vials." The following year's exercise was called "a convalescent pavilion for a tuberculosis center," thus correlating directly with his study for the Général Guisan Village in Chermignon. Tschumi conducted the sketch-sketch exercises through a pragmatic lens. In Lausanne he put his finger on the absences in, and needs for, civic architecture. He also made reference to Pontremoli's studio at the Beaux-Arts; for example, his program for "a house for a collector in a hot country" shares similarities with the master's Villa Kérilos.

Nevertheless, the majority of the programs attempted to anticipate the needs of the canton, Lausanne, and the school. Hence, "a communal village building," "a school campus for Montoie-Tivoli" or, in 1948, "the Polytechnic auditorium (*aula*)," a 600-seat space that accommodated "a good view onto the park and the lake from the foyer or lobby." Tschumi stirred his pupils' imagination by floating ideas that would encourage local debate. Thus he offered a fish-breeding farm, the underground entrance for a factory located inside a dam in a mountain (a program that paid homage to Stucky), a movie theater (conceived with a mind to the topography of the Rue de Bourg), a convertible swimming pool/ice rink, a museum on the lake shore, and an airfield. These types of drawings also ventured into "the recreational study of decorative elements." Assigned exercises for a circus entrance, a puppet show in a park, a nightclub, a postage stamp, or a buttonhole insignia for the school took a place within the playful and ephemeral atmosphere of the day. Again, it bears repeating that the sketch-sketch studies occurred during a restricted time framework and were an obligatory benchmark that was repeated throughout the whole program. One former

196
René Vittone, Restaurant Bar, circa 1952, "sketch-sketch" exercise

197
António Teixeira Guerra, project for a bank in North Portugal, circa 1955, involving a realistic program on a specific site

198
Alex Gerber, The Architect's House, winter semester exercise, 1956–1957, project for a specific site

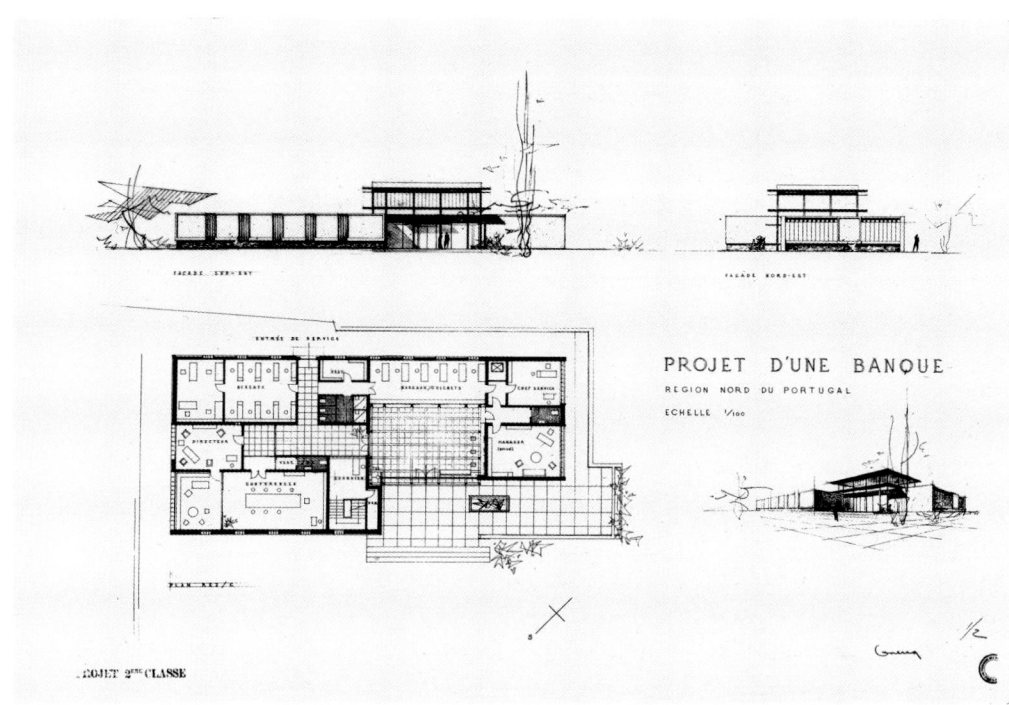

student remembers a test that consisted in drawing from memory and in freehand the elevation of the Lausanne railway station: "We trembled, but the time constraint forced us to look closely."[18]

"Quick studies," on the other hand, developed over the course of five, eight, or ten days and were subjected to the review of the *Patron*; Tschumi commented on and softened the proposals without offering a solution that could be interpreted as his own. Among the studies were a station terminus for a funicular, a weekend home, a farmhouse, and a lakeside restaurant and café. Every project was situated within a precise topography that could be verified on a map. Supporting coursework fell into two categories. The first concerned housing, confirming my view that the design of living spaces represented a required part of the curriculum.[19] Dwelling types corresponded to social housing, middle-income dwellings, and individual residences. Examples were inserted into an existing urban fabric or, in the case of the single-family home, into a suburban context. A second category focused on drawings for "practical buildings." Examples here ranged from a newsstand or pharmacy to a tearoom bar. Pupils ap-

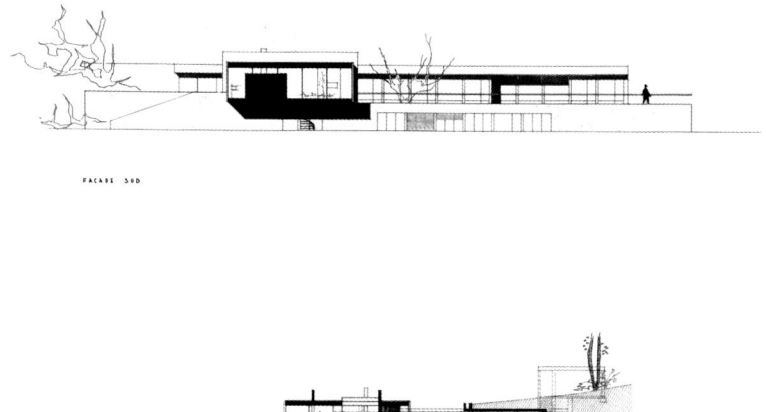

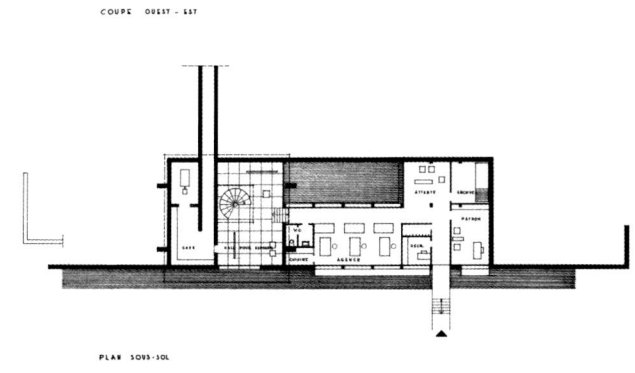

proached the studies through vertical and horizontal cuts at scales that allowed for the detailed design of material fixings. The exercises were supervised by a trilogy of professors from the disciplines of architecture, construction, and structures.[20] What resulted were working drawings in which the "objective" style of drawing entailed copying useful details by architects and manufacturers as published in magazines. The professional realism of the exercises served to illustrate the polytechnic value of the school (Plates 197, 198).

Two comments comprise a necessary digression. The first relates to the mythical prejudice that the Beaux-Arts system neglected technical considerations. Describing his years at the Parisian institution in the 1950s, Pierre Saddy referred to "the fallacious affirmation of an absence of training in construction." He continued:
Paradoxically, this accusation came from those who made much of their status as artists living it up at night; unlike the morning students, they slept through the classes taught by François Vitale, an architect who had authored several analytical works that elucidated construction technologies to the readers of architectural magazines. His lessons took place in the amphitheater from 8 to 9:30 in the morning, a schedule dictated by the situation of the hardworking students who were forced to pay their own way through school; at 9:30 they were then free to join their Patron's offices, most of which were in the area.[21]
During his Paris years Tschumi was always an "early riser" who made his way by working in construction workshops to cover his studies and supplementary fees.[22] Saddy's remarks confirm the costliness of obtaining a degree: "The diploma almost always entailed additional expenses that forced students to work part-time in an office to ameliorate their financial standing before undertaking their diploma studies."[23]

The second digressive component concerns the regulations imposed by the SIA. From the moment that the EPUL diploma would allow a student to take up individual professional practice, the SIA insisted on an obligatory internship period of one year, either in an office or on a construction site. Not everyone had the opportunity or desire to fulfill their training periods in offices run by their *Patrons*.[24] Some had their sights set elsewhere. In Paris a course of study took shape by which the firm of Herbé et Lecouteur served as a prime destination because of its effective orientation and training of interns. Other destinations included the firm of Lods et Le Caisne[25] or André Sive, a friend of Prouvé. In 1950 Mulhouse was regarded as a major architectural laboratory for postwar reconstruction. The Swiss architect Daniel Girardet worked there under the distant gaze of Perret. Perret had been in Lausanne in 1948, at the time of the inaugural congress of the UIA; Girardet, in turn, also hired interns and young architects in Mulhouse.[26] Students with an EPUL pedigree were sought after by virtue of their efficiency.

The final stage of diploma work engaged the EPUL's responsibilities in addressing the realities of the profession. Students chose their own individual programs, following a rule first introduced at the Beaux-Arts in 1888.[27] Tschumi described the project requirements as follows: "The project is elaborated on a real site, which corresponds to a particular program. The candidate will study all material at his disposal and undertake all relevant research in order to gain full knowledge of his chosen subject. The project proposal will include a site study, a model and, according to the nature of the program, a master plan as well as more detailed drawings at a larger scale, accompanied by special equipment and technical diagrams related to heating, ventilation, electricity, and structural analysis, along with a partial detailed estimate for construction costs."[28] The bar for the final project was set very high, taking into account all previous practical training. Its ambition was similar to that of a university thesis. Nevertheless, objectives were realistic, and students were under regular supervision by professors and had the help of assistants. The projects aimed to spur on specific discussions. The choice of the site and the motivation for the work depended on the origin of the pupils. For example, a student who came from Oslo chose to develop a maritime museum.[29] Another pupil tried to improve his father's rural farm.[30] Still another wanted to entice a potential client.[31] The initial relevance of some of the proposals had the potential to provoke actual buildings in the long- and medium-term.[32] Finally, the diploma projects served to feed local debate and took on the value of counter-proposals.[33]

199
Reconstruction of the railroad station in Lausanne, 1959, final-year exercise in urbanism displaying the radical proposals that resulted from Tschumi's *atelier*

Teaching Theory and Urbanism

"Modeling" a city, according to Tschumi, was "the highest act of the architect and town planner, and…the sacred act of any artist."[34] Tschumi was fond of using the metaphor of modeling as a way to define the practice of urbanism. From the school's first days in 1943, he insisted that architecture was the driving force that propelled urbanism. Once again, the dynamics of zoom are visible in Tschumi's thinking. The title and content of his inaugural lecture, "From Architecture to Urbanism,"[35] indicated that both disciplines were linked and could under no circumstances be viewed as opposing specialties. He again referred to Marcel Poëte and to his biological definition of the city as a "living being in perpetual transformation,"[36] all the while considering the functional and mechanical differentiation of the four urban functions that were outlined in the Charter of Athens as living, working, recreation, and circulation. Tschumi interspersed his lessons with numerous references. Le Corbusier, Perret, Alberti, Philibert Delorme, Gromort, and Guadet appeared in chronological order, along with Vitruvius and Choisy. Needless to say, the list clearly favored architectural theory.

Tschumi's pedagogical method unified architecture and urban planning within the same theoretical argument. His "Master Class" usually took place on Saturday mornings. The *Patron* showed the slides himself; the tempo was quick; and the examples were named and commented upon laconically. The division of built elements into successive chapters including bays, staircases, and load-bearing systems drew inspiration from Julien Guadet's presentation format in his *Eléments*.[37] Tschumi added in an extra chapter on "the city." He illustrated foundational cities, the new cities of antiquity, medievalism, and the Renaissance that he referred to as "created cities," as opposed to the ad-hoc dispersion of industrial cities. I have already stated that this theoretical lesson complemented the exercises that focused on other exemplary models. An additional possibility was offered: to choose the topic of the city in order to plunge into a comparative analysis (*analo*) (Plate 193). One student addressed the sites of Manhattan, San Gimignano, and Romont at 1:3400 and 1:1800 scales in a study of the architectural theme of the tower that aligned the skyscraper with the aristocratic Italian tower-house, among other typological structures. The graphic results were impressive.

Two exercises introduced in the second and first *classes* drew on typological studies of housing and neighborhoods. These "housing groups" were built as much in urban peripheries (Malley, Renens, Chavannes) as in the Lausanne town center (Riponne, Cité). From the second to the first *classe*, the size of buildings increased from three to fourteen or even eighteen floors. In the years between 1950 and 1953 the duplex apartment-type was a source of great fascination.[38] To address Lausanne's

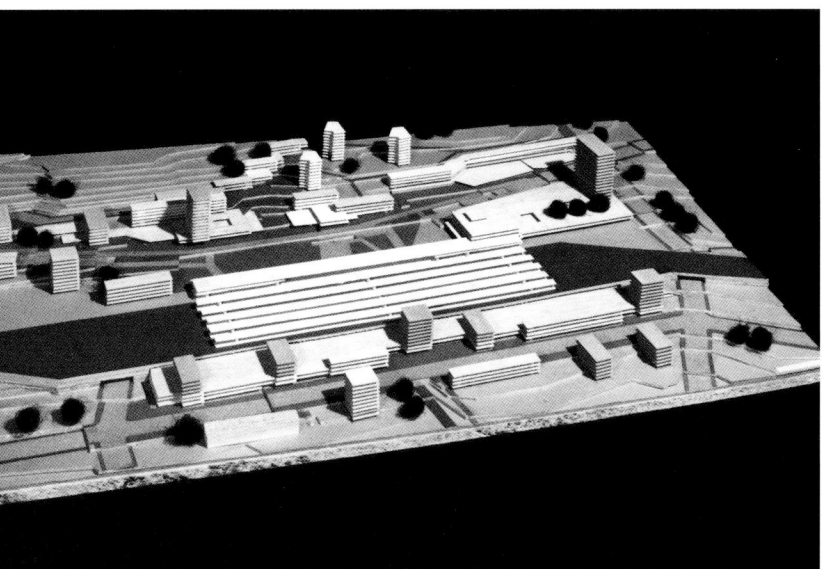
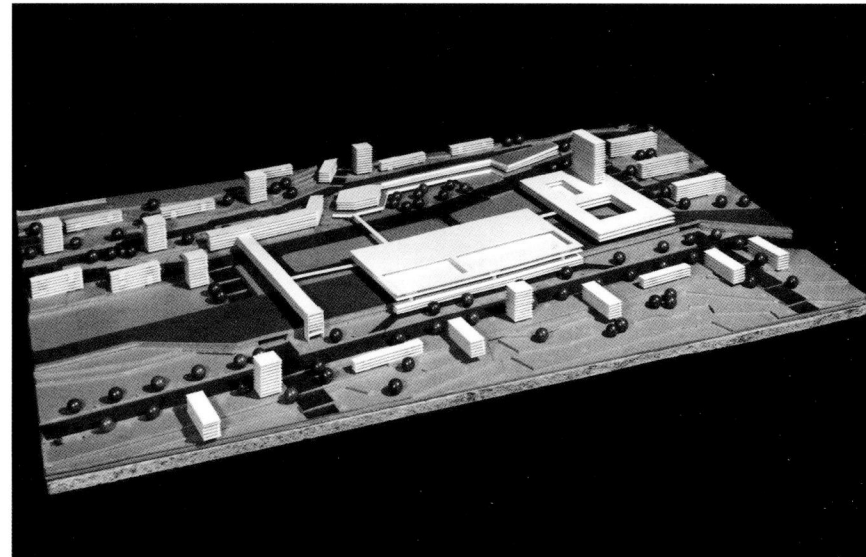

bumpy topography (as elaborated in Henri Onde's urban geography lessons), the "tower block" was placed atop massive plinths that were excavated into the slope, adding to the project's drama.[39] Tschumi established a distinction between the urbanization of a particular district or neighborhood and the programming of the "urban center." One major example involved the areas of Lausanne located along the upper and lower perimeters of the railway station. Radical proposals were studied (Plate 199). They postulated the installation of broad platforms staggered across the slope, whereby longitudinal buildings would follow the curves of the topography. Other buildings would be aligned transversally. Tschumi's intention regarding urban "modeling" was to play on ruptures in scale and on the singularity of buildings. For him, it was a matter of re-situating the city, starting from the zero meridian of the railway station, and of distributing commerce and living. All architecture proposals, by definition, include a major or minor utopian element. However, the project for Lausanne's station was more properly a product of academic rationalism. In accordance with the didactic procedures followed in contemporary architecture schools, the political question of feasibility was set aside. All that remained of the old city was the road and rail infrastructure. What was set forth for resolution over the course of the semester was the problem of the break that the railway imposed on the urban geography. This problem exists in all cities. In Lausanne, the population refers to the "*sous-gare*" or "below-station" district. This urbanism exercise was rational: the contrasting volumetrics of buildings corresponded to a precise architectural typography. At the same time, however, the exercise was also viewed as antithetical to diploma work. The realistic aspects of the diploma implied the possibility of an immediate solution. The plan for the new Lausanne re-established from the railway station was, more than anything, a stylistic exercise that was useful for observing the general phenomenon of infrastructural cuts through the city.

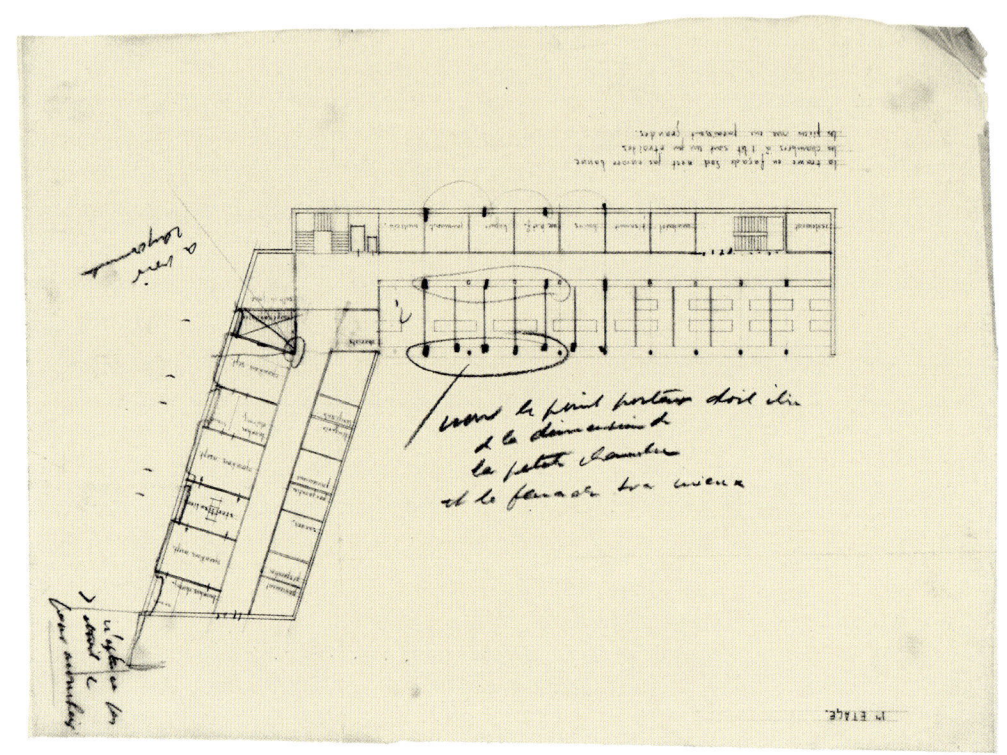

The Student Body

In the idiomatic lingo of the Beaux-Arts, the "*Masse*" referred to the student body, meaning the population of the various studios and their union representatives, in comparison with the *Patron* and the school authorities. Within EPUL, only the school of architecture had such an organ. The *Masse* challenged the director Alfred Stucky on questions that related to the curriculum, the administration of examinations, and specific requirements instated by some professors that were considered inadmissible. In his role as *Patron*, Tschumi appreciated the students' demonstration of their presence to the school leadership. He would address them himself by writing directly to the *Masse*. Within the EPUL, the *Masse* distinguished itself by organizing an annual ball.[40] A recurring problem for the students involved the night-time closing of school facilities. Stucky granted only rare infringements, and each time the *Masse* had to justify "pressing circumstances" (for example, a model that had became too large or unwieldy[41]). The *Masse* was always spelled with a capital "M." This detail pointed to an inherent sense of formality inherited from the Beaux-Arts. In addition to the honorary forms of "*mentions*" and "*demi-mentions*," "sketch-sketches," and the "*analo*," two other imports, the brass band and hazing, were among the customs transplanted from Paris. In Paris, the band was not required to play properly; its "music" was more a racket than anything. The more musicians, the better the entertainment. In Lausanne, in contrast, the band played in unison "as properly as possible."[42] Out of the EPUL a handful of true musicians emerged, all of whom liked playing jazz and performing as amateurs in an era when the "amateur jazz musician" was viewed as a semi-professional type (one who, in Switzerland, competed in the annual Zurich festival where prizes were distributed much like Beaux-Arts medals). The musicians' taste did not tend toward New Orleans revivalism, but rather toward "Bebop" and "Cool."[43] In a sense, this musical challenge hurled at modernity corresponded to the architectural values defended by Tschumi who, for his own part, listened to classical music programs on his car radio.

Starting in the winter semester of 1943–1944, women began to enroll in the school. Alice Ascher arrived first, and her 1948 diploma project was for an international university sanatorium in Leysin.[44] Certainly, the total number of female students remained a trifle; of the 141 certificates awarded between 1946 and 1960, only seven went to women.[45] Some marriages between pupils ended, perhaps under the convivial effect of shared charrettes. Over the years, the organization of the student body underwent a notable evolution that tended toward a less cosmetic trade unionism, beginning with the new curriculum introduced in the 1955–1956 academic year. The *Masse* obtained its own letterhead and organized a representative student delegation. The vertical studios that Tschumi created were replaced by the kind of horizontal stratification implied in the reforms. It became possible to speak about "student trade unionism" even if its actions produced only limited effects, such as the financing of study trips initiated by pupils.[46]

200
Corrections by the Master, 1952, lead and ink on tracing paper, competition for the Swiss Hospital in Neuilly. Notes traced by the Master's pencil read, "No, the load-bearing point should correspond to the dimension of the small room, then the facade will be better."

201
Competition for the Swiss Hospital in Neuilly, first round, 1952, pencil, India ink, and gouache on tracing paper. The filter of the trees introduces an element of seduction already evident in the competition for the MVA building.

202
Competition for the Swiss Hospital in Neuilly, second round, winning entry, 1952, pencil, India ink, and watercolor on tracing paper. Functional organization of the two blocks into maternity and general services

Growth and Crisis

In 1955 Stucky approached the architect Hans Brechbühler, by then a regular member of the school's jury before the Federation of Swiss Architects (FAS), to ask him to reform the curriculum. The director summarized their meeting: "Beginning with the basis that the current honorary system of *mentions* encourages lazy pupils as well as those wishing to work during their studies to interrupt them, hence prolonging their stay at the school, an alternative system of promotion at the end of every year has been proposed. To this end, a jury would evaluate the semester's work at the end of the semester."[47] The reactions to this change were muffled, but they effectively signaled the final rejection of the pedagogy advocated by Tschumi for more than a decade. Stucky referred to a "crisis of growth," and he was searching for solutions. He recalled that the school "had started with 20 pupils. In 1947, the number was 78; in 1952, 113. At the beginning of this year [1955], 116 pupils were enrolled. Fifty-five diplomas were awarded between 1947 and 1955."[48] While Tschumi had implemented the vertical studio, Brechbühler would introduce the horizontality of courses and workshops. Benchmarks, matched to the first-year foundation courses, would fall under the supervision of new teachers. Stucky pleaded with local political authorities to secure a new post specifically intended for Brechbühler; he would acquire two. The architecture school was going to have to conform to the plan of study in other departments at EPUL. Brechbühler's intention was to place Tschumi in the final-year curriculum while giving students the option of choosing their diploma professors. Brechbühler's plans reflected his education at the Zurich Polytechnic, just as the pedagogical model introduced by Tschumi spoke to his Beaux-Arts training.

Who was Hans Brechbühler?[49] At the time, he could boast three accomplishments: his training period in Paris with Le Corbusier and Jeanneret, the design and construction of Bern's *Gewerbeschule*, and the caliber of his representation of the FAS within the school's jury. Tschumi would feel bitterness during the imposition of the new curriculum.[50] It is curious to note that in the interwar period in Paris, the Swiss colony included three architects whose families originated from Bern. Tschumi was the first to arrive. At the Beaux-Arts he practiced speaking like a Frenchman. Alfred Roth came next in 1926 and joined Le Corbusier and Jeanneret's practice one year later. Roth charretted on two competition boards for the Geneva Palace of the SDN for Le Corbusier. He brought back from Paris a quick and talented expression of the French language, using melodic Art Deco intonations *à la*

203
Rough-measured drawing of the Hôtel Savoy, Lausanne, before transformation, south facade, April 1947

204
Field trip to Bern, Spring 1955. Tschumi's *atelier* paying a visit to a low-cost panel house built by Hans Brechbühler during World War II and premonitions of rivalries to come at EPUL in 1956–1960. Anonymous photographer

205
Transformation and extension of the Hôtel Savoy, Lausanne, south facade toward the lake, April 1947, ink on tracing paper, showing metalwork in front of the stone structure and an attic floor reserved for the school of architecture

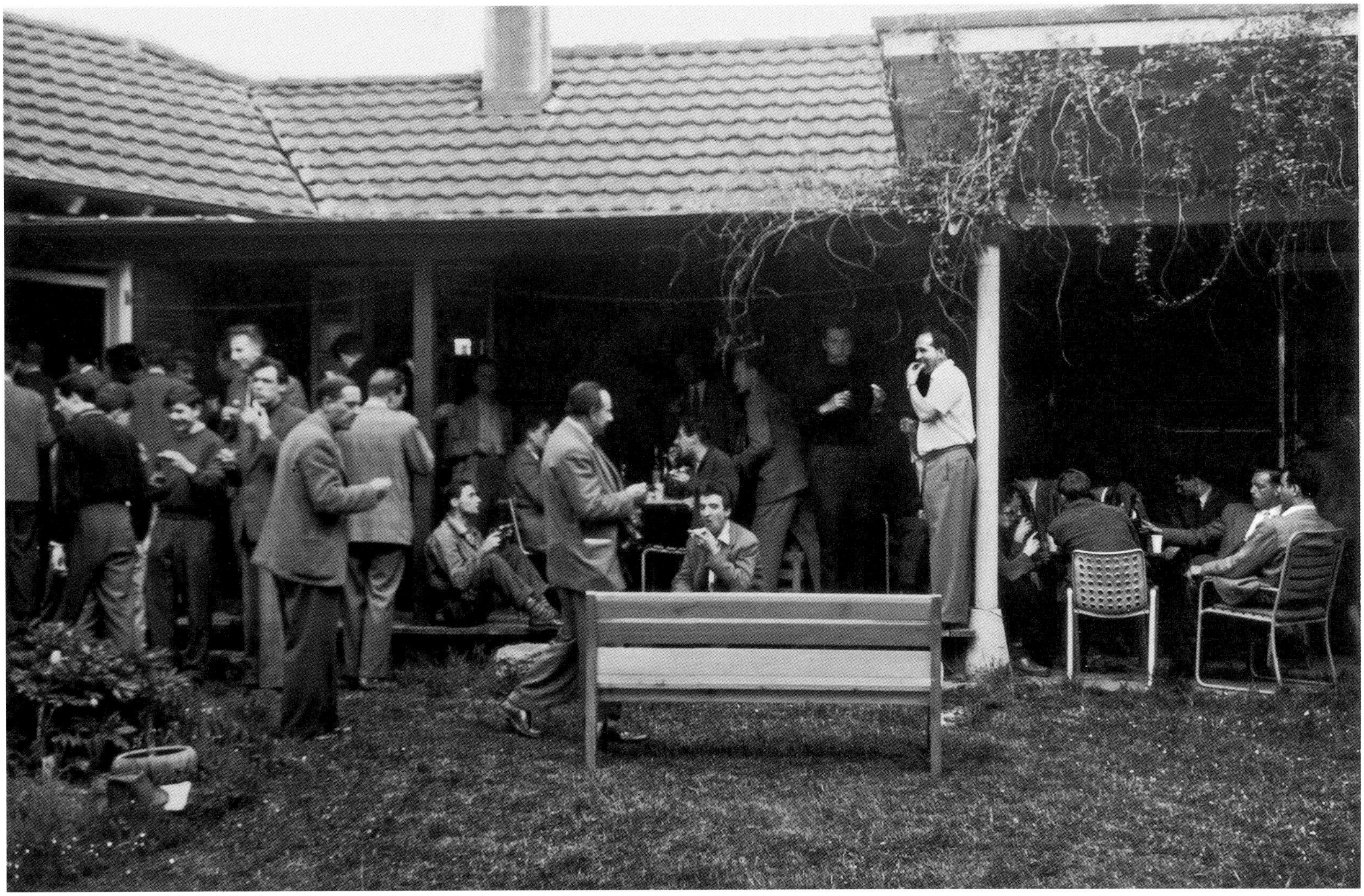

FACADE SUD
JEAN TSCHUMI · AVRIL 1947

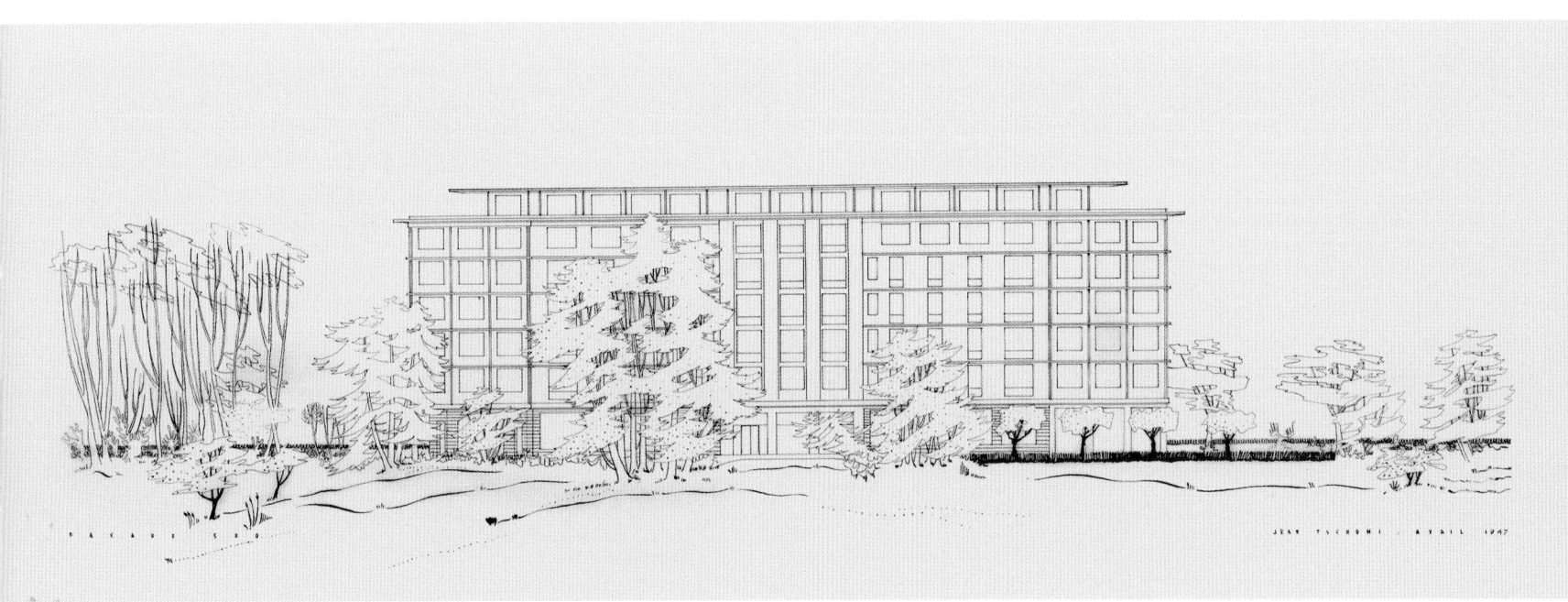

Maurice Chevalier. After receiving his diploma, Brechbühler left Zurich for Berlin in 1930–1931 before going to work for Le Corbusier and Jeanerret in Paris. "Corbu" put him charge of studying the tedious Parisian regulations governing the relative proximity of buildings, as well as ventilation courtyards, with an eye to a specific project. Le Corbusier set up his living quarters on top of the building in question, and Brechbühler recalled having worked on the project, particularly on the stone party wall.[51] Brechbühler returned from Paris having never lost his Bernese accent, but this did not stop him from winning the competition and job for the city's noted *Gewerbeschule*. To justify his gifted plan, he referred to the Corbusian orthodoxy described in the "Five Points of a New Architecture."

Corb's "Five Points" had first been published by a Stuttgart editor using a German translation by Roth, who had been Le Corbusier and Jeanneret's representative charged with supervising the construction of their two houses at Weissenhof.[52] Tschumi and Brechbühler, two men of Bernese origin in Paris, knew each other from a distance. Tschumi had also participated unsuccessfully in the *Gewerbeschule* competition.

Tschumi and Brechbühler would be forced to cohabitate at EPUL beginning in 1955. A photograph from spring 1955 permits some insight into their meeting[53] (Plate 204). What can we deduce from this particular moment, captured in an image by an anonymous photographer? The event, a local *Gar-*

206
EPUL buildings rising between public parks. Aerial photograph by Ph. Schuler, 1958–1959

207
EPUL west wing and auditorium, photograph by Würgler, 1960–1961. Reinforced-concrete vault of the auditorium visible in foreground, with attic floor for school of architecture behind the cornice to the left

tenfest, took place under the awning of a house that Brechbühler built in 1944 on the outskirts of Bern, between the railroad and the Köniz forest. The trip to Bern was intended to tour the city's modern architecture. In the photograph, thirty people, among them four adults, are shown eating and drinking. Tschumi has left his hat and a few sheets of paper on the grass in the left foreground. One can see him moving toward Brechbühler, who is leaning against a post and seems to have swallowed his sandwich in one bite. Hungry students have overtaken the chairs. Seated under the balcony is a group that clearly stands out from the others; these are the "Dark Ones," according to the testimony of Robert Monnier, who is visible on the left, holding a glass in his hand. What was the origin of this nickname and why go into the details of this story? To demonstrate the difficulties of an "oral history" based on survivors' testimony, and to illustrate the slippery notion of "collective memory." So in the studio, a small group of students was nicknamed "Dark Ones." Why? The recollections of former students offer varying explanations: the "Dark Ones" were sad, the most serious students, or Catholics (hence part of the black party). Perhaps they were on a pilgrimage to Bayreuth due to their adoration of Richard Wagner? More plausibly, they were the students who went to school dressed in white shirts and dark jackets and ties—drawing their inspiration from the *Patron*, always with his white shirt, cufflinks, dark blue suits. I wonder whether this photographic image of Tschumi and Brechbühler was an omen of

problems to come, when the curriculum reforms were put in effect later in the fall. Probably Tschumi's schedule, including his weekly back-and-forth trips between Paris and Lausanne[54] and his UIA presidency from 1955 to 1957, made his presence on the EPUL board unpredictable, a fact that could hardly have pleased Stucky. Tschumi tacitly followed the demands of the new schedule that relegated his teaching to the fourth year, but his authority had been questioned. It is unlikely that the new arrangement saved Tschumi any additional time to invest in his practice. Stucky entrusted him with an important commission for the school's auditorium. Other private commissions of interest to Tschumi would arise. A rarity in the annals of EPUL, he resigned voluntarily in July 1961. His achievements had grown by two: the Reynolds Prize and his winning entry for the World Health Organization competition.

The portrait of Tschumi's presence and pedagogy at EPUL is best rendered through the words of three former students, two of whom worked in his office. Their testimony reinforces Tschumi's impact: "Under his leadership the school had the opportunity to escape doctrine. Thanks to his remarkably liberal teaching style, everything could be questioned, everything was likely to spark interest, and the only *a priori* precondition was to have choice itself. Tschumi's suggestions for what choices to make were always relevant; his ideas about fashion were more balanced than his students', and basically more modern. His extraordinarily complete training enabled him to lead us in everything from construction details to urbanism on a large scale."[55] "He had a massive silhouette, yet he was shy....But above all he had a sharp eye....He was eclectic with his students. This meant a kind of generosity of judgment, an openness to what was presented to

208
EPUL auditorium, winter 1960–1961. Structure for reinforced-concrete parabolic vault calculated by François Panchaud, professor at EPUL, in a challenge to Saarinen and Nervi

him. And also, no doctrine."⁵⁶ Still another student recalled that "Tschumi would launch the ideas. We would work for a week, then pin up, and he would critique. We continued working with no preconceptions. This was pure empiricism; it was 'learning by doing.'"⁵⁷

In fact, through his work and his teaching, Tschumi sought an architecture that translated in industrial society rules that found their origins in Vitruvian classicism. To achieve this, he seized on the American definition of technology, one that was understood as a direct application of state-of-the-art tools to the realization of modernity. His buildings manifest a kind of elegance, much in the way that physicists and mathematicians speak of "elegant solutions."

209
Exterior view of the parabolic vault showing the cables of the prestressed structure calculated by François Panchaud

SALLE DES PROFESSEURS
ENTRÉE
SALLE DES COMMISSIONS
CENTRALE DE VENTILATION
LABORATOIRE
EXPOSITION

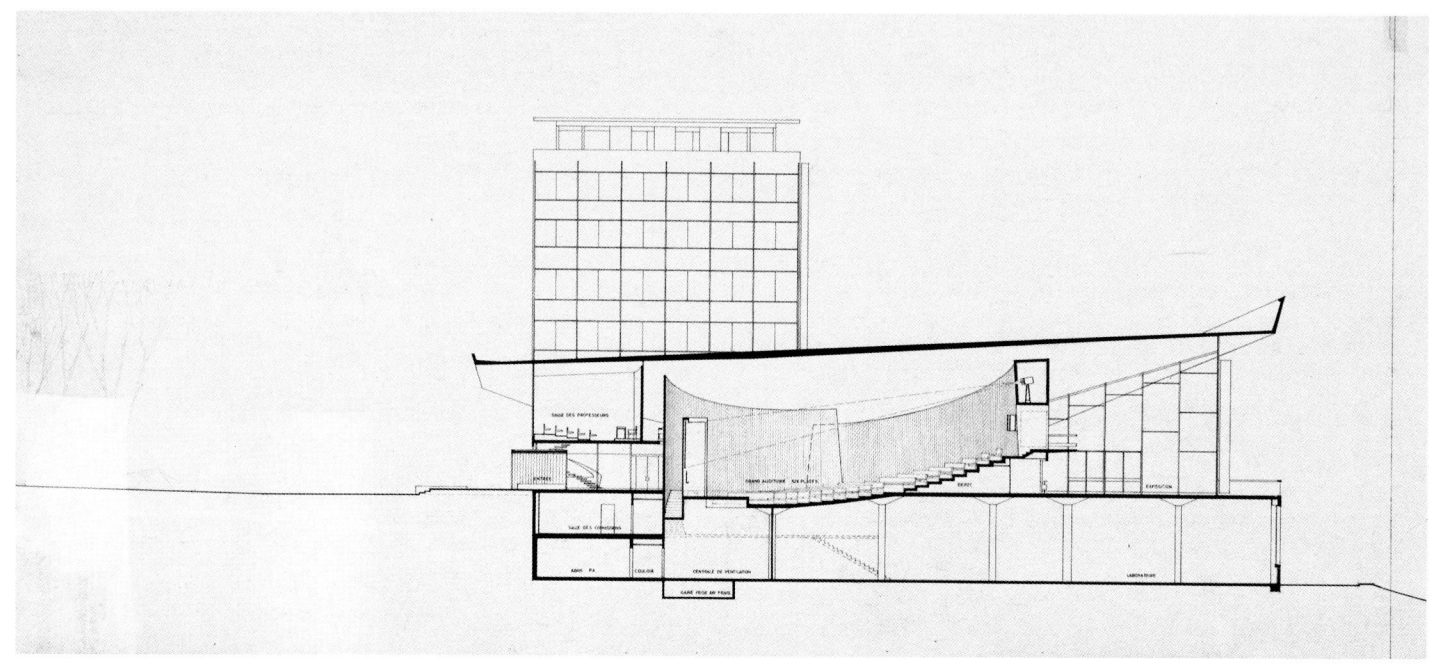

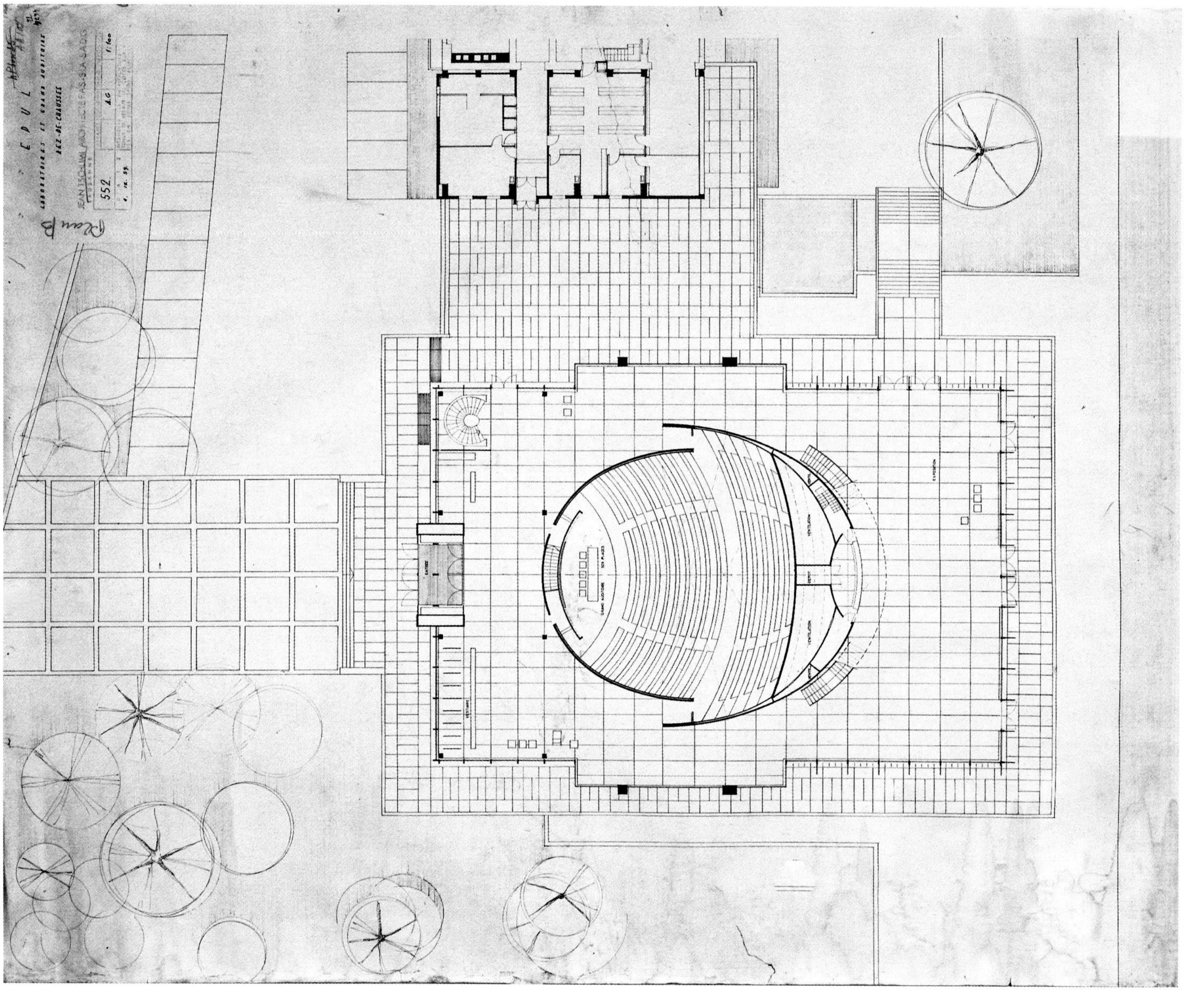

210
Transversal section through the auditorium and west gable of school, 4 December 1959

211
Plan of the auditorium, 4 December 1959

212
Entrance lobby, 1962. Photograph by Jean-Pierre Fleury

213
Southern ambulatory, 1962, photograph by Jean-Pierre Fleury. For Tschumi, a didactic demonstration of the combination of steel, glass, and concrete; for the school, a meeting room for events situated in front of the lake and mountains

214
Auditorium in relation to main EPUL building, with the profile of the vault as a monumental cornice, 1962. Photograph by Jean-Pierre Fleury

215
Auditorium and main building, circa 1969

216
Grain silo at Renens near Lausanne, 1956, blueprint, picturesque perspective drawn by employee and former EPUL student, Edouard Furrer

217
Grain silo (1956–1959) at Renens near Lausanne, photograph by M. Vuillemin, circa 1960, showing crystalline icebreaker profile on railroad, boardroom cornice toward lake

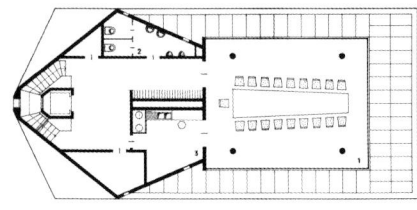
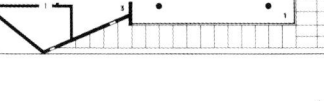
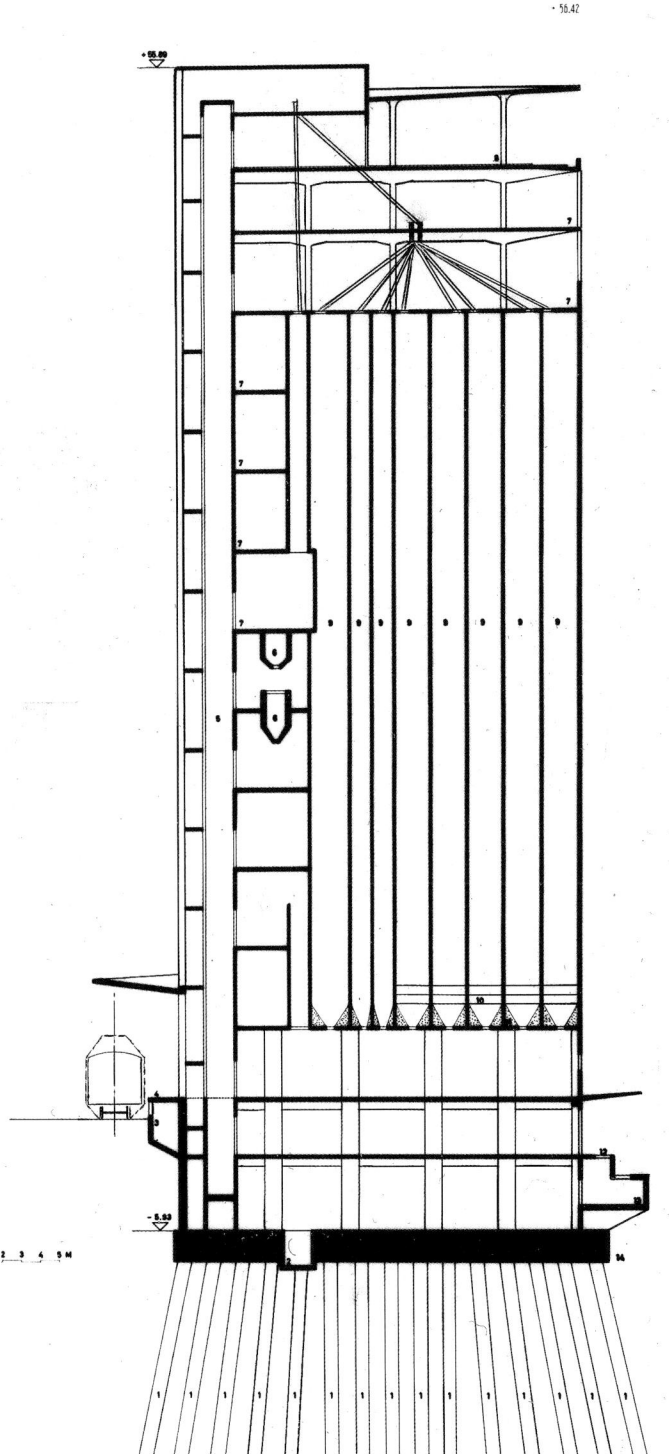

218
Grain silo (1956–1959) at Renens near Lausanne, plan of attic story, 1959. Boardroom, belvedere overlooking basin of Lake Geneva and the Alps

219
Grain silo (1956–1959) at Renens near Lausanne, cross section, 1959, height 210 feet, functional diagram

220
Detail of Plate 221. Jean Tschumi on building site in conversation with contractor

221
Grain silo (1956–1959) at Renens near Lausanne, photograph by Albert Revel, 1959. Building site seen from crane, pouring concrete for penultimate floor

222
Beaulieu observation tower, Lausanne, 1961,
India ink and gouache on photograph by
de Jongh showing compatibility between aerial
profile and existing residential typology

223
Beaulieu observation tower, Lausanne, 1961,
India ink and gouache on photograph by
de Jongh, outline of monument seen from
Chauderon Bridge

224
Beaulieu observation tower, Lausanne, 1961, pencil, stump, and wash drawing on tracing paper, project worked on with the engineer Alexandre Sarrasin. Shown located with a new residential structure and main pavilion of the Lausanne trade fair

Notes

[1] The former School of Engineering at the University of Lausanne, EIL, was re-named EPUL in 1946.

[2] Under the direction of civil engineer Maurice Cosandey, the transfer of EPUL to the Swiss Confederation took place in 1968, resulting in the re-named EPFL. See Maurice Cosandey, "Fil rouge: l'Ecole de 1953 à 1979," in Maurice Cosandey et al., *Histoire de l'Ecole Polytechnique. Lausanne: 1953-1978*, pp. 31–181.

[3] "Séance du Grand Conseil vaudois du lundi 31 août 1942," *GdL*, 1 September 1942. The opponents were from both the liberal and socialist camps. The radical Oscar Magnin, who had also trained at the Bienne *Technicum* and spent a brief period at the Beaux-Arts in Paris, defended Stucky's plans for the school. The liberal René Bonnard argued that the school served the same purpose as the one about to open in Geneva. He also defended those architects who did not have a diploma. The socialist Pierre Graber did not hesitate to reinforce the elitist status of a university, in which certain professors openly followed a Mussolini style of corporatism.

[4] Armand Brulhart, *Ingénieurs et architectes de Genève, Histoire de la SIA genevoise de sa fondation à nos jours*, SIA, Geneva, 1987, p. 120.

[5] Letter dated 29 September 1943, Archives Dir. EPFL.

[6] Jacques Gubler, "Enseignement de l'architecture, vie et avatars," in Cosandey et al., op. cit., p. 371.

[7] Colette Raffaele, *Une école d'architecture et son système d'enseignement (1942-1968), Eugène Beaudoin et Genève*, EPFL, 2004, Thesis no. 2943, pp. 29–53. I base my analysis of the Geneva-Lausanne comparison on this research, which is rich in interpretations, documents, and statistics.

[8] Tschumi's curriculum was drafted before 19 October 1942 and is kept at the EPFL archives in an unmarked dossier.

[9] In Geneva as well as in Lausanne, the impossibility of adapting to the university system of two *classes* led to the adoption of a third foundation ranking.

[10] Jean Tschumi, letter to P. Perret, head of the Department of Public Instruction, 19 October 1942.

[11] Tschumi and Beaudoin shook hands in Lausanne in 1948, at the time of the inaugural meeting of the UIA. Beaudoin wrote to the local Geneva government shortly afterwards, and stated that a collaboration between the two institutions would be beneficial. The letter was without consequences. See Raffaele, op. cit., p. 156, note 166. Tschumi was also the great uncle of Geneva architect Jean-Jacques Tschumi, who was 34 years his junior. Between 1954 and 1957, his nephew served as a guide and chauffeur in Geneva for visiting all the new administrative buildings, as well as for the housing district. As recounted on 11 June 2007.

[12] Raffaele's thesis retraces the Geneva-Lausanne confrontation in order to provoke a comparison between the ENSBA and the EPFZ. This research offers surprising conclusions that defy previous stereotypical clichés of the last 50 years.

[13] "*The National Library of Ankara*" was a diploma thesis completed in December 1946. Three years later, its author, Mukadder Çizer, built social housing for the city of Ankara as well as a bank in Istanbul the following year.

[14] As noted by Alice Ascher, who received her degree in 1948, and by Bernard Vouga, who graduated in 1957. Vouga's work has been published in Jean Tschumi, *Ecole d'Architecture et d'Urbanisme, Projets des élèves*, EPUL, Lausanne, 1953. This luxurious pamphlet was published on the occasion of the centenary of the School of Engineering. It is unpaginated.

[15] Letter to Stucky from Jean Tschumi, 8 March 1943, EPFL archives.

[16] Raffaele, op. cit., p. 82.

[17] The list of the programs for EPUL studios is conserved in a file. ACM 0060, Jean Tschumi.

[18] As recounted by Léopold Veuve, 28 February 2008.

[19] This first imperative disappeared in numerous schools of architecture, where students could slalom their way through the diploma without ever encountering housing projects, which were perceived as boring.

[20] Either Tschumi, the Geneva architect Jean Stengelin, who was responsible for the building construction courses between 1943–1955, or the Lausanne-based François Panchaud, who occupied the chair position for reinforced and prestressed concrete at EPUL.

[21] Pierre Saddy, "Le Roman des Beaux-Arts," unedited manuscript sent to the author, 22 March 2008.

[22] Ibid. Saddy insists that the diploma incurred expenses: "*C'est un examen lourd et coûteux.*"

[23] Letter from the student body to the director and professors of the School of Architecture at EPUL, 9 February 1960. EPUL archives.

[24] From winter 1951–1952 on, Roland Willomet was an intern in Tschumi's Paris office, where Max Richter, Jacques Felber, and Hubert Curchod also worked. It was in Paris that the charrette for the MVA competition took place. Willomet asserted Tschumi's competence at contractors' meetings as well as in his use of technical systems. At EPUL some professors and students cast doubt on his construction abilities. "This approach toward his character was, in my opinion, stingy and ridiculous," wrote Willomet to the author in a note dated 6 May 2008.

[25] Georges Van Bogaert states: "*Je suis parti en stage après la 3ème en automne 1948, à Paris, chez Lods et Le Caisne, puis Herbé et Lecouteur. J'y suis resté 2 ans,*" Letter to the author, 7 April 2008.

[26] Among the interns from Lausanne were Alin Décoppet (who stayed for 18 months), Paul Blondel, and Michel Weber.

[27] Jean-Pierre Epron, *Comprendre l'éclectisme*, Editions Norma, Paris, 1997, p. 73.

[28] Tschumi, introduction to *Ecole d'Architecture et d'Urbanisme*, op. cit.

[29] Liv Halle received her degree in 1952.

[30] Albert George, "*Une scierie dans le Jorat*" (1956), later built.

[31] Léopold Veuve, "*Une villa lacustre à Villette*" (1956), later built.

[32] Jean-Werner Huber, "*Une gare CFF-SBB à Bern*" (1948), Pierre Foretay, "*Une bibliothèque municipale à Lausanne*" (1949), and Pierre Margot, "*Un musée lapidaire pour la Cathédrale de Lausanne*" (1950).

[33] Roland Willomet's thesis project "*Un centre de jeunesse et de retraite à Crissier*" took the modern counter-position against the center at Crêt-Bérard built by Claude Jaccottet, a graduate of the EPFZ. The latter project is dominated by stonework modeled after a Roman cloister.

[34] Tschumi, introduction, *Ecole d'Architecture et d'Urbanisme*, op. cit.

[35] Jean Tschumi, *De l'architecture à l'urbanisme*, inaugural class, 18 November 1943, pamphlet, 24 pages, Université de Lausanne, 1944.

[36] Ibid., p. 17.

[37] Julien Gaudet, *Eléments et théorie de l'architecture*, Librarie de la Construction, Paris, n.d. (circa 1895). It was reprinted by Aulanier between the years 1901–1904.

[38] The contents of the report for 1953, *Ecole d'Architecture et d'Urbanisme*, op. cit. leave no doubt that the students had looked in the direction of Marseilles. A study trip was organized by the students in the Midi region of France, with stops in Donzère, Arles, Aix, and Marseilles along the way. As recounted by Roland Willomet, 6 May 2008.

[39] A professor at the UNIL, Henri Onde was a French geographer and glaciologist known for his work on the Savoie region. He gave ad hoc courses in urban geography at the EPUL in 1949–1950, using Annecy, Lyon, and Lausanne as case studies.

[40] "*La Masse des étudiants E.A.L. a l'honneur de vous inviter au bal qu'elle organise au château de Malley le vendredi 20 juin 1958 dès 21 h. Le bal est costumé sur le thèmes des 'dix Commandements.' Les vins et le couscous seront*

offerts." Card adressed to Jean Munier, general secretary of the EPUL. Munier sent his regrets on 15 June 1958.

[41] Letter from the *Masse* to Stucky, 18 March 1955, EPFL archives.

[42] As recounted by Alin Décoppet, 29 May 2008.

[43] Among the musicians at EPUL who made contributions to the discography of Swiss Jazz were Jean-Jacques Boy de la Tour (class of 1955) and the baritone saxophonist Alain Décoppet (class of 1954), both of whom played in Pierre Oguey's Lausanne-based octet. Oguey received first prize at a Jazz festival in Zurich in 1952. The group recorded for Phillips at the Radio-Genève studios. An arranger and composer, Oguey had been inspired by Miles Davis' "Birth of Cool" sessions in 1949–1950. Georges Van Bogeart (class of 1956) played the drums and the trumpet for a less adventurous jazz group. The architect in Lausanne who personified the tradition of continuity between the modernism of Jazz and modern architecture was the trumpeter Serge Wintsch, the founder of the "Onze Plus" festival. Listening to Art Blakey and the Jazz Messengers, Wintsch could also dream of an ideal model for a school of architecture.

[44] Alice (née Ascher) Biro, *Toujours en charrette*, Gockhausen, 2005. The first chapter of this illustrated autobiography is devoted to Tschumi's teaching.

[45] They were, in chronological order: Alice Ascher, Josette Lonchamp, Liv Halle, Anne-Marie Raccoursier, Irène Strebel, Josette Nicholas, Lydia Schaffner, Barbara Manttenfel-Szöge, and Liliane Sterea.

[46] In 1957 Bernard Meuwly pleaded with Stucky to finance a road trip to Berlin and Copenhagen. Upon their return, Hervé de Rahm sent Stucky a four-page report. According to de Rahm, they visited the Interbau district in West Berlin. Students also spent two enjoyable nights in East Berlin, where the Vodka cost ten Swiss centimes and chicken one Swiss franc. They wandered around the port of Hamburg before embarking for Copenhagen. On the return leg, they paid a visit to Ronchamp. Undated document, EPFL archives.

[47] Alfred Stucky, "Notes d'entretien avec M. Brechbühler," 1 February 1956, EPFL archives. Their first exchanges took place without the knowledge of Tschumi, who was confronted with the *fait accompli* of the new curriculum plan.

[48] As reported by Alfred Stucky to the DIP of the Vaud Canton, 8 December 1955, EPFL archives.

[49] See Ueli Zbinden's research in *Hans Brechbühler, 1907-1989*, gta, Zurich, 1991.

[50] "*Les jeunes m'ont trahi*," a phrase uttered by Tschumi that remained with Pierre Foretay, who was himself soon to become a professor. Another former student, Jacques Dumas, remembers Tschumi saying, "*Les meilleurs élèves m'ont trahi.*" The nuance in wording reinforces the teaching quality of the *Patron*. Stucky had alerted Tschumi in advance to the fact that the better students would turn their backs on their professors. The wildest rumor that was propagated in all sincerity, and which lasted for 30 years (1960–1990), claimed that Stucky had mistaken the firm "Brechbühl" for "Brechbühler," and that Stucky's teaching offer was actually meant for the fomer. The comedy of errors that fed this postal exchange entered the collective memory of the former students until their deaths and was continued later on by others.

[51] Recollections offered at La Chaux-de-Fonds in September 1987 on the occasion of a symposium commemorating the centenary of Le Corbusier's birth.

[52] Alfred Roth, *Zwei Wohnhäuser von Le Corbusier und Pierre Jeanneret, Fünf Punkte zu einer neue Architektur*, Stuttgart, Wedekind, 1927. See also by the same author: *Begegnungen mit Pionieren, Le Corbusier, Piet Mondrian, Adolf Loos, Josef Hoffmann, Auguste Perret, Henry van de Velde*, Birkhaüser, Basel, 1927.

[53] This photograph was sent to me in 2007 by Tschumi's faithful student, Robert Monnier. Monnier could not recall the origin of the document.

[54] As Bernard Tschumi recalls, "My recollection is that, in later years, Jean Tschumi spent two or three days a week in Paris and the rest, including the weekend, in Lausanne (spending two nights a week in the night train between the two cities). He would teach his theory course on Saturday mornings. I remember that he took it seriously, often preparing the slides from his various travels at home." 9 June 2008.

[55] René Vittone, address at Tschumi's memorial service, 30 January 1962.

[56] Jean-Jacques Gerber, undated letter to Robert Monnier regarding Jean Tschumi.

[57] As recounted by Léopold Veuve, 28 February 2008.

Epilogue

After six chapters and before condensing this research into a chronology, the author would like to admit that this publication reflects an obligation to correct errors in two previous efforts. The first is the *Album Jean Tschumi*, which served as a catalogue accompanying an exhibition in 1988. The second is the essay "Enseignements de l'architecture: vies et avatars," which appeared as a chapter integrated in the *Histoire de l'Ecole Polytechnique Lausanne: 1953-1978*, published by PPUR in 1999. Only a publication can verify or disprove dates, assumptions, and critical assessments. The current offering is equally provisional. It aims to trigger further research that is made possible in part through public access to drawings and correspondence at the Ecole Polytechnique Fédérale de Lausanne.

We went from the small sketch to full scale, the latter familiar to carpenters, to reconnect with the "postage-stamp method" that was advocated by Ruhlmann. For Ruhlmann, this format allowed small-scaled moments to inject maximum intensity and intelligence into the development of a project. We have seen that the practice of the *variante*, a comparative method that had its source in the Ecole Nationale des Ponts et Chaussées, entered the Beaux-Arts curriculum through the atmosphere of permanent competition that was instilled between *Patrons* and students. Hence a situation of confrontation and active emulation that produced alternative results: variants in *parti*, variants in "character," and even variants in the menu of graphic options for renderings that distinguished one *atelier* from another. In a somewhat obsessive manner, and perhaps because he financed his education by working with the industrialist Brandt who paid him to deploy a full range of contrasting models, Tschumi developed all of his projects *"en variante."* This *modus operandi* enabled him to achieve three results. When alone before a drawing board, he outlined design alternatives as a way of reflecting on the project. As head of his own firm, he expected his designers to submit various options in order to determine the "least bad" solution. Lastly, with his clients, he activated a strategy of seduction in the form of beautiful drawings that would provoke conversation themselves: "We could do this, or we could do that, but what do you want?" In this way, the client would come to identify with the ethos of a project. Commissions began streaming in when Tschumi, having assimilated the leadership mode of large capitalist companies, became the chosen architect associated with the corporations Nestlé and Sandoz.

While focusing on underground urbanism for the *Paris Souterrain* project, Tschumi was confronted with the large scale of the modern metropolis, as witnessed in the Stockholm competition. Tschumi did not view architecture and urban planning as a bifurcation of two specialist skill sets; instead, he was imbued with the French tradition of architects who redesigned towns by sublimating road infrastructure in an effort at "beautification." Gréber's proposal for Philadelphia was one such example; he placed road and rail networks at the center of his reflections. The Mutuelle Vaudoise Accidents (MVA) and the Nestlé headquarters in Vevey were designed with underground automobile networks. They were also projects that illustrated Tschumi's watchwords to his clients and to the population: preserve trees, build a portico in order to frame the horizon over the lake. But if we examine the private garden that Tschumi designed for the MVA, we discover, in Luigi Snozzi's words, a real "architecture of the ground," in which vegetal and mineral house the three-dimensional animation of volumes. Another demonstration is waiting in Vevey where, on the sixth floor, you enter a garden terrace on the north wing. In this space,

Jean Tschumi with the model of his winning entry for the Reynolds Prize 1960. Photograph by Pierre Izard

Nestlé headquarters in Vevey, north wing, construction of concrete portico and steel frame, 27 December 1957. Photograph by De Jongh

one witnesses an assemblage of material events: the metal structure of the pergola stands in place of a cornice. It occurs on a carpet that slices between mineral and vegetal. The green rectangular matt of finely combed grass refocuses the eye on the north gable, and a Japanese-inspired mineral garden rests on the reinforced-concrete elevator niche. Tschumi's architecture is one that proceeds by small and well-measured touches. I disagree with Bruno Zevi's laudatory analysis of the Nestlé building through the lens of mannerism—a term that undermines the Modern Movement.

I touched on the sentiments that led Tschumi to place himself in opposition to Le Corbusier. At the Beaux-Arts he competed against other Pontremoli students. Along the way, the ambition of his work defied other major figures of modernity: in France, Eugène Beaudoin and Bernard Zehrfuss, but also Marcel Breuer, Pierluigi Nervi, Eero Saarinen, Harry Bertoia. I think Tschumi wanted to occupy a title role in Paris; his sudden death on the night express train and his subsequent memorial service at the Lausanne Cathedral only served to dramatize this point. By way of a provisional salutation, I copy below the final lines of Chapter Six: *Through his work and his teaching, Tschumi sought an architecture that translated in industrial society rules that found their origins in Vitruvian classicism. To achieve this, he seized on the American definition of technology, one that was understood as a direct application of state-of-the-art tools to the realization of modernity. His buildings manifest a kind of elegance, much in the way that physicists and mathematicians speak of "elegant solutions."*

Nestlé headquarters in Vevey, inaugural ceremony, 1960

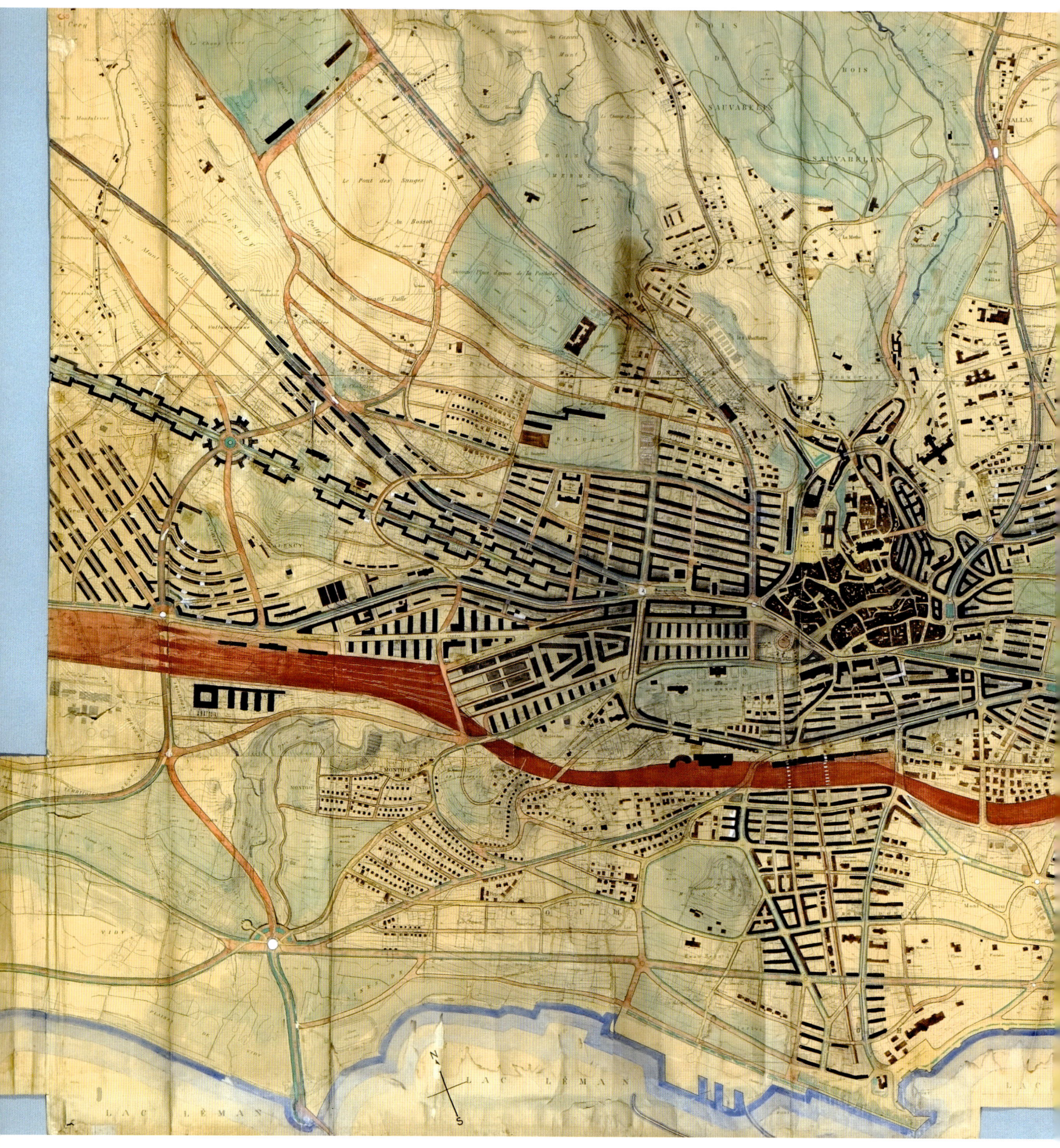

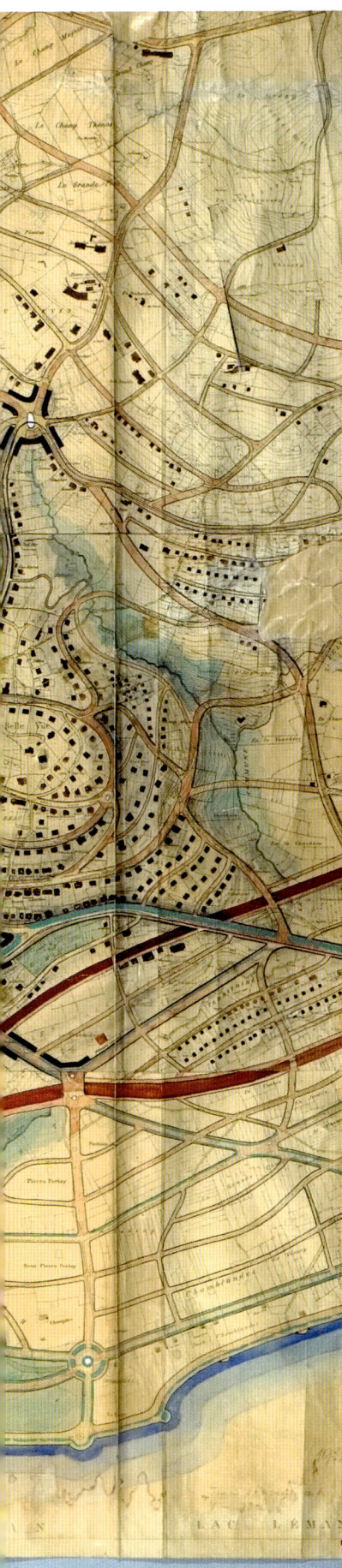

Competition for the revision of the plan to extend the city of Lausanne, 1932, ink, watercolor, and gouache on blueprint, third prize awarded to Tschumi and Vermeil. Plan shows railroad in red, lake shore in blue, medieval city in brown, blocks re-shaping the modern city in black and, to the west, a new monumental avenue intersected by a traffic circle.

Acknowledgments

The chronology of Jean Tschumi's life and work has resulted in a compilation that is destined to be incomplete. Early reference points were established by cataloguing around 4,400 drawings submitted by Bernard Tschumi to EPFL alongside the Archives of Modern Construction (ACM), whose inventory was conducted with Guy Nicollier, an architect at EPFL. Information relating to Tschumi's training at the Ecole des Beaux-Arts in Paris is a result of new research undertaken by Marie-Laure Crosnier Leconte, Chief Curator at the Musées Nationaux. Catherine Wegener-Tschumi allowed me to consult many of her father's documents that she had retained in Lausanne. This permission was granted to me before she turned them over to the ACM, where they now complete the drawing collection from the Paris office. I enjoyed the hospitality and support of three archival institutions: first, the Jean Tschumi Archive at the ACM (EPFL), administered by Pierre Frey and Jean-Daniel Chavan; second, the Novartis (formerly Sandoz) Archives in Basel, whose holdings administered by Carole Billaud and Walter Dettwiler contain material related to Tschumi's partner, the sculptor Edouard-Marcel Sandoz; finally, the Archives Historiques Nestlé, which contains a vast collection of correspondence and photographs, and where Lisane Lavanchy, Tanja Aenis, Carol Godard, and Albert Pfiffner attended to my requests. Joëlle Neuenschwander Feihl helped me complete the final version of Tschumi's Curriculum Vitae. Many previously unpublished facts were brought my attention by Pierre Saddy, architect (DPLG) and professor at the Ecole Nationale d'Architecture in Paris-Belleville and Grenoble, Alex Gerber, architect at EPFL, and François Neyroud, editor of the journal *Ingénieurs et Architectes Suisses*. Jean-François Semoroz, employed at the Service de la Population for the Commune of Renens, consulted his records in order to trace the Tschumi family's movements. Among Tschumi's former pupils and staff, I met with Alin Décoppet, Albert George, Robert Monnier, Léopold Veuve, René Vittone, and Roland Willomet. Jacques Felber and Georges Van Bogaert sent correspondence. The civil engineer Maurice Cosandey, active on the Vevey construction site, entrusted me with new details. Finally, Bernard Tschumi gave me access to Jean Tschumi's collection of drawings. My conversations with him, rich in theoretical impulses, resounded with questions regarding his father's œuvre.

Chronology

1904 (14 February)
Birth of Jean André Tschumi in Plainpalais, in the Commune of Geneva. His mother, Maria (*née* Krummenacker), was born in 1873 in Schüpfheim. His father, Johann, was born in Bern in 1871 to a family from Wolfisberg. In Plainpalais the elder Tschumi pursued a profession as a carpenter and cabinetmaker. Johann and Maria were married in 1899.

1906 (1 March)
Johann Tschumi establishes himself in Renens, near Lausanne, along the Paris-Milan rail route. The family lives on Rue de Simplon. Johann officially changes his name to Jean. He and Maria leave Renens on 30 July 1923 for the restorative climate of Heiligenschwendi, overlooking the Lake of Thoune.

1915
First drawing exercises under his father's guidance.

1917–1918
Drawing lessons at the Renens Ecole Primaire Supérieure. Exercises in perspective and in the representation of geometric solids.

1918 (18 April)
Receives certificate for completion of studies at Renens Ecole Primaire Supérieure.

1918 (April) – 1919 (April)
Apprentice at the office of Charles Braun, architect of Comptoir Suisse in Lausanne. Two presentation boards showing pen-and-ink wash studies of Ionic and Corinthian columnar orders remain from the project.

1918–1919
In parallel, Tschumi pursues professional courses under the direction of Charles Gilliard, an architect in Lausanne. Studies ornamental motifs used for the entry portal for the Lausanne Hôtel de Ville.

1919 (Summer) – 1922 (Spring)
Six semesters of study at the School of Architecture at the Biel *Technicum*. Full-scale charcoal drawings of friezes and capitols from antiquity and the Middle Ages. Courses included one semester of calligraphy using Roman and Gothic lettering and two semesters of technical drawing, including hyperboles, cycloids, and pierced cylinders. Projects included sight sketches of Biel monuments and Nidau Castle and lake landscapes rendered in pen and watercolor as well

as coursework in rural architecture. Examples of drawings of plans, sections, elevations, and perspectives composed on the same page and at the same scale include: a village fountain, an estate outbuilding, an "80-seat Protestant Temple," a villa on St. Peter's Island, and a mixed-use building on the Rue de la Gare in Biel. Meets Henri Vermeil and Oscar Magnin, whom he would encounter again in Paris. In 1943 Magnin, an architect in Orbe as well as an influential politician in the Radical Party of the canton of Vaud, was invited to teach rural architecture at the University of Lausanne's newly opened School of Architecture.

1920
The Société Industrielle et Commerciale de Lausanne grants Tschumi an award of excellence for two designs drawn at 1:10 scale for a living room and a worker's bedroom.
Ink and wash, showing skilled polychromatic rendering.

1922 (May)
Arrives in France. Employed as an architectural draftsman in a firm in Arras in Pas-de-Calais. The reconstruction of bombed French territories, subsidized by Germany as part of its war reparations, implemented rare capital investment to produce strong demand for new architecture.

1923 (February)
Arrives in Paris and takes up residence at the Hôtel de Paris on the Rue du Commerce in the 15th *arrondissement*.

1923 (June)
Takes entrance examinations for the Ecole Nationale Supérieure des Beaux-Arts (ENSBA). The next month, is admitted to the second *classe* in Emmanuel Pontremoli's studio.

1923 (July)
The architect's mother and father leave Renens for the pre-Alps commune of Heiligenschwendi.

1924
Tschumi moves to Rue Grégoire de Tours in the 6th *arrondissement*.

1925 (January)
Tschumi moves again to the Hôtel Diamant, 73 Rue de Dunkerque, in the 10th *arrondissement*.

1925 (September)
Finds lodgings in Courbevoie.

1925–1928
While a student, is employed part-time as an architectural draftsman with Jacques-Emile Ruhlmann. Studies models of beds and chairs destined for firm's furnishings catalogue, and (less often) customized ensembles for particular client needs. Another Pontremoli student, Henry Jacques Le Même, also worked at Ruhlmann's office during this period.

1925–1933
Employed by Etablissements Edgar Brandt, a firm active in armament production, metal casting, blacksmithing, locksmith work, ironworks, and lighting. Brandt's success at the Exposition des Arts Décoratifs in 1925 propelled him in the direction of the United States. His workshops were located on 88 bis Avenue Mozart in the 16th *arrondissement*, while his showroom was on 27 Boulevard Malesherbes in the 8th *arrondissement*. In July 1925 Tschumi designed a chair that resulted in 40 copies. That same year he executed projects for a bed, sofa, table, and wall lamp. Brandt's confidence in Tschumi is such that he entrusts Tschumi with orchestrating a "*grand salon Empire pour Mr. Duhem*" at 30 Rue Boissière. Sandoz is part of Brandt's circle of friends who enjoy animal sculptural motifs. In a 1942 CV submitted to the University of Lausanne, Tschumi mentions his role as artistic director and architectural advisor for Brandt's firm.

1926 (February–September)
Lives in Asnière.

1926
Meets the sculptor Edouard-Marcel Sandoz at Edgar Brandt's gallery on the Boulevard Malesherbes.

1926
Receives a first *mention* at the Beaux-Arts for a school for wine and fruit cultivation.

1927 (March)
Admitted to the first *classe* in Pontremoli's studio. As a student in the second *classe* from 1923 to 1927, Tschumi had obtained 21 notes of distinction (*valeurs*), including a third-place medal in perspective rendering. During his period in first *classe*, he received 17.5 *valeurs*, including a second-prize medal in *esquisse*, as well as a first-prize medal and a second prize for his Rougevin competition entry. Over the course of nine years in the same studio, the Swiss architect cultivated loyal connections. Among his close friends were Henry Jacques Le Même and André Aubert. Other classmates with whom he was cordial include Edouard Utudjian, Gaston Bardet, Marcel Lods, Paul Herbé, André Gutton, Paul Nelson, Jean Niermans, Jean François Hardel, André Leconte, Robert Camelot, and Eugène Beaudoin. Participated, among half a dozen "helpers," in the *charrette* for the Rome Prize won by Beaudoin in 1928. Tschumi admired the work of Beaudoin & Lods. In 1942 Beaudoin was invited to head architectural instruction at the University of Geneva; in 1943 Tschumi was appointed *Patron* of architecture and urbanism at the University of Lausanne. Placed in a competitive setting, the two former Beaux-Arts colleagues never succeeded in defining the cohesive strategy of exchange sought by Beaudoin, who recognized in EPUL a broader institutional capacity and consistency.

1927
Experiences pulmonary illness. Seeks relief in the high altitude of Heiligenschwendi (1,100 meters). Paints watercolors of mountain scenery.

1927
Takes up residence at 11 Rue de l'Echaudé in the 6th *arrondissement*, then at 59 Rue de Saussure in the 18th *arrondissement*.

1927–1928
As part of the first *classe*, wins a first-prize medal and a second prize in the Rougevin competition in the "foreigner" category. Financed by the French government, competitions, like the Prix de Rome, were in general limited to French citizens. The competition program was a postage stamp designed to celebrate the 1930 Exposition Nationale des Beaux-Arts.

1928
Resides at 119 Rue Lamarck in the 18th *arrondissement*.

1928
At the Beaux-Arts, produces a modernist rendering, a perspective of an office building located on a major avenue executed in charcoal and pencil on tracing paper, illustrating the effects of speed and light at dusk. The date "1928" and signature are retrospective additions. A 6B pencil becomes the tool of choice.

1929
Project at ENSBA for Pontremoli, namely a headquarters for a large company. The perspective of a large courtyard has the signature and title "Tchumy Vendôme." A fragment, the project's urban location seems to correspond to the Vendôme passage where it meets the Place de la Republique. Two variants of plans, facades, and perspectives. Mixed media: charcoal, wash, pencil, and gold powder.

1930–1931
Receives his membership card for the "*Grande Masse*," or student union of the Beaux-Arts.

1930
Draftsman for Robert Camelot on the 1931 Exposition Colonial competition. Work includes a large axial perspective of the entry.

1931
Travels to Sienna. Executes an ochre-yellow and red watercolor rendering of the city's silhouette, seen from above.

1931
Practices copying around 30 trees in elevation from the *Deutsche Baugilde*.

1931
Competition for a boys' school in Sion.

1931
Registers at the Sorbonne, enrolling in the Institute of Urbanism at the University of Paris. The foundation course, "The Evolution of Cities," is taught by Marcel Poëte and lasts two years.

1932
In conjunction with Henri Vermeil, enters a competition for an expansion plan for the city of Lausanne. Awarded third prize. Marcel-D. Muller, who participated in the *charrette*, would later attribute this award to the influence of a jury member from Basel, Hans Bernoulli.

1932 (16 February)
ENSBA Diploma awarded to "Mr. Tschumi, Jean André." Individual thesis program: a school in the canton of Geneva. The drawings seem to be lost. The Swiss architect is ranked 150th in his class and receives the official French title of DPLG.

1932
Opens an office in association with the Swiss architect Henri Vermeil, a former classmate from the Bienne *Technicum*, under the name "*Vermeil et Tchumi, architectes décorateurs*."

1932 (July 27)
Acknowledgment of entrance fee for Tschumi and

Vermeil in an international competition for the Nedere Norrmalm district in central Stockholm. 352 projects are in contention; the jury is overwhelmed. The jury report is printed in January 1934. In May the winners are approved by the municipal authorities. The contest was designed to stimulate political discussion in Stockholm at the time of a technical problem in the building of the subway. The infrastructure work eventually delayed the architectural solutions, which only began to take shape in the 1960s. Tschumi and Vermeil's project proposed cutting a diagonal avenue to the north, flanked by 23-story tower blocks referred to as the "backbone of the business district." The towers were to be planted in symmetrical pairs on both sides of the "New Avenue." Three traffic levels were devised, with a central elevated motorway. Elevated "promenades" were placed 5 meters above ground, with garages located in the basements of buildings. Down the avenue, bars and islands of high density were proposed. The architects presented two variants, of which the second more ambitiously proposed extending the avenue to install an additional two towers and a roundabout. The project makes reference to the radical designs of Le Corbusier and Ludwig Hilberseimer. The jury report states that the Tschumi and Vermeil submission (#6543) was eliminated from the second round and "could be considered as utopian." The same compliment was given to Le Corbusier and Pierre Jeanneret's project.

1932
In conjunction with Vermeil, enters a competition for the *Collegienhaus* at the University of Basel. The proposal is eliminated in the second round.

1932 (August)
Travels to Vieille Castille in the Valladolid, and executes a watercolor of the Saint-Laurent church.

1932 (September)
Takes up residence at 188 Boulevard Saint Germain in the 7th *arrondissement*, an address that would also become his office and remain unchanged until his death. In 1937 a new café, Le Rouquet, opens on the ground floor at the corner of the Rue des Saints-Pères. It is named after the owner, originally from Auvergne. Tschumi completes modifications to the café space in 1937 and 1953.

1932–1933
Second year at the Institute of Urbanism. In addition to Marcel Poëte's course, takes courses by Edward Fuster ("Social Organization of Cities"), Louis Bonnier ("Arts and Techniques of City Construction"), Gaston Jèze ("Administrative Organization of Cities") as well as the following related conferences: Joseph Barthélémy, "Organization of Capital Cities," Henri Sellier, "Organization of the Major Utilities in the Paris Suburbs," William Oualid, "Municipal Presence in Italy," Louis Rolland, "Maintaining Order in the City." It should be noted that the Institute of Urbanism was affiliated with the Faculty of Law at the Sorbonne, which offered a theoretical perspective on the subject. Tschumi meets other teachers, including Jacques Gréber, famous for the large diagonal avenue between City Hall and the Museum of Art in Philadelphia. The Sorbonne student develops his practical exercises through numerous competition submissions.

1933
As part of the architectural division at Edgar Brandt's office, Tschumi's monthly salary amounts to 3,000 francs, with a quarterly bonus of 1,500 francs. Works in conjunction with management under the official title of "consulting architect." His job description includes "the artistic development of studies or projects underway, and the creation of new models." His resignation becomes effective on 31 December.

1933 (June)
With Vermeil, enters a competition for the reconstruction of the National Temple in Renens.

1933 (September)
In conjunction with Vermeil, enters a competition for an expansion plan for the city of Bern. The submission is eliminated in the first round. The project proposed re-centering the train station to the west, a short-lived idea that he would be proud of for two decades.

1933 (December)
Furnishes a reception and "small office" for Etablissements André Citroën. The study is presented under Edgar Brandt's seal.

1934 (probable date)
The collaborative team "Vermeil et Tchumi" submits patent rights for a series of beds probably adapted to the Simmons mattresses used on *Normandie* ocean liner.

1934
Work exhibited at the Grand Palais as part of the Salon de la Société Nationale des Beaux-Arts.

1934
Work exhibited at the Salon des Arts Ménagers. Designs for offices of the president of the Comptoir Français de l'Azote. Work is presented under Edgar Brandt's seal.

1934–1935
"Vermeil et Tchumi" design a showroom for Omnium Central des Fours Electriques, located at 113–119 Boulevard Malesherbes.

1934–1935
Collaboration under the name *Vermeil et Tchumi, architectes décorateurs* changed to Huet Tchumi Vermeil. They design a first-class cabin for the *Normandie* liner. Francis Huet had served as chief designer for Jacques-Emile Ruhlmann, who died in November 1933. Ruhlmann received many orders for the *Normandie* project; begun in 1931, the transatlantic was launched in 1935 and represented the French nation in the face of British and German competition along the North Atlantic routes. The work involved a gigantic *charrette* of 20 architectural and decoration firms, including R. Bowens of Boijen & Roger Henri Expert, Pacon & Patout, P. Montagnac, J. B. Klotz (the only woman), Laprade & Bazin, Magnani & Masera, Robert Mallet-Stevens, Rene Herbst, G. H. Pingusson, M. Gascoin & Jean Prouvé, Frantz Jourdain & André Louis, as well as marble and glass manufacturers (including Lalique), and tapestry-makers such as Aubusson. Neither published nor credited, Huet Tchumi Vermeil's design for an "Honfleur" living and bedroom cabin suite drowns amid the collection of masterpieces on *Le Normandie*. Tschumi's collaboration with Huet and Vermeil ends in 1936.

1935 (April)
Collaboration with Vermeil on a competition entry for the Bern *Gewerbeschule*. Marcel-D. Mueller assists with the *charrette*. Their proposal is rejected in the first round. It is worth noting that the competition winner, Hans Brechbühler, applies Le Corbusier's "Five Points" to the letter. Ignoring each other in Paris, Tschumi and Brechbühler will be forced to cohabit at EPUL beginning in 1955.

1936 (January–February)
Tschumi and Vermeil submit a competition entry for the Casino in Bern. The program stipulates an underground parking garage located under housing and commercial structures. The project is eliminated, but in Paris Tschumi independently publishes his project for "an underground shelter to protect against aerial bombings in Bern," which integrates competition designs. The proposal accommodates a shelter for 1,800 people, along with a medical and surgical unit, not far from the location of the Parliament building. The realistic scenario is based on information obtained from the city's building department. The competition winner, the architect Emil Rüetschi, built his project from 1936–1937. Only a small shelter is located along three levels between the commercial building and the ancient Baroque monument of the *Hauptwache*. Tschumi wished to occupy the entire basement space, an area four times the size. His calls to the staff of the City Council were not returned. It should be noted that his project was ignored by the Swiss *Bauzeitung*, which nevertheless proclaimed interest in the role of the basement in passive defense. In Paris, Tschumi serves as secretary of the Executive Committee of GECUS, founded in 1933 by Edward Utudjian, another Pontremoli student. The proposal for the Bern shelter appears in the GECUS journal, *Le Monde Souterrain*, no. 5 (August 1936).

1936 (probable date)
Two festive polychromatic sketches for the transformation of the Kornhauskeller restaurant in Bern. The project involves the design of the basement vault, including lighting and furnishings. Is this an exercise in style intended to attract the city's attention to the proposed shelter for Casino Square?

1936 (February)
André Ventre and "J. T. Chumy" submit proposal for a competition to design a monument to Maréchal Foch.

1936
Collaboration with Emile Aillaud and André Ventre on a competition for a school complex on the Rue Baudin in Villejuif, Val-de-Marne, as well as a school in Antony, Seine. In researching this project, Tschumi consults a book by Julius Vischer titled *Der neue Schulbau im in-und Ausland*, published in Stuttgart in 1931.

1936
Beginning of regular collaboration with sculptor and board member of Sandoz SA France, Edouard-Marcel Sandoz. Under the motto, "*Suisse Vivante et Fraîche*," their competition project for the Swiss Pavilion at the Exposition Internationale des Arts et Techniques in 1937 is rejected by the jury in Switzerland. After this setback, the project continues outside of competition in the form

of an additional "Swiss Village" built above the Swiss Pavilion on the right bank of the Seine. Sandoz and Tschumi envisage an amusement locale called "*Alimentation Suisse*" ("Food Switzerland"). Exhibitors include the Bern *chocolatier* Tobler, famous for its triangular confection. A large Bernese farm is flanked by a mountain whose spiral accommodates a ski jump, perhaps recalling the Winter Olympics organized in 1936 in St. Moritz.

1936 (June)
Under the signature "*Jean T. Chumy, architecte DPLG, Ed.-M Sandoz, sculpteur*," Nestlé France receives commission for a "Pavilion for All the World's Babies" at the 1937 exhibition. The architect draws four variants, one using modern, spiraling dynamics, two with small, compact, symmetrical solutions. An intermediate solution, eclectic in character, seduces the sponsor. The main event in all proposals is a cylinder indicating the branded Nestlé box of powdered milk. The program has three basic elements: a coffee-tasting area, a diorama illustrating the firm's global presence, and a "*cinéma guignol Nestlé*." Sandoz designs murals for the diorama and theater. A dozen products will be exhibited and tasted. Built from December 1936 to March 1937, the final realization embodies a fifth, eclectic solution in which the spiral cylinder meets the box of the terrace, whose arcaded gallery leads to the *cinéma guignol*.

1937
Project titled *Voies souterraines pour l'amélioration et la protection de la capitale*, developed in conjunction with GECUS and overseen by Edouard Utudjian, is exhibited at the Exposition Internationale des Arts et Techniques. GECUS receives Grand Prize and Tschumi an honorary diploma for his personal contribution. Under the abbreviated title *Paris Souterrain*, the plan locates the intersection of north-south and east-west axes at Châtelet, then forms a 45-degree square whose angles create four interfaces, the Gares de l'Est and du Nord to the north, Denfert-Rocherau to the south, Bastille to the east, and Place de la Concorde to the west. The proposal is presented in plan and in section. The drawings' scales range from 1:2000 to 1:10,000, and were updated on the basis of topographic maps dated 1936. Tschumi designed and executed the luminous model for *Paris Souterrrain* that was exhibited in the dark cellars of the new Museum of Modern Art. He also hung a spectacular graphic rendering showing an underground crossroads with helical access ramps for cars.

1937 (September)
Brief respite in Heiligenschwendi. Tschumi's use of his parents' Bern address makes him eligible for entry in Swiss-sponsored competitions.

1937 (November)
Second individual construction site follows the Nestlé Pavilion: the transformation of Le Rouquet at 188 Boulevard Saint Germain, on the ground floor of Tschumi's apartment building. Plans are signed "J. T. Chumy." Project includes renovation of kitchen, heating and electrical systems, and furniture. A second-stage renovation occurs in 1953.

1937 (November) – 1938 (March)
Tchumi et Sandoz, architectes décorateurs unveils the *Miro-Mirage* and seeks to promote it. Made out of a rectangular mirrored table tilted and formed into a metal housing with a two-way mirror as its face, the device accommodates a photograph; when illuminated, it displays the image of a loved one, as if a magic lantern. Its principle reflects a wall application developed by Etablissements Baudet Donon Roussel, manufacturers of arms and metal works. Possibly the architects approached the same firm to launch their model, for which only one prototype version exists. Despite his commercial relationships and know-how, Sandoz was unable to produce the *Miro-Mirage* in series. The device was exhibited at the 1938 Salon d'Automne, accompanied by an elegant pouf and boudoir.

1939
Tschumi visits the Sandoz factories in Basel. The pharmaceutical company envisages building new laboratories in France in Noisy-le-Sec and Orléans. The calcium vial is its signature product.

1939 (January–May)
Design of furniture for administrative areas devoted to management at the Sandoz headquarters in Basel as part of the first stage (1937–1939) of construction of the L-shaped building designed by Brodtbeck & Böhny in association with Eckenstein & Kelterborn. Following Sandoz' invitation, Tschumi works on two sets of furnishings, one for Fritz Imhoff and the other for the boardroom. Pedestals are executed in Paris and the wool carpet is woven in France. Metal radiator housings are probably of French origin; the paneling and flooring are manufactured locally. BAG Turgi supplies the lamps.

1939 (27 June)
Presentation of *Paris Souterrain* to the Centre National d'Organisation Scientifique du Travail. First distinguished in 1937, GECUS's initial project has been developed according to analysis of its geological feasibility. The juncture of the central axes becomes known as the "*Croix des Halles*." Diagonal interfaces are now situated at Gare de l'Est, Gare du Nord, Observatoire, Bastille, and Concorde.

1939 (19 September)
Letter written to the Ministry of War requesting service in the Défense Nationale "for the duration of the war." Tschumi makes a simultaneous request for French citizenship. Emphasizing his experience with GECUS and expertise in underground shelters, he observes that, "Not put into action (*mobilisé*) in Switzerland, I feel I can render useful services to France." He is recognized as "physically fit" on 24 November 1939, but does not serve due to France's defeat in June 1940.

1939 (22 December)
Preliminary study for Sandoz laboratories in Noisy-le-Sec, Seine-Saint-Denis. Sited on the northern edge of the national highway, this structure took over operations for an evacuated plant in Saint-Louis, Haut-Rhin. Opens in 1942 as a first building flanked by a woodshop and a garage.

1939–1941
In 1939 Sandoz France purchases an industrial building on the Rue de Trudelle in Orléans. The structure requires adaptation in order to be converted to chemical production. The local architect, André Masson, offers an initial proposal. Tschumi meets Masson in December 1939 and modifies the project to accommodate the production of calcium vials. Construction is organized in three phases, with Masson on site and Tschumi administering construction. The factory opens at the end of 1940; despite cement and metal shortages, construction continues into 1941. The factory houses roughly 40 workers.

1941 (March)
Project for the transformation of the Villa Guiraud in Bignos. With a picturesque and regionalist image rendered in Basque taste, the project is left unbuilt due to its location in the "Free Zone."

1941 (March)
The hydraulic engineer Alfred Stucky, a specialist in reinforced concrete and director of the Engineering School at the University of Lausanne, submits a request to create an architecture school attached to the engineering faculty for the Canton of Vaud. Tschumi is announced as head of the new department. A recommendation from Sandoz, who was well known in Lausanne, probably played a role in the decision.

1942 (4 February)
Sketch for the boardroom of Sandoz France, located at 6 Rue de Penthièvre in Paris's 8th *arrondissement*. A brilliant polychromatic rendering is produced using red ochre, Indian red, sienna, and yellow-orange. Construction was postponed until after the war.

1942 (1 September)
By a vote of 61 to 59, the Grand Conseil of the Canton of Vaud agrees on the creation of a School of Architecture and Urbanism within the School of Engineering (EIUL). The school would later become known as the Ecole Polytechnique de l'Université de Lausanne, or EPUL, in 1946.

1943 (9 October)
Opening of the Haute Ecole d'Architecture at the University of Geneva at the initiation of State Counsel Adrien Lachenal. Eugène Beaudoin is called on to head the program.

1943 (18 November)
Opening of the School of Architecture and Urbanism at the University of Lausanne. Under the title "From Architecture to Urbanism," Tschumi delivers a long inaugural lecture, citing Vitruvius, Viollet-le-Duc, Choisy, Guadet, Valéry, Gromort, Marcel Poëte, and the charter of Athens. The lecture is dedicated to GECUS and its unspoken subtext centers on Le Corbusier.

1944
Home and office established at 7 Boulevard de Grancy in Lausanne. The birth of Bernard Tschumi. The office and home will later move to 5 Rue J.-J. Cart and 16 Avenue Tissot respectively.

1944 (April)
Competition for the hospital and veterinary faculty at the University of Zurich. Tschumi receives a *mention* and a prize of 1,200 Swiss francs.

1945 (May)
Competition for a new administrative building in the Werkhof district of Bern.

1945 (December)
Design of a temporary space in wood

(28 × 7.8 meters) dedicated to the manufacturing of calcium vials at Sandoz SA in Noisy-le-Sec.

1946
Competition for a cantonal hospital in Zurich. Project is eliminated.

1946 (1 February)
Tschumi's architectural license is validated by the State Council of the Canton of Vaud.

1946 (August) – 1947 (10 July)
Commission and execution of the Swiss Pavilion at the Exposition Internationale de l'Urbanisme et de l'Habitation, which opens in Paris at the Grand Palais on 10 July 1947. The project is sponsored by the Ministry of Reconstruction and Urbanism. The official Swiss section, conceived as a collective effort of the SIA, displays a contrasting journey, dividing the space according to four themes: the problem of Swiss housing, urban planning, habitation, and facilities and construction. The architectural promenade orchestrated by Tschumi plays with panels and pergolas to present a series of models, a niche for a 70-seat cinema, a diorama of living spaces equipped with bathrooms, kitchen, living room, and bedrooms, as well as a view onto a garden where four prefabricated houses are installed.

1946–1955
Expansion of the Sandoz Laboratories in Noisy-le-Sec at 171 Rue de Paris. The first stage was completed in 1946–1948, while the second stage was executed in 1953–1955. The heating units were installed by a Sulzer, a Swiss company with a factory in Saint-Ouen.

1947–1953
Work on a new Sandoz factory in Orléans, Loiret kicks off in the Lausanne office where, at the end of the war, the architect pays designers chosen largely from among his students. The preliminary project is submitted on 17 May 1947 and the project is developed in summer and fall 1948. Three variants are submitted at 1:200 scale and one at 1:100. The building permit is granted in 1949. The project was transferred to Tschumi's Paris office, where Henri Curchod, the only draftsman without an academic degree, scratched out a good number of the plans in the Boulevard Saint-Germain apartment in the company of Jean-Werner Huber and Charles Jeanneret. According to Max Richter, who oversaw the building site, 1,310 plans were needed. In spring 1952 furniture studies were produced at 1:1 scale. Construction costs, estimated in 1951 at 570 million French francs, rose to 644 million. A banquet celebrating the end of construction was served on the building's terrace on 2 June 1953. A second phase, designed as a wing running parallel to the Loire, was scheduled for 1953 but never executed.

1947–1950
Project for the central headquarters of Sandoz France in Paris on 6 Rue de Penthièvre in the 8th *arrondissement*. The work involved a radical transformation of a former *hôtel particulier*. The director, Yves Dunant, took over one floor, with his colleague, Jean Häuselmann, installed above him. For Häuselmann's office Tschumi developed a range of lamps drawn up in 6B pencil and "postage-stamp" format, according to the method advocated by Ruhlmann. Tschumi drew on blueprints for work that had been introduced in 1933 for the André Citroën offices under the seal of Etablissements Edgar Brandt. Other offices were designed for Th. Cacault, Geiser, V. R. Wallart, Chaland, Kordt, and Beyeler. In 1949 Tschumi developed a decorative Sandoz logo for the main entrance.

1947
Project for a residential building along the Langedoc road in Lausanne.

1947
Project for the Hotel Terminus, facing the Lausanne rail station.

1947
Following an introduction by Edouard-Marcel Sandoz, Tschumi presents a project for "Village Général Guisan" in Chermignon, near Montana. Sited to the west of the military clinic in an area known as Lavenire sur Sierre, the complex is designed to include ten houses for sick officers, 30 family houses, 15 single dwellings, a community hall, mechanical and craft workshops, a school, and a clinic. In December the architect compiles a building estimate of 1,027,500 francs, not including the purchase price of the site. The plan goes no further.

1947 (September)
Housing for agricultural workers in Sablonceaux, Charente Maritime, on the site of vineyards belonging to Jean Häuselmann, a director of Sandoz France.

1947 (September)
Bedroom and bathroom designed for Jean Häuselmann in Neuilly-sur-Seine.

1947 (February–April)
Survey study of Hôtel Savoy, Avenue de Cour in Lausanne, and proposal to transform the site with an eye to a future location for EPUL.

1948 (28 June–1 July)
Inaugural Congress of the International Union of Architects (UIA) in Lausanne. The presidency of the Union is reserved for Patrick Abercrombie, author of the *Greater London Plan*. The secretariat position goes to Pierre Vago. The honorary chairmanship falls to Auguste Perret, celebrated like a patriarch, and Tschumi assumes the role of chairman. Among the additional delegates are Vago and Perret, Helena Syrkus, André Gutton, Henry Jacques Le Même, Ralph Walker, Viacheslav Chkvarikov, Leslie Wilkinson, Bernard Zehrfuss, and Paul Vischer. Topics discussed include urban development, the industrialization of construction, the state and society. Tschumi exhibits his students' work at the Palais de Rumine. The Assembly officially numbers 50 members. Around 400 people from 38 countries attend. Many architects travel "in the company of their wives," and there are many excursions: to the auditorium of the University of Fribourg, Gruyere Castle, the Vaudoise vineyards of Dézaley, Rochers-de-Naye. In Lausanne Jean Pierre Vouga, architect DPLG, serves as commissioner and, with Robert Loup, coordinates all programs, including the trips.

1949–1957
Sandoz SA Laboratories in Saint-Pierre-la-Garenne, Eure. Various stages of work are organized. In 1950 Hubert Curchod designs a boiler room, hangar, and electric transformers. Laboratories and offices are built between 1953–1957. The extension is the subject of drawings until 1961.

1949 (20 October)
Purchases a Ford Vedette, V8, F492 E, a beautiful French-built American automobile with chrome lines. With a lit cigarette, left hand on the wheel and right hand on the gearshift, Tschumi loves to drive fast. In March 1957 the front of a truck meets the back of his second blue-colored Vedette. He then buys a Citroën ID, which he prefers to the DS; it is just as aerodynamic but more sporty. Tschumi's son would drive his father's Citroën in 1967–1968 during his internship with Candilis in Paris.

1950
Completion of work on the Sandoz offices in Lyon, on the corner of Rue Bonnel and Cours de la Liberté, in collaboration with Lyon architect Charles Vial.

1951
Villa for a Sandoz engineer at Saint-Pierre-la-Garenne, Eure.

1951
Becomes a "regular" professor at EPUL. Member of the Swiss Romande section of the Federation of Swiss Architects until his death in 1962.

1951
UIA Congress in Rabat, Morocco.

1952 (30 January–1 February)
Jury convened to judge an invited competition for the headquarters of the Mutuelle Vaudoise Accidents (MVA), on a site in Lausanne known as Le Cèdre. Other Lausanne-based competitors included Maurice Grivel, who located his proposal right in the middle of the park. Tschumi submitted his project in December 1951 and signed the contract for the commission in September 1952.

1952
Competition for the Swiss Hospital of Paris in Neuilly. Tschumi is declared the winner; members of the project team include Henri Curchod, Roland Willomet, Jean-Werner Huber, Charles Jeanneret, Jacques Felber, and Max Richter.

1952 (October)
Study and leisure tour of the United States with MVA clients Roger Bobillier and Marcel Delarageaz. Tschumi's interest focuses on New York City's Lever House, designed by Gordon Bunshaft of Skidmore, Owings and Merrill. Additional trips to Connecticut. Emphasis is placed on office building configurations and staff services, including self-service cafeterias and recreation areas. Discovery of furniture by Harry Bertoia and Charles and Ray Eames.

1952–1960
Pradet Frères factory for soccer shoes and balls in Saint-Jean-de-la-Ruelle, Loiret. Both project design and construction were difficult, involving two production units built in three stages with a single articulation of the final result. Today the building is partially abandoned, leaving behind beautiful relics.

1952
Probable date for a project in Orléans for the studios of the Cie Générale d'Electricité.

International competition for the WHO headquarters in Geneva, 1960, bird's eye perspective, India ink, watercolor, gouache, collage on photographic print. Winning entry

1953 (February–June)
Second transformation of Le Rouquet, located at the corner of the Boulevard Saint-Germain, adjacent to an antique shop. Both variants submitted to the client concerned the bar and the ceiling. Repair of technical and sanitary facilities on the ground floor and basement. Installation of a phone booth made out of a rounded section of wood. Neon-tube lighting built into a plaster hung ceiling. Sconces on the wall. Behind the bar, consoles for glasses and bottles set in a chrome frame. Formica veneered on hollow-core wood panels. Renovation of the facade and terraces. Neon-tube signage. Details were worked out at 1:20 and 1:1 scales. Today, Le Rouquet retains a few relics of this arrangement.

1953
Publication by EPUL of a pamphlet titled *Ecole d'Architecture et d'Urbanisme. Projets, esquisses, études des élèves de l'Ecole*, in commemoration of the tenth anniversary of the school's founding.

1953
UIA Congress in Lisbon.

1954–1958
Tschumi presides over the UIA.

1954
Farm workers' housing in Sablonceaux, Charente Maritime, domaine de La Chauvillère, on Jean Häuselmann's property. Vertical extension of an existing building: seven common rooms and sanitary facilities under a pitched roof, probably used by seasonal workers. Today La Chauvillère is owned by Häuselmann & Fils, producers of Pineau de Charentes and cognac.

1955 (circa)
Design of the Villa Gosselin in Orléans for one of the Sandoz directors.

1955 (circa)
Tschumi drops his Leica in the Atlantic tide at La Baule. He then buys an Alpa reflex camera manufactured in Sainte-Croix.

1955
UIA Congress in The Hague.

1955–1958
Site studies for administrative headquarters of SOPAD (Société de Produits Alimentaires et Diététiques) in Paris. Tschumi looked for a site around the Etoile, Boulevard de Lannes, and Pont de Neuilly areas. A draft was sketched for an Avenue Malakoff location. SOPAD would ultimately move to Courbevoie.

1956–1957
Project for the Cercle Volney, located at 7 Rue de Volney in the 2nd *arrondissement*. Sandoz presides over the club, which organizes exhibitions of contemporary art. The project is meant to integrate the gallery into an apartment block. The proposal remains unbuilt.

1956–1958
Study of variants for the EPUL auditorium and adjacent laboratories on Avenue de Cour in Lausanne. Built later, between 1960–1962.

1956–1959
Design and construction of a grain silo for the union of Syndicats Agricoles Romands in Renens, in collaboration with architect A. Cavin. The project entailed a beveled tower made out of reinforced concrete and located on the edge of the railway. The firm of Birchmeier & Matter served as project engineers. The silo perspectives, complete with picturesque anecdotes, were drawn by the student and employee Edouard Furrer. Tschumi wanted to turn the attic level into a public Belvedere, but the exceptional panorama over Lake Geneva would remain private. In 1972 the transformation of the space by Jacques Felber, a Tschumi student who was respectful of the *Patron*, would double the silo's capacity through a visual symmetry. The beveled elegance of the earlier project drowns in an opulent, almost amorphous mass.

1956–1960
Project and realization of the headquarters for Nestlé Alimentana, known locally as "En Bergère," on the grounds of the former Grand Hotel de Vevey. Nestlé sought out the services of the architect Willy Bühlmann, who defined and quantified program components, including the furniture, and researched the management of secretarial pools as practiced by Aluminium AG Zurich. At Nestlé's expense, Tschumi, Bühlmann, and their wives take a study tour to the United States, with stops in New York, Boston, Cambridge, and Washington. Tschumi develops and discusses the draft proposal before the two directors, Jean Constant Corthésy and Enrico Bignami. The architect presents an estimate that will not exceed the symbolic cost level of 40,000,000 francs. The reinforced-concrete portico is designed by the engineer Alexandre Sarrasin. The design of the curtain wall incorporates pivoting, openable aluminum windows. Many decisions are made by Bignami based on variants submitted by Tschumi; for example, Bignami wants a world map by Mercator (dear to Tschumi from his project for André Citroën) used as a projection to close the perspective view from the boardroom. The Nestlé corporate architecture is inspired by the "Olivetti model" implemented in Ivrea. Demolition of the Grand Hotel occurs in October 1956; the building site starts up in spring 1957; the completed building opens in April 1960. In November 1960 Nestlé writes to the Municipality of Vevey to submit a request for an extension in the shape of a hexagonal tower, to be located on the northeast part of the site.

1957
Invited competition to design the headquarters of Imprimeries Réunies in Lausanne. Receives third prize. Pierre Bussat and Jean-Marc Lamunière from Geneva are announced as the winners.

1957 (May)
Money is allocated by the Grand Council of the Canton of Vaud for modernization of the old Savoy Hotel, acquired by the state in 1943, to make it available for use by EPUL. Tschumi submits a proposal in 1947. The project is built between 1957 and 1959.

1957 (August)
Attends the UIA Congress in Berlin on invitation from the *Bund Deutscher Architekten*. Visits the pilot neighborhood Hansaviertel. Otto Bartning and Tschumi lunch with the young mayor, Willy Brandt, elected the same year.

1957–1961
Research in Paris to secure land for the new headquarters for Sandoz France. The preliminary draft outline from November 1957 designates no. 37–39 Avenue Pierre 1er de Serbie in the 8th *arrondissement*; other possible sites include Avenue Montaigne, the corner of Avenue George V and Rue Pierre Charron, Avenue d'Ilena, Avenue Marceau, Rue de Pressburg, Avenue de Villiers, Levallois-Perret, Avenue de Neuilly, Pont de Neuilly. In each case, the architect outlines possible *partis* and calculates square footage. In 1961 Sandoz settles on a different location in Rueil-Malmaison, Hauts-de-Seine.

1957–1963
Transformation and expansion of the maternity wing in Lausanne.

1957 (November)
Photographs the construction site for Choay pharmaceutical laboratories at 48 Rue Theophile Gautier in Paris's 16th *arrondissement*, architect unknown. This incursion suggests that Sandoz was aiming to take over construction of the building when Choay left Paris to relocate in Normandy.

1958
UIA Congress in Moscow.

1958 (September)
First installment of funds allocated by the state of Vaud for construction of the EPUL auditorium and laboratories. The second installment is paid in December 1960. The Confederation offers financial assistance equal to one-third of construction costs. In 1959 the civil engineer François Panchaud, who held the chair in reinforced and prestressed concrete, offers various solutions based on architectural variants proposed in 1957. The architect and the engineer struggle to coordinate their experiments with prestressed panels, as studied using laboratory models. Difficult construction-site conditions mar the realization of the vaulted ceiling between June 1960 and September 1961 as the contractor responsible for the masonry becomes confused by the combined complexity of the forms, the thinness of the shell, and the need to work in winter. The resultant defects are denounced by the architects. The building is completed in 1962.

1958–1960
Initial studies for the SOPAD headquarters (aka Nestlé) on Quai Paul Doumer in Courbevoie.

1958–1963
Design of laboratories, offices, and apartments for the northern France complex of Sandoz AG in Tourcoing, Nord, at the corner of Rues Derveaux and Soufflot. Begun in May 1958, the project was developed in 1960 but completed only after the architect's death.

1959–1962
Administrative building for André & Cie SA, in collaboration with the Lausanne firm of Pierre Bonnard. The building's triangular shape, which Tschumi saw as a reference to Marcel Breuer, would become the company's signature and logo.

1960, probable date
Preliminary proposal for the Paris headquarters of Helvetia insurance. Situated on a roundabout, the project was developed by Tschumi's Lausanne office before abandonment.

1960
Competition for the WHO headquarters in Geneva. Tschumi is awarded first prize and execution of the project. Following the architect's death, construction is overseen by Pierre Bonnard until 1964.

1960 March
Receipt of the Richard Samuel Reynolds Memorial Award for the Nestlé headquarters. With a $25,000 cash award, the prize recognizes "the innovative value and potential influence of construction in aluminum." The jury chair is Walter Gropius. In October Tschumi travels to San Francisco to receive the distinction.

1961
Expansion of the Paris firm into offices (unoccupied due to Tschumi's subsequent death) at 24 Rue d'Eylau in the 16th *arrondissement*.

1961 (February–July)
Centre Français de Protection de l'Enfance, 93 Boulevard Davout in the 20th *arrondissement*. Unrealized project for a wooden pavilion on two floors.

1961 (March)
Swiss Hospital of Paris. Final round of construction documents. Federal authorities in Bern were required to support the public funding of initiatives promoted by Swiss industrials in Paris, including Sandoz and Nestlé. In Switzerland, the architect William Vetter, who was eliminated from the competition, disparages the project, which collapsed following the death of the architect, who had already paid for the fence and signage for the building site. The hospital was later built in Issy-Les-Moulineaux.

1961 (29 March)
Attended the International Congress on Light Metals in Leoben, Austria, a conference concerning the "use of aluminum in architecture," and advocating for the nobility and universality of the material.

1961 (July)
With full international recognition, resigns from his post as professor at EPUL.

1961 (July)
The Lausanne press disseminates views of the model for the new Beaulieu district on the grounds of the Comptoir Suisse compound. A landmark observation tower, worked out in reinforced concrete by the engineer Alexandre Sarrasin, is intended for the occasion of the Swiss National Exhibition in Lausanne, scheduled to open in 1964. The singer Jean Villard Gilles, son of Montreux architect Louis Villard, publishes a mock poem titled "La Tour de Beaulieu." An excerpt: "*L'homme nouveau aura le cerveau dans les tripes et les tripes dans le cerveau.*" Joking with his son Bernard, Tschumi remarks that "*on en fera un moulin à poivre pour les touristes.*"

1961 (22 December)
Submission of the final report for "Lausanne Tower" to the board of Comptoir Suisse.

1962 (18 January)
Draft plans for a new headquarters for Sandoz France in Rueil-Malmaison, in Hauts-de-Seine. After the architect's death, the project is entrusted to Bernard Zehrfuss and the Basel-based Martin Burckhardt, who share the design of the buildings.

1962 (25 January)
Tschumi is found dead early in the morning at the Vallorbe customs checkpoint on the night train from Paris Gare de Lyon.

1962 (30 January)
Funeral ceremony at Lausanne Cathedral.

1962 (March)
Pierre Vago covers the posthumous settlement of blueprints for the SOPAD headquarters in Courbevoie and addresses the complex tax situation of the firm.

1962 (19 October)
Letter from André Aubert to the architect's widow. Aubert takes over completion of the SOPAD headquarters on 33 Quai Paul Doumer in Courbevoie.